ISBN 978-1-334-95972-1
PIBN 10783080

1 MONTH OF
FREE
READING

at
www.ForgottenBooks.com

By purchasing this book you are eligible for one month membership to ForgottenBooks.com, giving you unlimited access to our entire collection of over 700,000 titles via our web site and mobile apps.

To claim your free month visit:
www.forgottenbooks.com/free783080

English
Français
Deutsche
Italiano
Español
Português

www.forgottenbooks.com

Mythology Photography **Fiction**
Fishing Christianity **Art** Cooking
Essays Buddhism Freemasonry
Medicine **Biology** Music **Ancient**
Egypt Evolution Carpentry Physics
Dance Geology **Mathematics** Fitness
Shakespeare **Folklore** Yoga Marketing
Confidence Immortality Biographies
Poetry **Psychology** Witchcraft
Electronics Chemistry History **Law**
Accounting **Philosophy** Anthropology
Alchemy Drama Quantum Mechanics
Atheism Sexual Health **Ancient History**
Entrepreneurship Languages Sport
Paleontology Needlework Islam
Metaphysics Investment Archaeology
Parenting Statistics Criminology
Motivational

SPEECHES AND ADDRESSES
OF
WARREN G. HARDING
PRESIDENT
OF THE UNITED STATES

★ ★ ★ ★

Delivered During the Course of
His Tour
From Washington, D. C., to Alaska and
Return to San Francisco,
June 20 to August 2, 1923

★ ★ ★ ★

REPORTED AND COMPILED BY
JAMES W. MURPHY
OFFICIAL REPORTER
U. S. SENATE

𝔍𝔰𝔰𝔲𝔢𝔡 in tribute to the memory of One who gave the full measure of his talents and love to the service of his country

PUBLISHED UNDER THE PATRONAGE OF

CALVIN COOLIDGE
President of the United States

WILLIAM HOWARD TAFT
Chief Justice of the United States

CHARLES EVANS HUGHES
Secretary of State

ANDREW W. MELLON
Secretary of the Treasury

JOHN WINGATE WEEKS
Secretary of War

HARRY M. DAUGHERTY
Attorney General

HARRY S. NEW
Postmaster General

EDWIN DENBY
Secretary of the Navy

HUBERT WORK
Secretary of the Interior

HENRY CANTWELL WALLACE
Secretary of Agriculture

HERBERT CLARK HOOVER
Secretary of Commerce

JAMES JOHN DAVIS
Secretary of Labor

HENRY CABOT LODGE	ALBERT B. CUMMINS
FREDERICK H. GILLETT	FREDERIC W. UPHAM
WILL H. HAYS	JOHN BARTON PAYNE
ALBERT B. FALL	JOHN HAYS HAMMOND
JOHN ADAMS	EDWARD B. McLEAN
ALBERT D. LASKER	CHARLES G. DAWES
GEORGE HARVEY	WARREN F. MARTIN

TABLE OF CONTENTS

xi

TABLE OF CONTENTS—*Continued*

xii

TABLE OF CONTENTS—*Concluded*

Foreword

*I*N THIS *volume are included all the speeches and addresses delivered by President Harding during the course of his tour from
Washington, D. C., to Alaska, and return to San Francisco, embracing
the period from June 20 to August 2, 1923, the date of his untimely
and lamented death at San Francisco.*

*T*HERE *are also included the addresses prepared by him for delivery
at San Francisco, Calif., on July 31, and at Hollywood, Calif.,
August 2, but which, on account of his illness, he was unable to
deliver. The one at Hollywood was, at President Harding's direction,
delivered for him by his secretary, Mr. George B. Christian, Jr.
It is a melancholy but striking coincidence that President Harding's
death occurred almost simultaneously with the delivery of this address
which breathes so deep a religious spirit, so beautifully expresses
reverence for the Creator, and makes an inspiring plea for brotherhood and fraternity among men.*

*A*LSO, *there is printed in this volume the correspondence between
President Harding and the Directors of the American Iron and
Steel Institute, relating to the abolition of the 12-hour shift in steel
manufacturing. This correspondence was referred to in the President's Tacoma, Wash., address, and was released for publication at
the time when the address itself was released, and is published in
this volume because of its historical significance and its intimate
relationship to the theme of the discourse at Tacoma. Also, there is
incorporated in this volume an uncompleted address concerning reclamation problems, prepared for delivery at San Diego, Calif., but
never delivered, owing to the sudden death of the President.*

*A*S A *matter of historical information, there has also been included
in connection with President Harding's brief remarks at Seward,
Alaska, on July 13, the statement of Governor Scott C. Bone, of
Alaska, in reference to christening the entrance to Resurrection Bay
"The Harding Gateway."*

*T*HE *profound religious feeling, the warm affection for children,
the abiding love for humanity, the earnest longing for world
peace, and the highest ideals of devotion and service to the Nation,
so beautifully woven in these addresses and speeches, portray the
noble character of the man, the patriot—Warren G. Harding.*

President Harding's Last Speeches

WE ARE STILL AN UNDEVELOPED REPUBLIC

Speech at Grafton, W. Va., June 20, 9:30 p. m.

Ladies and Gentlemen:

IT IS very pleasing to me to greet you this evening. As I stand here I recall that the last time I was in Grafton, in 1920, I think, I spoke from yon stairway. We have been through various vicissitudes since then, but I think we have now entered upon more fortunate conditions. I hope they are more fortunate for you. Our political affiliations, after all, do not make so much difference. What we want is a country in which there are happiness and prosperity for everybody. That bespeaks a wholesome condition, and that is what I sincerely wish to bring about.

We have had a very interesting but exceedingly warm day, and all are a little tired. As you know, when one gets ready to go away he tries to clean up everything and leave matters in shipshape so that they may be readily taken up when he returns. We have had a pleasant day and have enjoyed riding through your wonderfully beautiful State. No one will ever be insincere when he tells you that West Virginia is not only a wonderful State in its resources but is beautiful to the eye and gives every manifestation of God's infinite touch in its mountains, its streams, its fertile valleys, and its ripening fields. You live in a favored part of the Republic, and I congratulate you upon being citizens of the great State of West Virginia.

17

We have started on a long period of travel. We hope to increase our knowledge of some portions of the United States that at present neither you nor I know very much about. I think it would be well for us all to know more about our country. It is so big and so wonderful that we have never come to a full realization of its greatness. I am going to Alaska so that the Government may know better, and may be helpful in revealing to you, this treasure land of ours which is nearly as large as one-third of the mainland of the United States and whose boundless resources are as yet undeveloped. We are still an undeveloped Republic. We want you in West Virginia to do your part, as we want every other community throughout the United States to do its part, toward making our common country even greater than it is. I know you will do it. Good-bye; good luck; and much happiness to you all. [Applause.]

INTERESTED IN PUBLIC WELFARE

Remarks at Mitchell, Ind., June 21, 9:15 a. m.

Ladies and Gentlemen:

I AM happy to see you this morning and to say a word to you. Nothing is more pleasing to those who are temporarily charged with authority than to meet and come in contact with the people whom they are trying to serve. I want you all to believe, because it is everlastingly true, that your Government is just as much interested in your welfare as you are yourselves, because, unless you are a fortunate and happy people, your Government cannot reach that height of efficiency, power, and helpfulness to which we aim to bring it. I thank you for this greeting. Good-bye and good luck. [Applause.]

OURS IS A FORTUNATE REPUBLIC

Speech at Washington, Ind., June 21, 10:20 a. m.

Ladies and Gentlemen, and Boys and Girls:

IT WOULD be a pleasure to shake hands with each and every one of you. I find just as much pleasure in the closer contact as you do, but there are so many of you and it comes so near breaking one's back to lean over the rail that I know you will excuse me if I am unable to shake hands with you all. I will take the opportunity, however, of saying for both Mrs. Harding and myself that we are grateful for your cordial greeting. It is heartening to those who are charged with the affairs of Government to go out over the land and see the reflexes of sentiment and the measurable contentment and hopefulness that come from the enjoyment of fairly fortunate conditions. After the tumult of the World War, when everything was put out of regular order, humanity had to set about the task of restoration. We are doing pretty well in the United States; we are doing better than any other people in the world. [Applause.]

America Representative Democracy

I think that we ought to have a measurable degree of sympathy with the other nations of the world. The burdens of war and the penalties of the great conflict have weighed upon other peoples more heavily than upon us. We were so well grounded in our institutions, we were so blessed by nature, and we had so much of resolute purpose to go on, that we are getting on the right track in this country. I should like to say to these boys and girls, who are always a joy, that we are hoping to insure for them a better Republic in the United States than you older people have ever enjoyed. [Applause.]

I would not wish anything to happen in America that would change the course of this great representative democracy. We must be a land of law enforcement; we must

19

be a land that reveres American institutions; we must be a land where everybody has a chance and an equal opportunity to make good in life. Furthermore, we must be a land where every boy and girl is made ready to embrace their opportunities.

It is a joy to see you amid the ripening harvests and the prospects of greater fortunes to come. It is a joy to get out and breathe the wholesome atmosphere of the expanding West. You in Indiana are "out West" to those who live in the East, but not to me, for my home is in Ohio; and Ohio has a very great pride in Indiana because so many people from Ohio came to Indiana to take the places of your forebears who moved westward with the Star of Empire in order to make a greater country.

Ours is a fortunate Republic. I am glad to bring to you a word of cheer, a word of confidence, a word of reassured hope that we are going to make the great recovery and we are going to go on to the fulfillment of the fine destiny which is set for this Republic of ours. [Applause.]

I like to look at these boys, for in the opportunities which America affords, there being no mark of caste, we cannot tell but that some one of them on the morrow may be the first citizen of the Republic. I am very glad indeed to have seen you. Good-bye. [Applause.]

WOULD PURGE GOVERNMENT OF EVILS

Speech at Vincennes, Ind., June 21, 11 a. m.

Ladies and Gentlemen:

IT IS a little bit difficult to shake hands with you all. I should like very much to do so, but, instead, I will tell you something I have been thinking about. As one rides across the country on a modern railway train, he is involuntarily and very delightedly absorbed in the panorama which everywhere meets his gaze. It is a very sweet and **grat**ifying experience to travel through the golden wheat fields, the waving timothy, the developing corn, and the fruiting orchards, and feel that there is in prospect that abundance which is essential to the happiness of a people.

As I was contemplating this wonderful picture this morning, with some recollection of the farm myself, I found myself wondering how, from the political viewpoint, we ought to apply the farming practices of the ages to our human affairs of today.

We till the soil; we plant the seed, and we look forward to the harvest with confidence. If the soil has been abused and made unproductive we try to help nature by adding artificially to its richness, and if we find that the growing crop is interfered with by insect life, we attack the grub or the cut worm or the boll weevil, or whatever it may happen to be, and give our energies to the destruction of the evils which impair the development and the realization of a bountiful harvest. We do not, however, quit raising wheat or corn or other products because we encounter difficulties in production, but apply our energies to the cure of the evil, to the removal of those things which interfere with ultimate satisfactory fulfillment. In the arid regions we try to help nature by means of irrigation. In some years there are surpassing disappointments and in other years there are abundant harvests.

His Ideal Democracy

Did any of you ever apply that thought to human affairs? Because at times something goes wrong, because at times there are periods when untoward conditions prevail, because sometimes we are discouraged, we do not put aside, and must not put aside, the institutions of this Republic. It is the duty of Americans in their governmental affairs to do precisely what they do in their productive affairs. We must diligently, conscientiously, and patriotically try to cure the evils which afflict us, and then go ahead. [Applause.] That is where government comes in.

21

The Government cannot make fortunes for its people; that is your business; but the Government can help and does seek to help. It is always endeavoring to strike at and destroy the evils which become apparent, and to bring about such conditions for the people that they may acquire and achieve for themselves. To my mind that is the ideal democracy. So I hope that you will help your government, as I know your government means to help you, in striking at, and if possible eliminating, the evils that sometimes menace our representative democracy. [Applause.]

It seems to me if you who live here in historical old Vincennes will look back and note what has been accomplished in this land of ours during a century and a third, you will find yourselves heartened in looking forward to a wonderful future for this State and for the entire Union. I wish to ask you, therefore, if you do not think that, instead of ceasing to plant the seeds of American ideals and civilization, we ought to go on hopefully, guarding against the things which impair development, and commit ourselves to a wholesome, helpful and promising program, looking to the betterment of all phases of human affairs? That is the thought that I wish to bring to you. [Applause.]

Hopes for Better Government

It is good to see you all. I am not on a speaking tour, although it has become a habit when the President travels to expect him to speak. [Laughter.] Perhaps, if I could just talk to you as my heart impels, we would be a little closer.

I envy you your freedom from the cares that come to those in high position. You think it is a wonderful privilege to be President, and it is, my countrymen, though the man who occupies that office cannot escape having at times a somewhat different feeling, one which he will never know in any other capacity, when he comes to realize his responsibility for the welfare of this marvelous land of ours; but you are care-free; you are confident of the morrow. I know you believe in your government. I do not care what party you may espouse—perhaps that is too broad a statement [*Laughter*], but I mean it in the big sense—for we are all of one purpose, we are all of one mind on the main thing. We have our different theories about government, but we are all concerned about the welfare of our common country.

I know that the parents in this assemblage, like all others in America, wish for their boys and girls a little better Republic than has been their boast. It is the habit of American life—perhaps it may be a fault—to want our children to start where we left off; we want better things for them than we have had ourselves. So far as I may speak, I, too, want them to have even a better government than their fathers have had, and I want them to live under even more inspiring and encouraging conditions than we of the present generation have known. The human tide is always flowing onward in America, and a conscientious citizenship will not only keep up with but will be in the vanguard, as it is today, in the procession of human affairs. It is good to see you all, and I thank you for this greeting. [*Applause.*]

REVERENCE FOR LAW AND AUTHORITY

Speech at Olney, Ill., June 21, 12 noon

Ladies and Gentlemen:

IT IS a very great pleasure to greet you. I like that spirit in America which, even without an engagement or promise to stop and make an address, shows such reverence for our institutions as you have indicated by the display of "Old Glory" on the occasion of the visit of the President. [*Applause.*] You know the President is not any different from anyone of you. He is just an ordinary citizen of our common country until you clothe him with authority to speak for you in government. When you bring out the flag it is a suggestion of your reverence for

23

authority in America. I pray to God that we shall always have a Republic reverent of the law and ready to maintain its authority. [Applause.] I also pray there will never come a time when we shall have a government which is not wholly just in the exercise of authority. [Applause.]

Did you ever stop to think what Government is? It is not some fancied, unreal institution; it is merely the authority which you have set up for the adjustment of your relationships one to another. And the law is merely a code for the adjustment of our mutual relationships. You would not want a government under which one community could thrive at the expense of another; you would not wish a Republic under which one group of citizens could prosper while another group could be enslaved. So, as we go along, seeking to provide the ideal government under which to live, we are constantly making adjustments in accordance with our conscience, our perceptions, and our better understanding of the legal relationships which make for the common good in this great Republic of ours. Do not those of you in overalls ever think the government is not concerned about you, for there are so many of you that we want you to be as fortunate and prosperous and happy as anyone else in America. Good-bye. [Applause.]

RAILROAD MEN AND COMPENSATION

Speech at Flora, Ill., June 21, 12:40 p. m.

Ladies and Gentlemen:

YOUR representative in Congress, Mr. Williams, asked me to stop at Flora and enjoy the very pleasing experience of knowing you better, of shaking hands for a few moments, and of saying a word of greeting to you; and I am happy to do so.

I understand yours is a railroad community; but railroad communities are not any different from other communities in the United States. The service of communication is an essential American service; and we are all interested in the affairs which are necessary for our common happiness. I like to talk with the railroad employees. I have been confronted with some trying problems. An unfortunate railway dispute occurred last year. I tried to bring about an adjustment of it, for we cannot have communication in the United States suspended at the dictum of either the railway managers or the railway workers, because—always remember this—the first interest of America is the interest of all the people and not of any particular portion of the people. [Applause.] Of course the President must always be for all the people, and I want you to believe that purpose is always in my heart, though I may at times be mistaken.

Good Wages for Railroad Men

I want the railroad men well compensated. When I ride on a train I want to know that the man who keeps the track in repair, though his is the humblest job of all, will insure the safety of those who ride over it; and I want the man in the cab to have a clear brain and a satisfied outlook upon life. I want everybody who is concerned with the safety of the American public to be satisfied in his employment and to give the best that is in him to an ideal service to the people of the United States. Beyond that I want, everywhere, community happiness.

Life is not in any sense one-sided, and should have no set bounds. Men should aspire always to reach an improved condition; to attain something of luxury, much of enjoyment, and all of happiness. If I may speak my heart to you today, I want to tell you with all the sincerity I can put in my words that the Federal government and those who speak for it want the citizens of the Republic to be blessed with the fullest measure of happiness. [Applause.]

It is good of you to extend this greeting. I am really trying to get to Alaska, which is a long way off, and in the course of the journey it is good to have your cordial

25

greetings; it is good to know of your interest, and heartening to know of your friendship. I should like you to believe that we reciprocate your very cordial greeting; we share your every hope, and we trust to have your support in everything worth while for the benefit and advantage of the United States of America. [Applause.]

TRIBUTE TO WILLIAM JENNINGS BRYAN

Remarks at Salem, Ill., June 21, 1:30 p. m.

Ladies and Gentlemen, Boys and Girls:

IT IS fine to see you; it is good to have you come out and greet us, and it is just as much pleasure for the President and Mrs. Harding to see you as it is for you to see them. I have been told that this is Mr. Bryan's birthplace.

Several voices: Yes, sir, it is.

The President: You have given a fine, lovable, worth while American to his country. [Great applause.]

AMERICA INSPIRATION TO WORLD

Remarks at Carlyle, Ill., June 21, 2:05 p. m.

Mr. Mayor, and Ladies and Gentlemen:

IT IS very good of you to think of us and be so considerate of us as we are passing through your city. It would be a joy to shake hands with each and every one of you, but our time is so short that that is not possible. I can do no more than thank you for coming out to greet us and giving us the opportunity of seeing you as examples of splendid Americans. [Applause.]

Not so many hundred years ago a great navigator came across the Atlantic looking for gold. He discovered America, and though he saw only some of the islands on the coast, yet he thought he saw a wonderland. Then we began to develop, and the tide of development moved westward until we conquered a continent; but there is nobody in the United States, the President not excepted, who understands the incomparable material wealth and possibilities of this great land of ours.

Our travels so far have brought us only to Illinois, not yet to the Mississippi, but it seems as though we have journeyed for a day through unending possibilities in material resources and among countless citizens of the Republic who, if they are not proud and happy under American conditions, have been pretending to be all along the way. [Applause.] We have just begun to realize the limitless character of our resources. We are young in America; but we have done so well that I believe God Himself must have intended that this great Republic of ours, this wonderful land, should be an inspiration to the world. Let us make sure of it for ourselves, and then give of our influence and sympathy to help all the world. Goodbye. [Great applause.]

SERVICE THE ONE GREAT IDEAL

Address before the Rotary International Convention, Coliseum, St. Louis, Mo., June 21, 4:30 p. m.

Mr. Chairman and Fellow Rotarians:

IF I ever make another application for Rotarian membership and a special class cannot be found in which to place me, I am going to propose that they admit me as the chief consumer of films in the United States. [Laughter and applause.]

It is a joy to come and greet you. You are not precisely on my schedule; but let me say that if I could plant the spirit of Rotary in every community throughout the world I would do so, and then I would guarantee the tranquility and the forward march of the world. [Great applause.] Statesmen have their problems; governments have theirs; but if we could spread the spirit of Rotary throughout the globe and turn it to practical application, there would not be much wrong with the human procession.

Story of the Blacksmith

I can understand how you have grown and how you have come to exercise a great influence. It is because, fellow Rotarians, no matter whence you come, service is the greatest thing in the world [Applause], and you are always performing some service, and doing so conscientiously. You are saving America from a sordid existence and putting a little more of soul in the life of this Republic. [Applause.] I do not pretend to say that you are alone in the good work; but I do not wish America ever to be without ideals. I do not want our America to be without some practical conception of service, and then I want that conception put into practice.

Nor do I come to recommend a service that shall be wholly free from compensation. Every service in life worth while has its compensation. Some of you, perhaps, have seen what I consider one of the greatest plays, if not the greatest, that was ever written. You may have seen Forbes Robertson, the great English actor, in "The Passing of the Third Floor Back." In that play he became a dweller in a boarding house where the boarders were ill-tempered, irritable, and living at cross purposes, and he brought to that unhappy place the spirit of service. He taught the dissatisfied house servant that after all there was a dignity to the humblest service in the world, and that honesty ought to attend it; he taught the dishonest gambler how honesty would elevate his life; he put an end to the snob, and everywhere, by the preaching of the dignity of and the compensation in service he transformed an unhappy household into one of the happiest and most harmonious.

My convictions came from the atmosphere of the small town in which I began my life. In that little town where I ran a newspaper for so many years—I will not recount their number—one day there came a modest little blacksmith, who had nothing in the world but genius in his head and courage in his heart. He did not have a dollar of money, but with his genius and his courage he convinced some other men that he could be of service in the upbuilding of that community by the establishment of an industry. He succeeded in establishing it, and it grew until the modest little blacksmith became the outstanding captain of industry in that community. As he served he profited in serving; he aided working men to acquire homes; he relieved the distressed; he offered sympathy. He was the outstanding figure in a community of twenty or twenty-five thousand people, and one day when, all too soon, his career of service came to an end, every activity in that community was stopped, and everybody halted to do reverence to the memory of a man who had come to the village to serve and to make it and his fellows better.

Put Ideals Into Practice

I can give you a more striking example than that, however. In a town in Ohio some years ago, there lived a veteran of the Civil War, whose heroism and whose capacity combined to make him a brigadier general in the war for the Union; but he, unfortunately, had his public career marred prior to the war without any fault on his part, and so he was obliged to forego public life for which he was eminently fitted. However, he gave of his eloquent tongue, unmatched in America, to service, and he gave of his great big heart to service, and he gave of his practical mind to service, so that he became the greatest contributor to the community in which he resided. One day when he came to his end, after ripened years, not only did the whole community stop to mourn him, but every tear that was dropped upon the bier of General W. H. Gibson reflected the rainbow that spanned the arch between reverence and affection. There was paid to this humble man of service the greatest tribute that community life may pay.

Oh, fellow Rotarians, your service is not alone in developing your ideals; it is in putting your ideals into practice. [Applause.] What the world needs today more than anything else is to understand that service alone will bring about restoration after the tumult of the World War. If we can all get down to service, ample service, honest service, helpful service, and appreciate the things that humanity must do to insure recovery, then there will come out of the great despondency and discouragement and distress of the world a new order; and some day I fancy I shall see the emblem of Rotary in the foreground, because you of Rotary, representative of the best we have in America, have played your big part in making service one of the appraised worth while offerings of humankind. [Applause.]

PORTRAYS VALUE OF PATRIOTISM

Address at the Laying of the Cornerstone of the City Club Building, St. Louis, Mo., June 21, 5 p. m.

President of the City Club, Ladies and Gentlemen of St. Louis, My Countrymen:

YOU little realize how much satisfaction there comes to the Chief Executive of the Nation in being able to participate in this civic function in your great city. It is a very genuine pleasure to me because we can only have a great Nation as we build up cities and communities. So those who are charged with the affairs of the National government have just as deep concern for the welfare of the city as those who reside therein. We can only make of America the reflex of the communities which in the aggregate constitute it, and, therefore, this manifestation of civic interest and civic conscience and the civic soul of St. Louis is of concern to all America, not for what you do among yourselves alone, but for what you inspire throughout the country.

As your president has stated, it has been my fortune to appear as the guest of the City Club in the past, and I confess with a little more pleasure, and a little less of anxiety than I have today, for then it did not so much matter what I said; I could speak with more or less freedom, and nobody cared. [*Laughter.*] Now, however, you are very watchful, as to what your President may say. [*Laughter.*]

There is one thought I wish to leave with you today: Knowing as I do the soul of the City Club, knowing as I do what it brings to your citizenship and to your virile, vigorous city-making force, and knowing that it brings into your councils and your discussions much of the best thought of the day, I ask you, what the value of it is, unless you translate thought into conviction, and then put the conviction into performance?

Teachings of Conscience

I like people in the cities, in the States and in the Nation to ask themselves now and then: "What can I do for my city?" not "How much can I get out of my city?" [Applause.] I like people to speak now and then in the same devotion to State and Nation, because, after all, my countrymen, whenever a man contributes to the betterment of his community, whenever he contributes to the enlarged influence of his State, whenever he contributes to the greater glory of the Republic and makes it a better place in which to live and in which to invite men to participate and aspire, he contributes to himself as he contributes to the welfare of his fellow men. [Applause.]

I have just spent a few moments at the Rotary Convention. I know you mean in this new edifice to center the various civic activities of the community; and Rotary teaches the lesson of service. In connection with that, I want to bring to your minds the teaching of conscience, for if you will give me service and conscience and patriotism in this Republic of ours, I promise you, my countrymen, we will make it better from day to day, and keep it the finest place under God's footstool in which to live. [Applause.]

31

INTERNATIONAL COURT OF JUSTICE WOULD AID
AMERICA IN RESTORATION "OF DESOLATE,
DESPAIRING WORLD"

Address on the International Court of Justice at the Coliseum, St. Louis, Mo., Thursday Evening, June 21

Mr. Mayor, Governor Hyde, My Countrymen All:

NO ONE could be insensible to the hospitality of your welcome. If I were not disposed to speak for myself of my gratitude, I could not resist speaking my appreciation of the kind references to and friendly interest in Mrs. Harding. I know it is not unseemly for me to say that she takes quite as much interest in seeing you as you do in seeing her or the President.

In an official journey from Washington to our great Territory of Alaska, our first stop halts us in your hospitable city, and affords an opportunity for renewed acquaintance and better understanding. I suppose it is perfectly natural to expect the President, when he travels, to stop and make report to the community he is seeking to serve. It has seemed to me that nearly every city and village from the Potomac to the Pacific has bestowed an invitation and a tender of hospitality. I like to say to you, because in saying it to you I am speaking to many others in this marvelous age of communication, that I very genuinely regret the impossibility of accepting all of them. Quite apart from the personal satisfaction and renewed assurance in direct contact with our people, I think there is vast benefit in bringing the government a little closer to the people, and the people a little closer to government and closer to those temporarily charged with official responsibility.

You view government from afar, and I am not surprised that you wonder now and then, because you receive occasional reflexes which are so erroneous that official Washington itself cannot understand them. And those of us who are in Washington live in an atmosphere of officialdom which often hinders our knowledge of the thoughts around the American fireside, and the activities which daily make the essential life of the Nation. These are conditions not easily to be avoided. Our government is the biggest business in the world, and like any other business it requires the management to be more or less diligently at work.

Congress has been more or less continually in session for eight years, and under our coordinated form of government the President must be more or less "in session" at the same time. So I have welcomed this opportunity to see the great Central Valley, the Mountain West, the Pacific Coast, and our treasure land in Alaska. I am rejoiced to speak to you as your President, reporting on the state of affairs to the stockholders of this Republic.

After Effects of War

I do not come, my countrymen, with a partisan report, though I am politically a partisan and believe in the utter necessity of political parties. One only serves his party by first serving his country well, and good service to his country ought to be the aspiration of every citizen of our land.

The present national administration came into responsibility at a very difficult time. Our country found itself in a bad way in the aftermath of World War. We had expended in heedlessness; we had inflated in madness; we had rushed into the abnormal, and found ten thousand difficulties in resuming our normal stride. There was the inevitable business slump. It follows every war. It applies to business in every line—finance, industry, agriculture. And business reflexes are felt by every citizen, no matter how humble or how great. We found in the inevitable reflux of the war tide threatened financial ability, agricultural distress, and vast unemployment. A survey of unem-

33

ployment revealed four and a half to five millions of workers without jobs. I leave the appraisal of all relief efforts, legislative, executive, or administrative, to your own judgment. The thing I want to say is that this distressing situation has been wholly reversed, and today employment is calling for men. There is complaint about that, too, but, since we cannot always preserve the actual balance, I prefer a land which is seeking workmen to a country where discouraged men are hunting for jobs. [Applause.]

Financial Stability of Nation

I like to believe that the recovery is based mainly on confidence in the American policy and the fundamental righteousness of our institutions. I like to believe we have recovered because we avoid the paths of destructive experimentation, ignore mad theories, and cling tenaciously to the foundations of business and property rights and human rights, which have made ours the most rapidly and most safely developed representative democracy in all the world.

We have done more than banish unemployment; we have made our way to financial stability, without which there is little permanent employment. And we halted the extremists who caught their inspiration in European madness, and proposed to destroy our social order because of temporary ills, rather than cure the ills.

I believe America tonight, with confidence in herself, is a fine example to the world of a people capable of laying aside their arms, grappling a reconstruction problem, and digging down to hard work to effect the needed restoration, rather than to fling aside all they had wrought in a century of hopeful progress, and thereby subscribe to destruction in the name of social democracy. We gave business a chance to resume, and assured it that honest success is no crime in the United States. We assured it that the government was not going into business, but that we meant to get out of it. Then, to prove that we meant to have more business in government, we struck at the extravagance which grew in war's fevered activities, we pruned government expenditures, and reduced the government personnel, not by thousands but by tens of thousands, and went a long way in reducing government outlay. [Applause.]

Accomplishments Enumerated

Measures were adopted to lighten the taxation load and distribute the burdens more equitably. We sought to substitute for the exactions of war the convictions of peace. We inaugurated the budget system of government financing, and thereby effected reductions in government outlay amounting to billions. Of course, this enormous reduction was made possible mainly because we suspended war activities and ended war commitments, but we drove at the ordinary expenditures in the peace-time business of government, and lopped off hundreds of millions at a time, and we have proven to the world, in spite of a gigantic debt and its interest burdens, that here is a government resolved to live within its income.

The fiscal year, now near its close, threatened a $800,-000,000 deficit when its financial budget was in the making, but we cut and trimmed, and insisted upon reduced expenditures, and it will close with a $200,000,000 surplus. [Applause.]

These are rather dull facts, but they are interesting to the Government because they afford the proof that government itself joined in the tremendously essential task of striking at its own cost. We were always keeping in mind the people who pay in lifting our country out of the slough of depression and despondency.

In the simplest expression possible, we were trying to get this great country of ours on the right track again. The anxiety was in behalf of no one interest, but for all interests. We were anxious alike for the great captain of industry and his working army. We had concern for him whom we sometimes call the little chap, who makes up the great industrial procession, who is little noted because he walks in the ranks, but whose good fortune is a foremost essential to national happiness and contentment. We safeguarded against our own destruction being

35

effected by the world's demoralization, but we never hindered the world's honest efforts at recovery. On the whole, we contemplate fortunate conditions today, and I believe they are going to abide. We are the most prosperous people in the world. I do not share the belief that we have effected only temporary relief. I never did share the convictions of many men that our permanent recovery could only come after complete collapse, which we have so happily avoided.

International Obligations

It is too early now safely to appraise the competition of the world restored, but the world must take cognizance of the new order as well as we. War wrought an emancipation of men and changed conditions of production which the Old World must recognize before a stable order is restored to it. Our recovery is based on a prompt recognition of the new order, socially just and economically sound, and I am sure we will "carry on." [Applause.]

It is very gratifying to contemplate our conditions at home, wrought amid many manifestations of impatience, but, in spite of discouragements, the record is made. I share your gratification, and have full confidence for the morrow.

These things, briefly related, with great satisfaction in progress made, are meant to serve as a foundation for a wholly frank statement to you of St. Louis and Missouri, and to all the United States, concerning my convictions about the attitude of this Republic toward other nations of the world. The President's impressions concerning international relationships are necessarily founded upon official experience which can come, because of the duties of office, to none other except the Secretary of State.

The endless problems of foreign relations are relatively little revealed to the world. Most frequently they are more readily adjusted because they are not revealed, though it is fair to assure you that nothing of vital importance is unduly hidden from the people for whom the government speaks. Week by week, day by day, often hour by hour, there are problems in our international relations which are no more to be avoided than the vital questions of our own relationships at home. The citizen who believes in aloofness is blind to inescapable obligations, insensible to the twentieth century world order, and unmindful of our commercial interdependence about which the modern business fabric has come to be woven.

In his never-to-be-forgotten Farewell Address, in which the first President compressed the gospel of our mutual interests at home and our proper relations abroad, he said:

"Observe good faith and justice toward all nations. Cultivate peace and harmony with all. Religion and morality enjoin this conduct. And can it be that good policy does not equally enjoin it? * * * The experiment, at least, is recommended by every sentiment which ennobles human nature. Alas, is it rendered impossible by its vices?"

This solemn admonition was addressed by George Washington to his fellow countrymen one hundred and twenty-seven years ago. That it has been heeded scrupulously we are proud to assume the world believes. That we have, indeed, observed good faith and have exalted justice above all other agencies of civilization, barring only Christianity, surely none can deny with truth.

Opposes League of Nations

And we have cultivated peace, not academically and passively merely, but in practical ways and by active endeavors. Even as Washington appended his signature to his most memorable and far-reaching declaration, a new principle had been written into the treaty of peace between Great Britain and the United States, had been sustained by the Congress, at his resolute insistence, and was in full force and effect. That principle was arbitration, which was not only employed successfully at the time, but became from that moment an established policy of the Republic, from which, to this day, there has been no departure.

Thus, clearly, by the method already operative in substituting reason for prejudice, law for obduracy, and justice for passion, the Father of his Country bade us, no less than his contemporaries, not merely ·to countenance and uphold but actively to cultivate and promote peace. It is with that high purpose in mind and at heart, men and women of America, that I advocate participation by the United States in the Permanent Court of International Justice.

Two conditions may be considered indispensable:

First, that the tribunal be so constituted as to appear and to be, in theory and in practice, in form and in substance, beyond the shadow of doubt, a world court and not a league court.

Second, that the United States shall occupy a plane of perfect equality with every other power.

There is no consequential dispute among us concerning the *League* of Nations. There are yet its earnest advocates, but the present administration has said, repeatedly and decisively, that the league is not for us. [Applause.] There admittedly is a league connection with the world court. We can not hope to get anywhere except in the frankest understanding of facts. The authors of the court protocol, cooperating with a brilliant American leadership, turned to the league organization for the court electorate to solve a problem in choosing judges heretofore unsolvable. Though I firmly believe we could adhere to the court protocol, with becoming reservation, and be free from every possible obligation to the league, I would frankly prefer the court's complete independence of the league.

Argument for World Court

Just as frankly, let me say that I have not held it seemly, in view of oft-repeated declaration favorable to the world court establishment, to say to the nations which have established very much what we have wished that they must put aside their very commendable creation because we do not subscribe to its every detail, or fashion it all anew and to our liking, in every specific detail, before we offer our assistance in making it a permanent agency of improved international relationship.

38

Government can never successfully undertake the solution of a great problem unless it can frankly submit it to the people. It is for these reasons that I confess these objections. I recognize the constitutional requirement of Senate ratification, and I believe that the tide of public sentiment will be reflected in the Senate. I am so eager for the ultimate accomplishment that I am interested in harmonizing opposing elements, and am more anxious to effect our helpful commitment to the court, than I am to score a victory for executive insistence. Let us, therefore, appraise some of the determining factors which must be considered in hopefully mapping our course.

The Hague Tribunal

Nearly three years ago, by an overwhelming majority, the people rejected the proposal of the administration then in power to incorporate the United States in the *League of Nations*. To assert that those 16,000,000 voters did not know what they were doing is to insult their intelligence, and to deny the facts. Whatever other considerations may have influenced their judgment were purely incidental. The paramount issue, boldly, defiantly advanced in unmistakable terms by the Democratic Party and espoused by the Democratic candidate for President, was indorsement of the demand of the then Democratic President. I dislike the use of party names in dealing with a problem which has now passed far beyond party association, but I want the world court proposal utterly dissociated from any intention of entrance into the league, and I recite the history in order to paint the background. Moreover, I am so earnest in my desire to have the United States give support to the court that I would gladly wipe out factional difference to effect the great accomplishment.

If the country had desired to join the league, in 1920 it had its opportunity. It most emphatically refused. It would refuse again, no less decisively today.

There has been no change in condition. It is the same league. Not a line in the rejected covenant has been altered, not a phrase modified, not a word omitted or added. Article

X still stands as the heart of the compact. Article XI and all other stipulations objected to and condemned by the American people remain untouched, in full force in theory, however circumspectly they are being ignored in practice.

In the face of the overwhelming verdict of 1920, therefore, the issue of the *League* of Nations is as dead as slavery. [Applause.] Is it not the part of wisdom and common sense to let it rest in the deep grave to which it has been consigned, and turn our thoughts to living things?

But let there be no misunderstanding. I did not say three years ago, and I do not say now, that there is no element in the league organization which might be utilized advantageously in striving to establish helpful, practical cooperation among the nations of the earth. On the contrary, I recognized generally then, and perceive more precisely now, rudiments of good in both the league and the Hague Tribunal. Having marked the fundamental difference between a court of international justice, which I espoused, and the council set up by the league covenant, which I disapproved, as "the difference between a government of laws and a government of men," I said plainly on August 28, 1920: "I would take and combine all that is good and excise all that is bad from both organizations."

The World Court Principle

That is exactly what I am now proposing to do. The abstract principle of a world court found its genesis in The Hague Tribunal. The concrete application of that principle has been made by the league. Sound theory and admirable practice have been joined successfully. The court itself is not only firmly established but has clearly demonstrated its utility and efficiency.

It is a true judicial tribunal. Its composition is of the highest order. None better, none freer, from selfish, partisan, national, or racial prejudices or influences could be obtained. That, to the best of my information and belief, is a fact universally admitted and acclaimed. I care not whence the court came. I insist only that its integrity, its independence, its complete and continuing freedom be safeguarded absolutely.

The Sole Question Involved

The sole question is whether the requirements which I have enumerated as essential to adherence by the United States can be met. My answer is that where there is a unanimous will, a way can always be found. I am not wedded irrevocably to any particular method. I would not assume for a moment that the readjustment of the existing arrangement which appears to my mind as feasible is the best, much less the only, one. But, such as it is, I submit it, without excess of detail, as a basis for consideration, discussion, and judgment.

Granting the noteworthy excellence, of which I, for one, am fully convinced, of the court as now constituted, why not proceed in the belief that it may be made self-perpetuating? This could be done in one of two ways; (1) by empowering the court itself to fill any vacancy arising from the death of a member or retirement for whatever cause, without interposition from any other body; or (2) by continuing the existing authority of the Permanent Court of Arbitration to nominate and by transferring the power to elect from the council and assembly of the league to the remaining members of the court of justice.

The fixing of compensation of the judges, the supervision of expenditures, the apportionment of contributions, etc., could also be transferred from the league to either the court of arbitration or a commission designated by the member nations. Thus, incidentally, would be averted the admitted unfairness of the present system, which imposes a tax upon members of the league who are not subscribers to the court.

His Deference for the Senate

The exclusive privilege now held by the league to seek advisory legal guidance from the court might either be abolished, or, more wisely perhaps, be extended to any member or group of member nations. Thus all would be served alike, subject as now to determination by the court itself of the kind of questions upon which it would render judgment.

The disparity in voting as between a unit nation and an aggregated empire, which now maintains in the assembly of the league, to which many object because of apprehensions which I do not share, would, under this plan, disappear automatically.

These observations are not to be construed as suggesting changes in the essential statute of the court, or the enlargement or diminution of its numerical strength, or modifying the proper provision that a nation having a cause before the court, which is not represented among the judges, may name one of its own nationals to sit in that particular case.

Such, in brief, is an outline of the basis upon which I shall hope, at the opening of Congress, for the consent of the Senate to initiate negotiations with the powers which have associated themselves with the Permanent Court of International Justice. I should like to say to you, in passing, my countrymen, that the usual order has been reversed —I hope somewhat to your satisfaction—so that the President, instead of negotiating arrangements abroad and then asking the assent of the Senate, has in this important matter gone first to the Senate for its assent before undertaking negotiations abroad. [Applause.]

Two Schools of Thought

No program could be devised that would win unanimous approval either at home or abroad. We can not hope to attain perfection or to satisfy extreme demands. The best and the most we can do is to appeal, let us hope successfully, to reasonable minds and, with sturdy faith, be true to ourselves and ready for our duties as liberty-loving, duty-realizing Americans. [Applause.]

There are those who openly advocate our proposed association with the court of justice as a first step toward joining the League of Nations. Their number is not large, and they can not hope to prevail. There are those who, in fear and trembling, proclaim their opinion that this mighty Republic should live as a hermit Nation. They, too, are few and hold to an impossible position. Both are extremists. In an endeavor to obtain actual results, both may be safely omitted from serious consideration.

But two great groups, comprising a vast majority of our people, need to be considered, and between these there lies no difference in professed desire. I am striving for fulfillment of that expressed desire. Both urge participation of the United States in a World Court of Justice, in fulfillment of our age-long aspiration and in conformity with our unbroken tradition. They agree that in order to achieve its fundamental purpose of substituting justice for warfare in the settlement of controversies between nations, such a tribunal must be its own master. The distinction between the two is not one of essential principle or of avowed intent, but one only of fact and opinion.

Sentiment for World Court

There are those who hold that the creation of the existing court under a distinct protocol, instead of directly under the covenant of the league, removes every tincture of subservience or obligation. For present purposes, granting its correctness, there can be no real objection to clarifying the fact in plain, simple terms, to the end that all doubts shall be dispelled and that all minds shall be wholly convinced by ready understanding instead of being only partially persuaded by intricate exposition. If, as we all believe, the corner stone of every judicial structure is unquestioning faith in its integrity, I am unwilling to deprive it of any particle of strength which would enhance popular respect for and confidence in its decisions. Surely no harm, but rather much good, might spring from simplification of an admitted condition.

The other large group comprises those who, while equally earnest in advocacy of an international tribunal, regard the present court with suspicion because of its origin. This objection, for reasons which I have noted, is unimportant. Indeed, from a practical viewpoint, I consider it a matter of distinct congratulation that there is in existence a body which already has justified itself, upon its merits, by demonstration of its character and capabilities.

If American adherence could be made effective in the reconstruction of the court, with respect to its continuing operation, that would seem to dispose conclusively of all other cited apprehensions of danger from the exercise of any influence whatsoever, either open or furtive, by the League of Nations or by any other organization.

A Test of Sincerity

The whole question of support or opposition on the part of these two controlling groups clearly resolves into a test of sincerity. When once American citizens have comprehended that vital point, I shall have no doubt of their answer.

I have taken very frank cognizance of the avowed objections, because we have come to this very test of sincerity. Except for the very inconsiderable minority, which is hostile to any participation in world effort toward security, which our better impulses are ever urging, there is overwhelming sentiment favorable to our support of a world court. But I want the United States to give its influence to the world court already established. Since any adherence must be attended by reservations, I am willing to give consideration to our differences at home and thereby remove every threatening obstacle worth considering, so that we may go whole-heartedly to the world with an authorized tender of support.

So much for the domestic phases of this problem. But there is another phase. I hear the voice of the doubter: "This is all very well, but it can not be done. The forty nations which have signed the protocol will refuse to make these changes. They have formulated their plans, have arranged their procedure, have constructed their machinery, have established a going concern; they are not only themselves content, but they can see no reason why the few remaining powers should not be equally satisfied with the result of their endeavors. They will resent the mere suggestion of such proposals by the United States as an

44

attempt at dictation. It would be an act of discourtesy, if not indeed of unfriendliness, on the part of the American government to approach them along these lines. They will spurn the offer. They will not brook interference from an outsider. They will not consent to upset or modify their *fait accompli*. The whole project will fall to the ground."

This is the voice of the pessimist, to which I reply: Primarily, at this time, it is to satisfy the acknowledged hope and to comply with the earnest wish of our sister States that we are striving to find a way to join and strengthen the one body created by them which bears promise of eliminating the need of war to regulate international relations. We wish no more of war. To submit terms which we consider essential to the preservation of our nationality is not an act of discourtesy; it is the only fair, square, and honorable thing a great, self-respecting nation can do. So far from being unfriendly, it springs from a sincere desire, through frank and intimate association, to help to restore stability, and, in the words of Washington, to "cultivate peace" throughout the world.

The United States Is Not a Suppliant

Manifestations of resentment at our pursuing this natural and usual course would appear far less as evidences of indignation than would attend a course of aloofness, or an utter disregard for so notable an international endeavor.

The United States is not a suppliant. Nor has it the slightest desire to become a master. It is and must be an equal, no more and no less, regardless of its relative material power or moral authority, ever conscious of its own rights, but never denying the like, in even proportion, to another.

And what is the crux of conditions which I have ventured to suggest as constituting a basis for negotiation?

The making of the world court precisely what its name implies, and for which we have so earnestly spoken.

Can it be possible that, despite their protestations to the contrary, this is not what some of our sister States at heart desire? Must there be a test of sincerity abroad as well as at home? Then the more quickly it can be made, the better for them and the better for us. There is nothing to be accomplished in ambiguity. We want to know; and the only way to find out is to inquire.

Very recently a striking message was flashed through the air from Rome to Washington. "Tell America," said the vigorous Prime Minister, "that I like her, like her because she is strong, simple, and direct. I wish Italy to be the same and shall try to make her so." God speed him! And God grant that America shall never forfeit the high honor borne by that sentient tribute from Mussolini!

No Attempt at Coercion

I can not doubt that you will accord, at least, the merit of simplicity and directness to what I have said. Understand clearly, I do not advocate compromise. I merely reiterate and stand squarely for every pledge I have made. I still reject as unwise, untraditional, and un-American any foreign political alliance or entanglement. I still "favor with all my heart association of free nations, animated by considerations of right and justice, instead of might and self-interest, so organized and so participated in as to make the actual attainment of peace a reasonable possibility." I strongly urge adherence to the Permanent Court of International Justice as the one and only existing "agency of peace," to which we can safely subscribe without violating the basic principles of our national being.

I neither advance nor retreat from the position which I assumed in my recent message to the Senate. My sole purpose tonight has been to amplify the constructive suggestion which, at what appeared to be a proper time, I placed before the country for consideration and judgment. Broadly, and yet I trust with sufficient particularity, I have indicated ways and means for realization of our common aspiration.

Further than that I shall not go. I shall not attempt to coerce the Senate of the United States. I shall make no demand upon the people. I shall not try to impose my will upon any body or any person. I shall embark upon

46

no crusade. Hereafter, from time to time, as tonight, acting strictly within, but to the full limit of, my constitutional authority, I shall make further exposition of my matured views and maturing proposals, to the end that we may not only "remind the world anew" by our words, but convince the world by our deeds, that we do, in fact, stand "ready to perform our part in furthering peace," and in regaining the common prosperity which can come only through the restoration of stability in all affairs.

But I shall not restrict my appeal to your reason. I shall call upon your patriotism. I shall beseech your humanity. I shall invoke your Christianity. I shall reach to the very depths of your love for your fellow men of whatever race or creed throughout the world. I shall speak, as I speak now, with all the earnestness and power of the sincerity that is in me and in perfect faith that God will keep clear and receptive your understanding.

"My Soul Yearns for Peace"

I could not do otherwise. My soul yearns for peace. My heart is anguished by the sufferings of war. My spirit is eager to serve. My passion is for justice over force. My hope is in the great court. My mind is made up. My resolution is fixed.

I pass from Washington to Lincoln. "With malice toward none, with charity for all," accurately depicts our attitude toward other nations. All in equal measure hold our sympathy in their distress and our hope for the quick coming of better days. We would make no invidious comparisons.

It is but natural, nevertheless, that we should feel, and it is proper that we should express due appreciation of conduct which conforms notably to our own conceptions of what honor, integrity, sagacity, and gratitude require of self-respecting nations. I consider it eminently fitting at this time to voice the keen admiration and enhanced regard of this country for Great Britain as an immediate consequence of her frank acknowledgment and sturdy assumption of a financial obligation which, though incurred for the preservation of her very existence, added materially to her already heavy burdens.

Nor can I withhold from the German democracy just recognition of its new Government's clear manifestation of faith in our consciousness of fairness as the chief requisite of a peace settlement between her government and ours, and of our disinterestedness in all matters pertaining to the adjustment of European affairs.

It has ever been an irresistible impulse of our liberty-loving people to welcome a triumph of democracy over autocracy and a substitution of popular government for monarchical domination. Hence our earnest hope that a just settlement, the terms of which we do not pretend to indicate, will be made in Europe, satisfying the just dues of democratic and heroic France, so that Germany may make good in her promises of reparations, and therein German democracy may establish a national honor which the monarchy had not conceived, and then take her place in support of the Permanent Court of International Justice.

Germany, Mexico and Turkey

Our neighbor to the south, for whom we have only good will and good hope, will soon, I trust, be in a position to make practicable resumption of fraternal relations with this country, and, following that happy consummation, what more natural than that Mexico, too, along with Germany and, let us hope, Turkey, should accompany the United States, upon terms equally essential to her welfare, into the great tribunal. Then it will become indeed a true world court.

Thus, briefly, my friends, I have revealed the hopeful anticipations of my mind, and the trustful longing of my heart. I feel that the time for America to take the first, long stride in restoration of a desolate and despairing world has come, and that the way stretches clear, though far, before our eyes. May our vision never be clouded by spectres of disaster or shadows of dismay! If, in our search for everlasting peace, we but let lead, and follow humbly but dauntlessly, the "Kindly *Light*" of divine inspiration to all human brotherhood, gleaming like a star in the heavens, from the most beautiful hymn ever written, God will not let us fail. [Prolonged applause.]

PEOPLE ENTITLED TO PLEASURE WITH TOIL

Speech at Municipal Theater, Forest Park,
St. Louis, June 21, 10:20 p. m.

Ladies and Gentlemen:

IT HAS been a happy but strenuous day for those of us who have come westward from Washington. I have thought, perhaps, in extending to you my greetings, most cordial and sincere, that I could convey to you the thought which is in my heart and mind if I told you something of the day. Throughout the daylight hours until four o'clock this afternoon, we were travelling across the wonderful States of Ohio, Indiana and Illinois, noting the rural and agricultural life and that infinitely indescribable charm which comes just before the wheat harvest. We noted the seeming good fortune and contentment and happiness of the agricultural districts.

Then, after coming into your great city of St. Louis, the first thing I encountered was the spirit of Rotary at the International Convention, assembled from some thirty nations, to preach the gospel of service—men unto each other and nations unto each other. From there, it was my good fortune to participate in the laying of the cornerstone of the City Club, which is to be a monument of civic spirit and a symbol of your determination to make a bigger, better, and finer St. Louis.

Believes in Pleasure With Toil

Then, tonight, after speaking before an audience of my fellow-countrymen on the question of our international relationships, I find myself here where a typical American audience is enjoying a splendid performance. I wish we might have more of such delights in the United States of America. I believe in a country where the people can have a full measure of diversion and wholesome entertainment; I believe there should be something of pleasure as well as of toil in this land of ours.

In all the events and happenings of the day there have been evident so much of fine spirit, so much of courtesy, so much of hopefulness, and so much of assurance, that I like to stand before you tonight, my countrymen, and tell you that, in spite of the tumult of the World War, in spite of social upheavals throughout the world, in spite of the distress and restlessness and rebellion which the World War brought to mankind, we in the United States of America at least are on a firm footing and are finding our way back to stable conditions. [Applause.] With God's help, you and your government will join together in making of the United States the best Republic in which to live under the shining sun. [Applause.]

RAIL SYSTEMS MUST BE EXPANDED WITHOUT IMPOSING "IMPOSSIBLE" BURDEN ON INDUSTRY AND CONSUMPTION

Address on the Transportation Problem at Convention Hall, Kansas City, Mo., Friday Evening, June 22

My Countrymen All:

I THINK I may say in every meaning of the word that you have given me a warm reception. Your mayor has referred to Kansas City as the "heart of America." To that I cordially give my sanction, but if you were to ask me for a designation appropriate to Kansas City, recalling my meeting with you three years ago and again this morning, and then appraising the picture which filled my eye and stirred my soul as I came into this auditorium tonight, I believe I would call Kansas City "the sanctuary of the flag." [Applause.] I love "Old Glory," as do you, and it is the fortune of the incumbent of the presidential office to see it, perhaps, more often than any other individual in America; but I have never seen it in fuller, freer, more enthusiastic, and becoming use than in Kansas City. [Applause.] While I am indulging this preface, may I express the hope, my countrymen, and to you of Kansas City in particular, that you will always in a civic and national sense be a fine reflex of all that the flag stands for; that you will be confident of yourselves as citizens of America, and unafraid to have our country play its becoming part in the world. [Great applause.]

Our National Interests Mutual

My countrymen, stopping as I am, en route across the continent, to make an official visit of inquiry to the vast territory of Alaska, I stand before you to offer greetings,

51

and bring, if possible, the Federal government a little closer to you and the people of the United States closer to their government. I confess it has been something of a problem to select subjects for localities, and take cognizance of the territorial interest in the spoken word, and at the same time keep in mind that the printed speech, in the days of modern publicity, is available to all America. I do not mean that there are any circumstances under which the President would say a thing in Kansas City that he could not say in New York, New Orleans, or San Francisco, because our varied national interests are wholly mutual in their last analysis, and the President would not be worthy of his high office if he did not speak in the utmost sincerity whenever he addresses an audience anywhere in these United States.

Ours Is a Common Country

Ours is a common country, with a common purpose and common pride and common confidence. I am thinking rather of the enlarged audiences made possible by the marvels of the radio. I was speaking to you last night in St. Louis, precisely as I am speaking to Denver, Chicago, and elsewhere tonight. We have come into very close communication in the United States, and we shall infinitely profit if it brings us into closer and fuller understanding. I know of nothing which will so promote our tranquillity and stability at home and peace throughout the world as simple and revealing and appealing understanding. [Applause.]

Production is the very lifeblood of material existence and commerce is its vitalizing force. Put an end to commerce and there will be no cities, and farm life will revert to a mere struggle for subsistence. And there can be no commerce without transportation. In all the exchanges which make for commercial life, transportation is as essential as production.

Farm Prices 80 Years Ago

Not long ago, while discussing the distressing slump in agricultural prices which threatened the very existence of farm industry, a caller drew from his pocket an old

52

Ohio publication, a weekly newspaper of the early forties of the last century, and turned to the quotations on live-stock, dairy, and farm products. Wheat was 40 cents a bushel, pork 3 cents the pound, butter 5 cents the pound, potatoes 8 cents the bushel. There could not be many automobiles in returns like those. But that was before the age of motor cars; that was in the flatboat era, when a cargo of farm products had to be floated down the Scioto and Ohio Rivers 250 miles to market. The prices were a reflex of the crudity of transportation. And manufactured products were correspondingly high to the consumer, because there was the same crudity of transportation in distribution.

Earnings and Consumption Costs

I should like to say to those of you who complain now-a-days about the disappearance of earnings in consumption costs that my mother taught school for one month in order to earn enough to buy herself a calico dress, and the sum that is now paid for a silk dress does not exceed that paid for calico fifty years ago.

The stage coach, the wagon train, and the flatboat were speed wonders of that day, and the canal boat was the last word in luxury on many waters. The great Missouri Valley was then unrevealed, and only awakening transportation was the revealing agency. In the infinite bounty of the Creator the measureless riches of the West were bestowed, but they availed little until the whistle of the steam locomotive proclaimed its westward march with the Star of Empire.

It is a curious trait of human nature that we acclaimed railroads in the building and then turned to hamper them in the operation. Missouri and Kansas were doubtless like Ohio. We gave from our purses to contribute to needed building funds; we donated vast areas for right of way; we witnessed financial exploitation with little protest, because of our eagerness to acquire, and acclaimed the acquisition. Marvelous development attended, but we omitted the precautions which would have avoided many present-day difficulties.

Everybody knows how necessary transportation is in this modern world of specialized industries and extensive exchanges. Everybody knows that our very social scheme, as now organized, is dependent on the maintenance of adequate transportation media. A great many people, indeed, have latterly come to wonder if it might not be possible even that we have committed our welfare and prosperity too largely to the assumption that it would always be possible to provide all the transportation that the community might desire at costs which would not be prohibitive, if, indeed, we have not even staked our very existence on the daily continuity of transportation. There is a new, and I think increasing, school of thought on this subject. Its adherents are beginning to ask whether, in the long run, it would not be better to attempt making local communities more nearly self-dependent, by diversifying their range of production, and thus reducing the amount of transportation and exchange of products over long distances. But such a course would be a reversion to the old order, which no modern community willingly would accept, back to the farm self-contained, back to the restricted community, with its candle burning beneath the half-bushel measure.

Need for More Facilities

Of one thing we may be reasonably assured, and that is that since railroads first began to be built in the world there never was a time when so many people, in so many communities, were frankly and intelligently questioning the future as regards instrumentalities of transport. They are asking very frankly and pointedly how they can secure sufficient railroad facilities in the next few generations to supply them, along with other agencies, with the transportation they will require. No live community is ever satisfied. Only today one of your foremost citizens was boasting to me that Kansas City, although presumably the best equipped with railroads of any city in the world, is to have still another system brought into its midst.

I doubt if there is a country in the world in which railroads have come to be a considerable transportation factor which has not some sort of a railroad crisis on its hands right now. There are some countries which merely need more railroads, and are willing to pay almost any price to get them, just as we would have done a generation or two generations ago. There are others which have more railroads than current traffic and insistent demand for lower rates make profitable, so that they have been made, in some fashion or other, a burden on either industry or the Public Treasury. There are still others which have excellent railroad systems but have found, in the increased cost of capital and operation which came with the World War upheaval, that the cost of transportation is threatening to become too heavy for the producing industries to bear.

Conditions in America

Our own country, although it possesses something like 40 per cent of the world's railroad mileage, is confronted with all of these difficulties. In much of our territory we need more railroad facilities, and somehow will have to supply them in the near future. It is stated on high authority that the indirect losses in industry and commerce due to insufficient transportation run into figures equal to the burdens of Federal taxation. On the other hand there are some railroads in this country the building of which would better have been deferred, for they were born out of misguided enthusiasm, or unjustifiable speculation, or the mere purpose of levying a sort of transportation black-mail upon systems already in the field. Finally, we have railroads which, though apparently well managed and abso-lutely necessary to the communities they serve, are finding it difficult to earn a living and quite impossible to provide the necessary maintenance and the means of expanded facilities.

Every passing year adds to the cost of producing new railroads. Most of our railroads were begun at a time when land was the most plentiful and least valuable thing we possessed, and their rights of way and terminals cost, as compared with the present expense that would be involved in reproducing them, very little indeed. Everybody is doubtless familiar with the story that a few years ago a great engineer was commissioned to make preliminary calculations of the cost of a complete new trunk line system between New York and Chicago. He is said to have reported that the purchase of real estate for terminals on Manhattan Island alone would require as much capital as would the physical construction of the entire line from New York to Chicago.

The Problem of Expansion

There could hardly be a better illustration of the increasing difficulties which the country must face in any considerable expansion of its railroad system. Of course, this hypothetical new trunk line from *Lake* Michigan to the Atlantic coast was not constructed. If it had been, it could not have earned returns on its enormous cost unless rates had been greatly increased for its benefit. But if rates had been increased for it, they would have had to be increased also for the lines competing with it; otherwise, the new road would have no business at all. An increase of tariffs which would have permitted such an expensive new property to earn even a moderate return on its investment would have enabled the older and less expensive properties to earn absolutely preposterous returns.

It is worth while to bear in mind, in the face of current agitation, that we could not replace our railroads for a vastly larger sum than the valuation placed upon them by the Interstate Commerce Commission, and it is fortunate for our people that we do not have to contemplate a rate structure founded upon replacement cost.

I have referred to the previously recited instance because it so perfectly illustrates the whole situation which the country must meet in dealing with its railroad problem. Events of the last few years have made us all realize that the railroads must be administered under some policy that will make it possible to find the capital wherewith to expand the existing systems as business shall require, without imposing an impossible burden upon industry and consumption.

It is no theoretical problem. It is not an imaginary thing to be swept aside with a wave of the hand. When the government undertook operation during the war, and standardized wages, and was caught in the sweeping current of mounting cost, it created a situation to ignore which would quickly develop a national menace. At an awful cost we learned the extravagance and mounting burden of government operation. Yet there are today very insistent advocates of government ownership. Frankly, I do not share their views. [Applause.] Our political system has not reached such a state of development that we can insure proper administration.

Opposes Government Ownership

I believe it would be a colossal blunder which would destroy initiative, infect us with political corruption, create regional jealousies, and impose incalculable cost on the Public Treasury. But we must find a solution of the rate problems and the necessary expansion of facilities, and find that solution in spite of the prejudices of the present-day sponsors for operations and the present-day destroyers who would bankrupt, or confiscate, else government ownership and operation will become an accepted necessity. Nor do I share the views of those who would lower rates without regard to railroad good fortune. The prosperity of the railways is the prosperity of the American people, and the property rights in railway investment are entitled to every consideration under our Constitution which is due to property rights anywhere. Any tendency toward confiscation will lead to confusion and chaos, and destroy the very foundation on which the Republic is builded.

Competitive Carrying Charges

It is easy to understand how many people contemplate the abolition of competitive carrying charges, and the elaborate machinery of government regulation, and argue that the logical step is to put the railroads all in one common pool under government ownership. That would effect an adjustment between the fat and the lean, if it did not make them all lean. It would equalize profits and losses between favored lines and less fortunate ones; it would abolish profits and saddle all losses on the Public Treasury. More, it would completely disarrange the economic relationship between our different communities, upon which our present-day commerce is builded. It is preferable to preserve initiative and enterprise, to maintain the inspiring competition of service, and it is vital that the cost of transportation be borne by the commerce which is served.

Not Proposing Nationalization

No, my countrymen, I am not proposing nationalization, nor a renewed experiment in government operation, the cost of which we have not yet settled. The Federal Treasury can not well bear any added burdens until we have lifted many of those already imposed. I had rather solve a difficulty than embrace a danger.

I do believe there is a rational, justifiable step, full of promise toward solution. It will effect a diminution in rates without making a net return impossible, and will make sound finance possible for expansion. I refer to the program of consolidating all the railroads into a small number of systems, the whole to be under rigorous government supervision, and the larger systems to be so constituted that the weaker and unprofitable lines would be able to lean upon the financial strength of the stronger and profitable ones until the growth of the country makes them all earn a just return upon capital invested. The transportation act of 1920, known as the Cummins-Esch law, contemplated this kind of a consolidation, but made it permissive rather than mandatory. In effect, it left to the railroad managements, subject to the master plan set up by the Interstate Commerce Commission, to arrange the system groupings of the roads.

That provision was adopted only after long and detailed consideration by men of wisdom and experience, and seemed to represent the best judgment of leaders in both political parties. Its weakness was that it was doubtful whether the railroads would be able, of their own volition, to reconcile all the conflicting interests involved in so enormous a reorganization. It was frankly recognized when the legislation passed that it was necessarily somewhat experimental. Likewise, it was extremely uncertain whether the wisdom of a dozen Solomons, sitting as railroad presidents and chairmen of boards, and as financial backers of these great properties, would be equal to the task of organizing a group of systems which would represent fair treatment of all the interests involved, including those of the public.

There now appears to be no difficulty about any constitutional inhibition to the voluntary consolidation as authorized by Congress. But the problem of reconciling the interests of the hundreds of different ownerships and managements of lines to be merged into systems has proven a task for which no solution has been found.

Consolidation of Roads

It is, therefore, being seriously proposed that the next step be to amplify further the provisions for consolidation so as to stimulate the consummation. It is my expectation that legislation to this end will be brought before Congress at the next session. Through its adoption we should take the longest step which is now feasible on the way to a solution of our difficult problems of railroad transportation.

There has been undue alarm in many communities, Kansas City included, concerning the effect of such consolidations upon commercial centers like yours. Let me allay the alarm by reminding you that the whole question is one of adjustment, and the whole program is to be constructive, looking to enhanced service, and destruction is as much to be avoided as failure is to be prevented.

Though no other nation in the world offers a parallel in railway development, those of us who believe that this program of regional consolidation would produce highly beneficial effects find our belief sustained by recent experience in Great Britain. The railroads of that country have in the last few years passed through an experience which, considering the vast differences between the two countries as to area, geographic configuration, and industrial and social organization, has more or less paralleled that of American railroads. The United States and Great Britain were, when the World War flamed, the only two great countries which had clung unalterably to private ownership of railroads.

In every other important country a considerable portion or all of the railroad mileage was owned or operated by the government. In Britain, as here, the necessities of war persuaded the government to take over the roads, place their operation under more rigorous control than before, and extend financial guaranties. In both countries, the results were expensive from the viewpoint of the treasury, and highly unsatisfactory from that of the public's convenience and the accommodations of business. In both countries, agáin, the experience went far to dispel whatever illusions had been entertained about the desirability of government railroad management.

Transportation Problem Pressing

The parallel does not end here. When the war ended opinion in both countries urged return of the railroads to corporate management as soon as possible. In both this was affected, and—here comes the most striking coincidence of all—in both the return was accompanied by a legislative provision looking to consolidation of the many systems into a small group of great ones. The difference was that in Great Britain the legislation was mandatory, requiring that by January 1, 1923, the roads should be consolidated into four great systems; here it was permissive, and, of course, a much larger number of systems is proposed. The British program has been carried into effect; there are now four systems in the country, all organized around the same general idea of increasing efficiency and providing their financial stability.

While this reorganization has been in effect only a few months, its early results are reported to justify fully the expectation of better conditions under it. It is regarded as a long step toward permanent settlement, on a basis fair to the owners of the properties and to the public interest in good service at the lowest possible rates.

The necessity for early adoption of this or some other program to place the railroads on a sound basis is so pressing as to make it a matter of deep national concern. I would not discuss the question before you did I not consider it of exceedingly great importance to the Republic. There is no other issue of greater importance, for herein lies in large part the solution of the agricultural problem, and with it the assurance of our industrial position. No other industry can possibly prosper with agriculture depressed; and agriculture is calling loudly for relief from present transportation burdens.

Must Find a Way to Aid

Quite recently Senator Cummins, the veteran chairman of the Senate Interstate Commerce Committee, made the startling statement that probably 75,000 miles of our railroads are earning so little and costing so much to operate that with scant incomes they can not be adequately maintained and expanded in facility to meet traffic requirements. If we realize that this means nearly one-third of the country's railroad mileage, we will appreciate the gravity of the situation. Yet there it is, grimly staring us in the face, challenging our statesmanship and business capacity.

Not long ago the Interstate Commerce Commission actually granted the necessary authorization to tear up and abandon one piece of over two hundred and thirty miles of railroad. It was no frontier line, in an undeveloped, uninhabited section; it was in the rich and populous State of Illinois. If the spectacle of a railroad literally starved to death in such a community is alarming, it is yet less a calamity in some ways than it would be in a region possessing fewer lines capable of taking over the public service. A majority of the people tributary to it will, by going a few miles farther, get transportation from other roads; but there is no such solution of the problem for many extensive communities now served by roads in financial distress.

There are some roads—many of the smaller ones in fact—whose continued operation is absolutely vital to many thousands of people, to considerable towns, to large areas of country, whose revenues simply can not provide financial facilities through earnings pending a considerable growth in community population, to say nothing of earning

61

any return whatever on capital invested. No legerdemain of court processes, receivers' certificates, or financial juggling, can save them. They must get more revenue or stronger support or quit operating until the country is more largely developed. We shall contribute nothing to solving their problem by agreeing that they ought not to have been built so soon. Nor shall we help by talking about the wickedness of men who, years ago, exploited the public, watered stocks, and did other reprehensible things. No panacea will be found in statistics proving that some other roads are earning more than they need, unless we find an equitable way to coordinate the activities of the strong roads to develop the weak ones.

Three Plans Outlined

The railways have become publicly sponsored institutions, and government must find a way to avoid confiscation, avoid starvation, and maintain service and a proper return upon capital which will assure them a growth commensurate with the country's development.

We are all agreed that to abandon any important share of railroad mileage is inconceivable. We can not do it because people already dependent on the railroads would be ruined; and because, further, in a not very distant future we should be compelled by the country's development to put them back, or their equivalent in capacity for service. They must be saved. There are just three possible ways to do it:

1. For the government to take and operate the weak roads, and thus bear all the loss without any of the profits of railroad management.

2. For the government to take all the railroads, convert them into one gigantic pool, and plunge into the enormous responsibility thus incurred. In the present state of the Public Treasury and of tax burdens, and in the light of recent sad experience with government management, I do not think this is to be considered. I believe it would be politically, socially, and economically disastrous.

3. The plan of consolidations already outlined, bringing economies in operation, financial stability, ability to secure needed capital, adjusting rates and regulations to the necessities of the position, and preserving the real advantages of competition in service, while avoiding the evils of government ownership.

Problem of Car Destruction

As among these possibilities there can be little doubt of the public preference for the third program. It is not unjust to the strong roads, for the prosperity of these, like the prosperity of all industry, depends on keeping the country as a whole prosperous. Every mile of railroad trackage in the land helps to make business for every other mile. The transportation system must be considered as a unity precisely as the Nation itself must be considered. In this manner we will best help to insure the credit of the railroads, assist them to new capital for future expansion, and insure, for the future, against the sort of wildcat and competitive railroad construction which in the past has been responsible for giving us a great share of the trackage which now proves economically unjustified.

There is another particular reason which urges the early adoption of the larger-system plan. It would be a long step toward solving the problem of keeping the railroad equipment adequate. Many financially weak roads are unable to provide all the rolling stock they need. Inadequacy of car service hindered the relief of the coal situation last winter; it denied the farmer a market when prices were most advantageous, and has impeded manufacturing industry time and again. It is fair to say the railways were helpless because they were financially and otherwise unable to keep up with the demands for service. Prevailing practices further embarrassed the situation. Roads inadequately equipped make up their deficiency by borrowing the cars of other roads. When a foreign car comes to one of these parasite lines it is not returned promptly, but often is deliberately retained. The free movement of cars is prevented; no company can be certain of commanding even its own equipment when it is needed; seasonal congestions or shortages of cars follow; and an unfair burden is imposed on those roads which sincerely try to meet the demands of this demoralized situation.

To meet this condition, the proposal of a nation-wide car pool has lately attracted much attention. The Pullman company fairly illustrates what is meant. This great corporation provides most of the railroads with certain kinds of cars, on a rental basis. Applying the same idea to the furnishing of freight cars, you have a rough notion of the proposed car pool. It is urged by advocates that it would unify the rolling-stock organization; make possible the enlistment of adequate capital to provide for the weak and strong roads alike; place the entire organization under a single centralized control which would insure equity to all roads and sections. There are others who insist it would not correct the present evils, and would divide responsibility and make regulation and supervision more difficult. In any event the system of consolidation would in effect clear up many difficulties in car distribution.

Position of Employees

We come now to an entirely different phase of the transportation question. Quite regardless of its cost, the continuity, the assurance of service at all times is absolutely necessary in transportation. Business that is done today depends on the certainty that the goods can be delivered tomorrow. If there is doubt about the trains running and the deliveries being made tomorrow, there will be unwillingness to buy and sell today. All of which brings us to a consideration of the relations between the transportation organization and its employees.

There is no other business, so far as I know, in which suspension of operations can produce such disastrous results as in transportation. The vital importance of this service has brought many people to the conclusion that it ought to be possible absolutely to forbid and prevent railroad employees from striking. I do not believe it possible under our form of government to compel men to work against their will [Applause], and do not think it desirable under any form of government. I say this, fully recollecting my vote in the Senate in favor of the antistrike provision of the railroad act of 1920. That was not a provision denying men the right to strike. It was merely a requirement that before the men should strike or the employer should lock them out, both sides should submit their differences to a properly constituted and impartial tribunal, empowered to consider the facts, determine the merits, and make an award.

It was believed that in the vast majority of cases this procedure would prevent lockouts and strikes; and, in view of the enormous loss to the carriers, to their employees, and to the public resulting from strikes, I profoundly regret that it should not have been possible to give the plan a fair trial. When I say a "fair trial," I mean a trial under conditions fully and frankly acceptable to all interests. I do not believe that in such a situation a fair trial is possible unless both sides have absolute confidence in the fairness of the tribunal and are sincerely willing to accept its verdict. If human wisdom shall ever be capable of setting up such a tribunal as that, and of inspiring both sides of the controversy with complete confidence in it, we will have traveled a long way toward industrial peace.

The Railroad Labor Board

Personally, I have confidence that the thing is possible. I believe so firmly in the underlying common sense of both organized industry and organized labor, and in the fairness toward both on the part of the great public on which both of them are finally dependent, that I believe at last it will be possible to arrive at settlement of industrial disputes in public services by such a method. Let me say so plainly that there will be no misunderstanding, that in most disputes which end in strikes or lockouts I do not believe the difference which at last divides the two sides very often represents any underlying question of human rights and human justice.

There was an interesting illustration in the strike last year of the railway shopmen. The government sought to effect a settlement that had for its firm foundation the pledged acceptance by both managers and employees of the decisions of the Railway Labor Board. To such a settlement the spokesmen of managers and employees gave their pledge, but the managers rejected the agreement on the ground that it did not do justice to the new employees who were taken on after the strike began. Much was made of the issue, but in the end all settlements were effected on precisely the terms the government proposed. Yet the agreement to abide by the Labor Board decision was lost in the days of anxiety and the separate settlements which were effected.

Continuity of Transportation

It is inescapable that the government feels the importance of public interest and right in connection with the settlement of such questions. The vital existence of the Nation now depends upon continuity of transportation. In recent years it has come to be accepted that there are three parties, rather than two, to every controversy between the employer and employee of a public-service corporation. The employer is one, the employee is another, and the great public, which must have the right to consume and to be served, is the third. If we are quite frank among ourselves we will have to admit that in dealing with such controversies the third party in interest has, down to this time, decidedly received the least consideration. Yet the public is the party on which finally must be placed the burden of whatever adjustment is effected.

As a means of making possible righteous adjustment between railroads and their employees, with due regard for the interest of the public which pays, the government established a Railroad Labor Board. It was assumed that this organization, required to represent in equal numbers the employers, the employees, and the public, would command the confidence of all sides and that its determinations would be accepted. Unfortunately, for reasons which are the subject of no little controversy, the board has never had the cooperation of employer and employee for which its authors hoped. For myself, I am not convinced that the test has been a complete or entirely fair one, and I favor, not its abandonment, but its continuance under such modifications as seem most likely to make the plan successful. But there is little to hope for until all concerned are ready to comply promptly with the board's decisions. I am frank to say I do not hope for compliance on the part of employees so long as decisions are ignored by the managers.

Utilization of Inland Water Ways

There is another highly important phase of the transportation problem very much worth our attention. I believe the use of our inland waterways offers the one sure way to reduced carrying charges on basic materials, heavy cargoes, and farm products. [Applause.] Probably all of us acknowledge the urgent need of diminished cost on agricultural shipments and many bulk cargoes essential to manufacturing industry. While it is well established by the Boston Milk Case decision that public necessity justifies carrying a commodity at less than cost, the service at less than cost on the larger tonnage of the country does not offer the righteous solution. We ought to try the experiment of coordinating rail and water shipments; we ought to avail ourselves of the waterways developed through enormous expenditures of public funds, and we ought to give the waterway carriers a chance to prove their capacity for helpful service. [Applause.] I cannot tell you how impressed I was as our train ran along the Missouri River for miles and miles this morning with the thought that that great highway ought to be controlled and harnessed and made to serve the great community through which it flows. [Applause.]

The Federal Government has expended approximately $1,130,610,000 on river and harbor improvement. Only last spring the Congress appropriated $56,589,910, in spite of a budget recommendation of less than half. For the sums spent on harbors we have most beneficial results. The millions expended on inland waterways, on rivers and canals, have brought small returns because we have put them to no practical use. Though we expended to cheapen carrying charges and to facilitate transportation, we have failed in coordinating service and have allowed the railroads to discourage every worth while development. Where barge and packet service has been established there has been such an unfair division of the joint carrying charge that waterway development has been impeded, and where service lines by water have been established the hoped-for diminution of rates has been denied or avoided until the plea of cheapened transportation by water has seemed a mockery.

I believe we should encourage our water service; we should encourage and enforce coordinated service; we should see to an equitable division of rates, and exact rate reductions whenever practicable to operate successfully under rate reductions.

It is a very discouraging picture to contemplate the expenditure of $50,000,000 of public funds on an inland waterway such as the Ohio when the tonnage on that waterway has diminished more than half, while the waterway itself is made better and better year by year. We have either wasted many hundreds of millions in blind folly or have been inexcusably remiss in turning our expenditures to practical account, and I think the latter is true.

Will Not Tolerate Ruin of Roads

I wish the railway leadership of the country could see the need of this employment of our water routes as an essential factor in perfected transportation, and join in aiding the feasible plan of coordinating service and cheapening charges, not alone as a means of popularized and efficient public service, but as a means of ending the peril of their own fortunes.

No thoughtful sentiment in America will tolerate the financial ruin of the railroads, but the people do wish, now that exploitation has been ended, to have their transportation adequate to the country's needs, and desire all our facilities brought into efficient service. They wish to make sure of ample agencies, and they demand the least carrying charge which will make an adequate return to capital and at the same time permit extensions and additions and more ample equipment essential to the best transportation in the world.

We have not fully appraised the evolution from the ox-cart to the motor age. The automobile and motor-truck have made greater inroads on railway revenues than the electric lines with their intimate appeal to the local community. There will never be a backward step in motor transportation; but we shall do vastly better if we find a plan to coordinate this service with the railways, rather than encourage destructive competition. Indeed, the motor transport already promises relief to our congested terminals through better coordination. We have come to the point where we need all the statecraft in business, to find the way of making transportation in its varied forms adequate to the requirements of American commerce, to afford that transportation its due reward for service, without taking from production and trade a hindering exaction.

I can not too greatly stress the importance of this great problem. It can not be solved by those who commend the policy of confiscation or destruction, nor can it be solved by those who make a prejudiced appeal for political favor. We must frankly recognize the exactions imposed upon the American farmer during the war expansion of rates, take note of the wage development which will yield no reduction in the principal item of operating cost, and seek conditions under which we may have the requisite reductions in fixed charges which will afford encouraging relief. If the system consolidations, with diminished overhead costs, with terminal advantages largely improved and terminal charges greatly reduced, will not afford the solution, then our failure will enforce a costlier experiment and the one great commitment which I hope the United States will forever escape.

United States Prosperity Not Temporary

We are dwelling now amid a gratifying return to prosperous conditions. I do not share the feeling that the recovery is a mere temporary one, with impending relapse. The guaranty of permanence lies in our doing the things essential to the equitable sharing of our good fortune. There can be no abiding prosperity in industrial centers,

69

in transportation or elsewhere, unless it is properly shared by American agriculture. Government can make no direct bestowal of good fortune, but it is the duty of government to maintain conditions under which equal opportunity for good fortune is the heritage of every American everywhere. [Applause.]

Under our representative democracy we find ourselves absorbed in issues which more or less concern us in our individual affairs, but we lose the aspect of government as a whole and take it as a matter of course. It is our accepted practice rather than a deliberate intent.

Americans ought ever to be asking themselves about their concept of the ideal Republic. I take it to be one of universal good fortune, where freedom is as complete, under the law, as justice is unfailing within the law—a land where the equality of freedom's opportunity and the reward of merit are held as sacred inheritances and citizens are made fit to embrace beckoning opportunity.

Above all else, since we are the great exemplars of representative democracy, ours should be a land of unquestioned loyalty to the great fundamentals on which we are builded, to which Americans are committed by birth, or declare allegiance when they are adopted. We have achieved most notably in development. Let us make sure of the preservation and hold ourselves equipped for the continued triumphs of progress at home and unafraid to play a great people's becoming part in the affairs of the world. [Prolonged applause.]

FREEDOM AND JUSTICE OF AMERICA TYPIFIED

Address to the Assembled School Children,
Hutchinson, Kan., June 23, 10:30 a. m.

Young Ladies and Young Gentlemen:

THERE are so many of you that I hardly know which way to turn to address you. I believe I will come over here first of all and say "how-do-you-do;" and then I will turn to this side and say "hello;" and then I want to ask, "how are you?" over here; and then turn to this side and say, "greetings" to you all. The President sometimes can do wonderful things; he thinks so, at any rate; but it is difficult to speak to so many people when they surround you on all sides.

There is not a finer picture in the world than the one you present here this morning. [Applause.] It is made up of the typical childhood of America, the schooling youths of this free land of ours. I never look upon such a body of young folks without experiencing a new happiness and a new pride in being an American citizen. We are so accustomed to it, it is so much a part of our lives, we are so familiar with the picture of the bright-eyed, smiling boys and girls of America that we do not stop to appraise it at its true value; but I like to think that here is the proof of the freedom and the justice of America, and here is the hope of a greater tomorrow than we know today. Perhaps there may be other lands, but I know of none other in the world, where there is such an utter freedom from caste, such complete lack of any class; where opportunity is beckoning all to grow into the full realization of the privileges and possibilities of life.

Hopeful American Childhood

As I look out upon these wonderful boys and girls, I do not know which is the child of a working man, which is the child of a captain of industry, or which is the child of a financier. They all look alike; they are dressed very much alike; they laugh alike, and they join alike in the sparkling music of hopeful American childhood. That is the finest reflex of any government in the world; nothing can surpass it. I do not say that life will treat them all precisely alike. I do not think God Almighty ever intended that to be the case. If He had meant us to know life precisely alike, I rather think He would have created us all just alike. Then this would have been a very unhappy world in which to live. But in our free America every boy and girl develops into manhood and womanhood and is prepared under our school system to embrace the equal oppor-

71

tunities of American citizenship. Once they are ready to embrace them, it is up to them to determine how greatly they shall attain and acquire.

The duty of America, the duty of Hutchinson, and of every other community throughout the United States, is to prepare the boys and girls to embrace the equal opportunities of the Republic. It is not enough to have a citizenship; it is essential to have a citizenship fit for the duties and obligations of life and ready to make use of the privileges and advantages thereof. So in America we are finding in our educational institutions and facilities great satisfaction; but we are also looking forward to a finer and greater and better tomorrow. I hope that may be your fortune, because, unless it is your fortune, America cannot attain that position which we all hope for her. The destinies of this land of ours are a common concern. Whatever happens to Hutchinson, Kan., is bound to be reflected in other great communities throughout the Union.

An Inspiring Picture

I am more than happy to greet you. As I told you a moment ago, you make the most inspiring and the most attractive picture in all the world, and you do more—you make the President of the United States, as you ought to make every public official charged with responsibility throughout the land, more and more eager and earnest and more and more serious in the desire to perform well the duties of office in order to make this government of ours in every way worth while for its developing citizenship. Oh, I am happy to see you, and I wish you, under the Stars and Stripes of America, the best gifts in God's bounty. [Applause.]

AGRICULTURE THE NATION OVER PASSES THROUGH WORST OF DEPRESSION; DETAILS RELIEF MEASURES ENACTED BY CONGRESS

Address on Agriculture, Fair Grounds,
Hutchinson, Kan., June 23, 2 p. m.

Mr. Mayor, Governor Davis, and My Countrymen All:

I WISH you might see yourselves as I see you. You present to one who comes from Ohio a very appealing picture this afternoon. Somehow we have been enjoying appealing pictures ever since we awakened this morning. We were first able to look out upon the great promising fields, almost ready for the harvest, when we saw Kansas as the wonderland it truly is. Then we came to your city and saw the school-children in their promise of the morrow; and I saw the harvest fields a little more intimately than I had in many years. [Applause.] Then, most wonderful of all, although many Kansans came from Ohio, to my delight and surprise this day I saw for the first time in forty-five years a lady who, as a girl of twelve, seemed to me to give promise of being the most beautiful and wonderful woman in the world. Just think of coming to Kansas and finding your first boyhood sweetheart still living, married, having grand-children, and doing her part in the making of America! [Applause.]

A half score of years or more ago, I was making a number of addresses in your State, and had the good fortune to make a more or less intimate survey of several thriving Kansan communities. While driving in the outskirts of a county-seat town, not a hundred miles from here, we noted in the distance a structure rather more imposing than the average home, and I made inquiry as to its

73

ownership. My host said: "Well, sir, I'll have to apologize. That's the county poorhouse, but it is out of commission. We discontinued its public operation for we had no inmates." "Omit the apology," I replied, "and make it a boast. I never saw an unoccupied almshouse before. If this is a reflex of the life of Kansas, it is a glorious chapter in human progress." [Applause.]

My host had spoken truly. I doubt not there are some in this assemblage who knew him. I refer to Mr. Robinson, the wheat king, who first proved that the cultivation of wheat could be substituted for that of corn in southern Kansas. More interesting still, before my speaking tour was finished, I saw two other county almshouses which had been abandoned as public institutions, and made into eloquent monuments to a community's good fortune. A civilization without a public charge is not the supreme attainment in human progress, but it is a lofty achievement, and I know there can not be very much wrong with the fundamentals of the government under which it is recorded.

Burdens of Readjustment Period

Probably the fortunes of agricultural Kansas are not today precisely what they were a dozen years ago, and agricultural fortunes are invariably reflected in the fortunes of all other industries, because they are so closely related and interdependent that there can be no good or ill fortune of one without influencing the other. The whole world has been in a social, industrial, financial, and political upheaval since then. The very fabric of civilization has been sorely tested. Dynasties have fallen; monarchies have failed; revolution has reigned in various sections of the world, and disasters have exacted their toll nearly everywhere and in nearly every way.

The losses to American agriculture are universally admitted and deplored, but it is not an experience peculiar to American agriculture alone. Nor was the readjustment following war's inflation a burden to agriculture alone. It came to the railroads, to bankers, to manufacturers, and to the mercantile world. The miracle is that we all escaped with relatively so little of disaster. It is characteristic of human nature that we magnify our own ills and too little appraise the ills of others; but the eyes of the government are attracted to them all. I hesitate to tell you how seriously vast interests, presumably unendangered by the changing tides of business, were affected, and at what sacrifices disasters were averted. Looking backward, I find my confidence in the social and industrial fabric of this Republic strengthened by our wonderful emergence from threatening disaster.

Weathered Period of Depression

Ever since the earlier processes of deflation which began after the World War we have been studying and talking about the rehabilitation and the better organization of our agricultural industries.

I confess a very frank pride in the government's part in bettering a situation against which you justly complained and which all the people of the Nation deplored. The cooperation of all the governmental agencies, and with them the cooperation of the fine forces of leadership which the great national farm organizations have developed, made it possible to secure a measure of helpful results in this department of our endeavors which has been especially gratifying. Moreover, it has found prompt reflection in the improved status of every agricultural concern. We have been officially informed that owing to improved conditions the farm products of the country for 1922 were worth $2,000,000,000 more than they were in 1921. Clearly, we are through the worst of the depression and can reasonably expect gradual improvement. [Applause.]

The balance within the industry, as between livestock and grain production, has been restored. The disturbance of that equilibrium, so highly important to a properly adjusted agriculture, had been one of the unfortunate and unavoidable results of the war-time necessities. Called upon to feed a world, American farmers had willingly responded to the demand for special efforts in certain lines of production. Relationships between supplies and demand for some staples were badly disrupted and could not be instantly restored when peace came. That was in considerable part responsible for the violent fluctuations which imposed so much hardship on the farmer. Along with this distortion of the production ratios went an even more acute and difficult disturbance of the factors which determine foreign demand.

While the war lasted there was no possibility of overproduction of such staples as wheat and cotton, for example; and when peace suddenly burst upon the world, the farmer had plans for a long future which he could not readjust instantly. No human wisdom could possibly have foretold the course that would be taken by supplies and demand; and it is as futile as it is obvious to us now to say that wisdom would have dictated at least a less precipitate policy in removing the war-time restriction and guidance in dealing with some aspects of production and distribution.

Government's Aid to Agriculture

When the present administration came into responsibility, agriculture was in the lowest ebb of depression. The immediate need was for measures to meet an emergency. There was urgent call to keep open and so far as possible enlarge our foreign markets, and this was accomplished by a prompt policy of placing necessary credits at the disposal of those engaged in finding foreign markets for our foodstuffs; by arresting and reversing the drastic deflation which had the seeming, under the former administration, of being aimed especially at the destruction of agriculture's prosperity; by recalling the War Finance Corporation from its state of suspended animation, giving it a credit of $1,000,000,000 in government funds, and recommissioning it to afford relief to the American farmer. The wisdom of this action has been demonstrated by results.

Four hundred million dollars have been loaned by this institution, three-fourths of it to the farming and livestock interests. At the same time the emergency tariff measure was passed, by which to secure the farmer's home market against the flood of competing articles from distant corners of the earth. During the war vast quantities of farm products had been dammed up in countries so distant that shortage of shipping made transportation to Europe impossible. With the seas again free, these sought, at whatever price could be obtained, the one market where there was real buying capacity and cash to pay—the great market of the United States. We took prompt measures to stop this movement; and the combination of effective protection, easier credits, and the operations of the War Finance Corporation quickly arrested the downward trend and started agriculture upon the upgrade once more.

It is only fair to pause a moment and emphasize the value of these measures of agricultural relief so promptly put forward by the Congress. The new tariff schedules saved for the American farmer a vitally important and gravely menaced home market. The resumption of the War Finance operations, backed by the resources of the only Government on earth that was able to summon such a credit, enabled the American farmer to compete for sales abroad.

Legislation in Behalf of the Farmer

Along with these measures, prompt steps were taken to put the Federal Farm Loan Board back into business. Like the War Finance Corporation, it had been in a state of suspended activity for want of money to loan. It was given a credit of $50,000,000 and resumed loaning on farm property.

A bill to facilitate cooperative marketing of farm products was passed. Legislation to prevent harmful gambling in agricultural futures was passed, held by the courts to be unconstitutional, and quickly repassed with the defects removed. The act for the control and regulation of the meat packers was enacted. Important reductions of freight rates on agricultural products were effected. Certain restrictions upon the operation of the joint-stock land banks, which had prevented them from doing their share in financing the farm, were removed. The loan limit of $10,000 which had formerly been imposed upon the Federal Land Banks was increased to $25,000, a change which is certain greatly to increase the practicable usefulness and range of operations of this system.

Important to Farmers

A measure of the utmost importance to farmers in those parts of the country where irrigation is the very basis of agricultural life is the act authorizing formation of irrigation districts, whereby the water-using settlers are brought together in associations to conduct their relations with the Federal Government. Formerly the settlers had to adjust all differences of this kind as individuals, at great expense and inconvenience to themselves. These water-users' organizations promise to become nuclei of highly useful cooperations in assembling, shipping, and selling the products of the irrigation districts. Further encouragement was extended to the irrigation farmers by amending the farm loan act to provide terms on which the land banks could make loans to farmers on the irrigation projects, whose conditions and necessities require special treatment.

Yet another provision in behalf of this same community is made by the new law which authorizes extending the time on payments due from irrigation farmers to the government. This measure has given a new chance to thousands of farmers in the irrigation areas who have fallen under the same misfortunes that have afflicted other farmers, and who had been unable temporarily to meet their commitments to the government.

If the recital of this long list of accomplishments in the farmer's behalf shall have seemed to suggest that Washington has been devoting itself with a special and perhaps partial assiduity to the agricultural interests, I shall reply that the farmer has received nothing more than was coming to him [applause]; nothing more than he needed; nothing more than was good for him, and nothing that was not also good for all of our national interests, bound up as they are in the nation-reaching mutuality of dependence and interdependence. I tell you frankly that I am proud to be able to come to you today and tell you of what has been done, because in doing it we have served not only the farmer but everybody else in this land. [Applause.]

But that is not all. I have reserved till the last what we may well appraise the crowning achievement of the entire list. I refer to the code of agricultural credit legislation known as the agricultural credit act of 1923, which became law in the closing days of the last Congress. It has not been possible yet to perfect machinery for administering this act, but I do not hesitate to express confidence that this scheme of agricultural credits, taken in connection with the other enactments I have described, furnishes the basis for the most enlightened, modern, sound, and efficient scheme of agricultural finance that has been set up in any country, and will enable the farmer in no distant future to free himself from obstacles which have made it difficult heretofore to conduct farm operations upon a sound, business-like basis.

Benefit of Agricultural Credits

Before describing this program of advancement in agricultural finance, permit me a word by way of bringing before our minds the background of the agricultural problem. Farming is the oldest of all industries. It has supported the community in peace, and has been the most essential line of industrial defense in war; commonly, too, the first victim of war. In olden times the conqueror distributed the subjugated lands to his favorites, and his prisoners as slaves to till it. Thus land ownership became the mark of favor and aristocracy. Later, the feudal régime substituted the somewhat less severe conditions of serfdom and villanage for those of slavery on the soil. Then came the modern institution of an agricultural peasantry, politically more free, but economically still held in fetters of old tradition.

Merchants and manufacturers, in the Middle Ages, devised banks to help them finance their ventures. Banking methods developed which served their purposes, but were not adapted to the farmer. The farmer's way of life made him an individualist. He could not organize the great cooperations which we call corporations. The banks did not furnish credit of the kind and on the terms he needed. The manufacturer and merchant, doing a large gross business in proportion to capital, having a short turnover period, wanted to borrow working capital for short periods. The farmer, with a long turnover period, wanted working capital on very different terms.

The Agricultural Credit Act

The bank of deposit and discount is easily the most completely cooperative institution that human society has devised. But it got started dealing primarily with industry and commerce, and the farmer never quite caught up with it. The railroad or industrial corporation raises plant capital by selling bonds; the farmer, by the essentially similar operation of selling a mortgage on his land. Both still require at times, to supplement this capital, by making less permanent loans with which to pay operating costs.

These loans the banks make out of the funds intrusted to them by great communities of depositors. In order to keep their resources as liquid as possible, against the possibility of heavy demands from depositors, banks have preferred to loan for short periods, commonly one, two, or three months. This precisely suited the commercial or industrial borrower; but it did not fit the farmer's case, because he requires a full year to produce most crops; two or three years, even, in case of livestock.

So, as the ordinary banking practice did not meet the farmer's needs, the idea arose of establishing intermediate credit institutions, which should advance money for longer periods than the merchant or manufacturer desired it, but yet not on the long-time basis of the farmer's mortgage or the corporation's bond. Various forms have been taken by these institutions in different countries and under different conditions; but I doubt if there has ever before been set up a system of intermediate farm credit so well adapted to serve the needs of the farmers in America.

This legislation designed to furnish necessary intermediate credit for production purposes, taken in connection with the Federal Farm Loan system, which provides long time mortgage credit, and with the new law making easy the organization and conduct of cooperative associations, and with the amended Federal warehouse act, provides what seems to be a complete, scientific and well-rounded, efficient and workable system of agricultural finance. Quite possibly experience may show the need of minor amendments here and there to the credit act, but the principle underlying it is sound and needed changes can readily be secured.

Under the agricultural credit act, which became law last March, two classes of corporations are authorized. First come the Federal Intermediate Credit Banks. They are 12 in number, just as there are 12 Federal Reserve Banks and 12 Federal Farm Loan Banks. Each Intermediate Credit Bank is to have $5,000,000 capital, subscribed by the Secretary of the Treasury in the name of the United States and paid for from the Treasury. There is to be one of these banks in connection with each Federal Farm Loan Bank, and they may be under the same or separate managements.

Operation of Intermediate Credit Banks

The Federal Intermediate Credit Banks are to make loans to banks, or to cooperative marketing associations of farmers, which associations are carefully provided for. The loans are to be made specifically for agricultural purposes.

Whenever the loans made from the original capital reach an aggregate justifying it, the Farm Loan Board, which supervises the system, may issue debenture bonds against the securities which the Intermediate Credit Banks have taken. The sale of these debentures will put the banks in funds once more for a new loaning campaign; and so, in the revolving-fund fashion which has been made familiar through the operations of the Farm Loan Board in real estate mortgages, the endless chain goes on and on, drawing in with each sale of debentures a new supply of capital for loaning to the farmers.

The Intermediate Credit Banks are fundamentally different from the Farm Loan Banks in that, while the Farm Loan Banks advance money only on real estate mortgage security, the Intermediate credit institutions are to discount farmers' notes taken by local banks and to loan on personal and chattel security—livestock, farm equipment, growing crops, and the like. The debentures sold by the Intermediate Credit Banks are tax-exempt precisely as are the debentures of the Farm Loan Banks.

The debentures will be sold to the public at a rate sufficiently below that charged the original borrower to insure that all expenses will be met by the margin of difference. These banks are authorized to make loans on these debentures to the amount of ten times their capital; that is, each bank may carry $50,000,000 of business, which places the total for the system of twelve banks at $600,000,000.

National Agricultural Credit Corporations

Under the same law, another and entirely distinct set of corporations are provided for, called National Agricultural Credit Corporations. These are to be set up, their capital furnished, and their management controlled by private capital and enterprise, under the general supervision of the Comptroller of the Currency. A National Agricultural Credit Corporation may be formed with capital not less than $250,000, and national banks are authorized on proper conditions to subscribe for stock in such corporations, in the aggregate not exceeding 10 per cent of their capital and surplus.

The National Agricultural Credit Corporation is authorized to make loans for agricultural purposes on chattels, livestock, growing crops, and personal credit up to a period of nine months; except that in the case of breeding stock and dairy herds the period may be extended to three years. They may issue debentures against the securities they have received, and these may be marketed up to whatever amount may be determined by the regulations prescribed by the comptroller.

To facilitate the marketing of the debentures issued by these corporations, a class of rediscount banks is provided. A credit corporation may subscribe, up to 20 per cent of its stock, to the capital of the rediscount bank. A minimum of $1,000,000 paid-up capital must be provided for a rediscount bank. The rediscount bank, on the responsibility of its own capitalization, will enter the general money market, float the debentures that have been turned over to it by the credit corporations, and thus provide them with new funds for further investments. It is simply another application of the revolving fund or endless credit chain idea which we found illustrated in the case of the Intermediate Credit Banks.

Every Possible Safeguard Established

The utmost care has been taken to surround these various institutions with every possible safeguard that can be afforded through skilled supervision, ample responsibility, and sound methods. It is the judgment of financial experts that their debentures will find just as ready an acceptance among investors as have those of the Federal Farm Loan Board.

There is thus created at last a complete farm credit system which, drawing together the aggregated responsibility of the greatest single industry in the land, backed by the security of the land, and of livestock, warehoused and growing crops, all kinds of agricultural equipment, and, finally, by the character and high responsibility of the men and women who constitute the great agricultural community, will be capable of furnishing the American farmers, for the first time in the history of agriculture in any country, adequate investment and working capital on terms as favorable as those accorded to commerce and industry anywhere in the world. [Applause.]

Many people have been inclined to be skeptical of benefits which might follow the enactment of legislation to give the farmer a better system of credit. They have said that the farmer needs better prices for his crops and livestock, rather than easier ways to borrow money. That is true, but these friends do not seem to understand that prices of crops and livestock are directly influenced by credit facilities.

In the past, farmers have been obliged to finance their productive enterprises by borrowing money for short terms. When times are good they have no difficulty in renewing such loans, but in periods of financial stress too many farmers have found themselves under the necessity of pushing their crops or their livestock on the market, not infrequently before the latter is fully fitted for market, in order to pay notes which they had expected to be able to renew, thus at times flooding the market and seriously depressing prices. Under a system of intermediate credit, administered with reference to the farmers' seasonal requirements, they should be able to market both their crops and livestock in a more orderly fashion, and this in itself will be a potent influence in keeping prices more stable and reasonable.

Agrees That Fair Prices Are Essential

I thoroughly agree that what is needed is fair prices; and I very well know that the farmer wants to get out of debt rather than to get further into debt; but it is my opinion that both these ends will be much more quickly accomplished through this new system of agricultural credits.

The legislation enacted by Congress does not by any means measure the attention Congress has given during the past two years to the needs of agriculture. People who have not been familiar with what has been going on in Congress can little appreciate the exhaustive study which the appropriate committees of Congress have given to our agricultural problems.

Day after day, and week after week, and month after month these committees have held hearings. They have considered every conceivable measure suggested for relief They have listened patiently to all who came to them. Congress enacted legislation which seemed to promise real help; but did not enact nearly all the measures which were suggested, because after the most exhaustive study they became convinced that such measures would not only be of no help but might aggravate an already bad situation.

Go back with me for just one glance, in conclusion, at the steps which have marked the rise of agriculture to this, its new estate. We need to go back but a very few generations to the time when the title to land represented no more than the whim of a despot or the shifting and uncertain fortunes of a military adventurer. The agricultural worker was a serf, a mere human chattel, bound to the soil on which he lived and to the service of the particular adventurer who at the moment, in the permutations of fortunes and of favor, chanced to hold the land.

In the view of his masters, he had no rights which could command respect, his political status was nil, and he was permitted the least possible share in the fruits of his toil on which he could keep together his soul—if indeed it were conceded that he had a soul—and his body, so as to perform the grueling toil of tasks that were regarded as utterly menial. All agricultural operations were crude, inefficient, barbaric. The great light with which science and organization and efficient methods have illumined the art of agriculture had not yet cast its first feeble rays over the desolate and dehumanized landscape of the rural countryside. The old-time picture is one to make women weep and men despair of their kind.

Period of Emancipation

But somehow the life of the open places, under a sky which inspired always the longing for a fair chance; somehow the daily touch with the mighty forces of mother nature in all her wondrous moods; somehow the dim realization that there was yet something beyond and above the squalor and misery of his immediate surroundings— somehow, through the centuries of his serfdom, these things kept the farmer mindful of possibilities for better times and friendlier fates; kept him longing for liberty; inspired him in the age-long struggle to lift himself up to a wider vision of life; moved him to eternal revolt against the fetters which bound; gave him courage for the seemingly hopeless conflict with destiny.

The centuries passed, and untold millions went to their graves despairing. But other millions followed, to seize the torch and bear it a little farther on the road. The slave became a villain, the villain a peasant; and yet the grim struggle went on, with political rights and economic emancipation as its twin goals. Painfully, doggedly, the men of the soil toiled under their dual burden of furnishing sustenance for humanity and keeping alight the flame of that consuming purpose to achieve freedom and human equality.

Dawn After Dark Hours

Down to times so near our own that they are but the yesterdays of history, the outcome of the struggle seemed in doubt. But mankind's darkest hour was followed by the dawn. The vast structure of artifice and selfishness which had been built and supported by the soil at length crumbled under its own weight of futility and corruption. The revolutionary movements of the eighteenth century, the reformations of the early nineteenth, the spread of knowledge, the rise of invention and growth of industrialism —all these combined to extort from tyranny the recognition of human rights. The man of the land had won his first battle; the battle for a place in the political system.

The economic struggle was longer and harder, because it had to be waged against preconceptions and prejudices which through the ages had driven their roots deep into the very fundamentals of human nature itself. It was not possible, all at once, to establish the conception that the tiller of the soil, ignored through centuries, must now be taken into full fellowship with the favored of the earth.

Sometimes I think it more interesting to recall the more modern processes of emancipation, because it will bring reminders to quell needless insurgency and suggest at least that moderate contentment which will tend to bless.

I can well recall the making of Kansas, and the nearby States of the Mississippi and Missouri Valleys. That was when farming was more a struggle for subsistence than a contest in industry. That was before the days of harvesting machinery like that which I saw this morning. That was when men swung the cradle with bended backs and toiled as the farmer does not have to toil today. That was back in covered-wagon days, when the men of Ohio, and bordering States, migrated westward. Too poor to come with family and possessions by rail, where rail travel was possible, they builded their wagons, loaded all their material possessions which the wagon would carry, crowned the cargo with the family, and drove westward under the glow of the Star of Empire. A few returned, but the great majority "dug in," battled with nature and her elements, and conquered.

In those grim days there were no motor cars, no electric lights. The cracky wagon, now forgotten in our lexicons, or the spring wagon, double seated, was the luxury of travel, and the kerosene lamp had recently put the tallow dip to shame. Ten dollars in cash in the family purse was an inordinate excess, and a hundred dollars cash balance for the year's trade was success extraordinary. Nowadays we expend more money for gasoline going to and from town in one week than was spent for kerosene to illumine the home for a whole year a generation or two ago. The farm emancipation in this country has been apace with other advancement, though there are inevitably periods of unbalanced price relationships, the reflexes of supply and demand, which have vexed and discouraged.

Relativity of Outlay to Income

There is no escaping the relativity of outlay to income. The sane practice is to make sure that the outlay is less than income, but it is somehow inherent in our lives that we pay more or less as we receive. I can recall when my annual offering to the church was one dollar, and it was considered ample. But it cost me more, and I gladly paid, when my annual earnings expanded. We live very much according to our incomes. It is proper that we should. The citizen who skimps and denies while the tide of good fortune is flooding is often acclaimed a miser and an undesirable citizen; in the slang of the day he is appraised as a "tightwad."

Tribute to the American Farmer

My point is that agricultural emancipation has brought its problems as well as liberation. The blue-sky stock salesmen can dissipate a farm surplus with ready facility, and extravagance on the farm is no less costly than in palatial city homes. I am sorry that simple rural life is too often giving away to modern extravagances. In the rise and fall of nations, in the peaceful conquest for human advancement, the simple-living peoples will make the long survival and record the notable triumphs.

It is good to contemplate the political, social, economic, and financial equality of the American farmer, good to confirm his title to all the instrumentalities and facilities which make for success in other activities, because he is the supreme contributor to human welfare. And he brings another invaluable asset to our Republic. He has been and must continue to be the anchorage of dependable public opinion when ephemeral whims are appealing and storms of passion play. The farmer, better than all other toilers in our community life, has learned that only the rewards of endeavor spur humanity on to larger achievement. He fully appraises property rights and the necessity of their preservation. In spite of his adversities, the farmer has never failed as the stalwart defender of the American heritage. In his fuller participation, the American farmer must continue to be the stabilizer of sentiment and the defender of our fundamentals upon which is builded the Republic which wrought his emancipation. [Applause.]

COMMUNITY COOPERATION NEEDED

Speech at Dodge City, Kan., June 23, 8:30 p. m.

Ladies and Gentlemen:

WE HAVE been riding across the wonderful State of Kansas, and a great many people have been telling us what is the largest city in Kansas. Now I know. [*Laughter.*] You have given us a splendid and a very happy surprise by coming out in such numbers to greet us. I can assure you it is a very great pleasure to see you.

I speak truly when I say that all concerned with the affairs of Government are always refreshed and newly inspired and more firmly committed to the public service when they come in contact with the great American people, and there is no place in the United States where the American people are seen to better advantage than in the State of Kansas. [*Applause.*] It will be disparaging to no one else if I say that you are very distinctly American, because those of us who come from sections further east know of the parent stock and the character of the men and the women who made this great State; and that same sturdy stock has created the Nation.

Welfare of All a Common Concern

I remember it used to be considered that Dodge City was about the "Jumping-off place" going west. I know you do not now so consider it, and I share your opinion. I recall reading with very great interest many of the romantic stories of the cattle days and the days when the buffalo roamed the prairies, when Dodge City was really away out on the frontier; but in the making of a productive country and applying the modern methods of present-day civilization, you have made your community similar to those we find in Ohio, Indiana, Pennsylvania, and other States. We have common habits, common aspirations, and a common devotion to flag and country, and that, indeed, makes us one people everywhere throughout the United States.

89

I like to come to you in an official capacity and say that we in Washington are just as much concerned in doing the things that will make for your good fortune as we are in doing those things which will benefit any other section of the country. No matter what is sometimes said by the politicians, the government is deeply interested in every section of America. We know we cannot have a fortunate, happy country, unless all the people are prosperous and contented. We can never build up one community at the expense of the impoverishment of another; we must always be thinking of the welfare of all the American people. Sometimes it is difficult to maintain such conditions as will enable all to prosper precisely alike, but the government undertakes to bring about adjustments, so that all, as nearly as possible, may share alike in progress, in material wealth, and spiritual advancement.

Wants America "Best Land"

I know you of Dodge City are doing your part, and as your President I want your help. I am not here campaigning; I merely want you to help those of us who are in authority to make America the best land in the world in which to live—an America that is confident of herself at home, an America that is unafraid to play the part of a great, progressive nation in her relationships with the other nations of the world.

I happen to know you are a railroad city. I was talking about railroads in Kansas City last night and I shall be gratified if you will take occasion to read what I then said. We cannot have a fortunate country unless we have railroad good fortune; we cannot have a fortunate country unless we have agricultural prosperity; we cannot have a condition of complete national well-being unless there is good fortune among the great mass of American working men who live by daily wage. We have come to a time when conditions among men have advanced greatly over any which have prevailed heretofore. The war gave mankind a new emancipation. The wage earner receives a higher compensation and he aspires to more than ever

90

before, as he has a right to aspire to more. We are adjusting ourselves to the new conditions. I think we are doing extremely well in the United States; I know we are doing better than any other people in the world.

I wish you a continuance of happiness and good fortune, and, with all my heart, for Mrs. Harding and myself, thank you for the cordiality and the cheer you have shown in your greeting tonight. [Applause.]

URGES FRATERNITY AMONG NATIONS

Address at Colorado Springs, Col.,
Sunday, June 24, 6:55 a. m.

Ladies and Gentlemen:

IT IS very good of you to come out and greet us this morning. I am very frank to confess to you that ordinarily we are not ready to receive visitors at 7 o'clock in the morning, but when someone telegraphed Mr. Christian that you wanted to extend greetings at Colorado Springs and that you would come down at this hour to do so, I said that "people who are so hospitable as that cannot very well be denied."

I am glad to stand before you this Sabbath morning. I wish I could preach you a sermon, for it is in my heart to do it. I tell you, my countrymen, the world needs more of the Christ; the world needs the spirit of the Man of Nazareth. If we could bring into the relationships of humanity, among ourselves and among the nations of the earth, the brotherhood that was taught by Christ, we would have a restored world; we would have little or none of war, and we would have a new hope for humanity throughout the globe. There never was a greater lesson taught than that of the Golden Rule. If we could have that one faithfully observed, I would almost be willing to wipe out the remainder of the commandments. [Applause.]

91

I should like to say further that if we are going to make of this America of ours all that the fathers sought, if we are going to keep true to the institutions which they builded, we must continue to maintain religious liberty quite as well as civil and human liberty. [Applause.] As you remember, we builded on the foundation of civil liberty, and we capped that with the stone of human liberty, and the third fundamental was religious liberty. We can never afford to deny religious freedom in this Republic of ours.

Urges Religious Devotion

One more thought: I should like to have America a little more earnest and thoroughly committed in its religious devotion. We were more religious a hundred years ago, or even fifty years ago, than we are today. We have been getting too far away from the spiritual and too much absorbed in our material existence. It tends to make us a sordid people. The World War lifted us out of the rut. We in America found ourselves consecrated to the defense of the Republic and fighting for our ideal of civilization, and we were put on a higher plane. But when the war was ended, we started to drift back, thinking only of our selfish pusuits.

I tell you, my countrymen, that we can never be the ideal Republic unless we pursue great ideals and know something of the spiritual as well as of the material life. That is one of the reasons I have been so zealous in the last few weeks in trying to have our country committed to something more of international helpfulness, so that it may be ready to play its part in the uplift of the world and in the movement to prevent in the future conflict among the nations. I think that is an ideal worth pursuing. [Applause.] So long as we have something of that kind to think about and to strive for and to inspire us to go on, I know we are going to be a better people than when we occupy ourselves merely in digging, digging, digging for the dollar. There is, my countrymen, something else in life than that to think about. I do not under-appraise the desirability of material good fortune. You must be able to subsist before you can begin to aspire; I should like material good fortune to be the portion of every man and woman in America; but I do not choose material good fortune alone.

Deplores Suspicion and Hate

One of the troubles with the world today is that it is torn with suspicion and hate. Europe is in a condition of feverish restlessness and is feeling the effects of the poison engendered by old-time passions, envies and rivalries, so that one people will not trust another. Would it not be better if somehow we could bring into the lives of those nations the spirit of Him whom the Father gave to the salvation of men, and exerted ourselves to spread brotherhood and new trust and new confidence among peoples, so that they might live in that fraternity which tends to solidify and cement together mankind? I should like more of fraternity amongst ourselves in the United States; I should like more of fraternity amongst the nations of the world, and if we could apply the Golden Rule, about which none of you will dispute, for we all believe in it and admire it—the only trouble is we do not practice it as we believe it—if we could bring the Golden Rule into every phase of American life, we would be the happiest people in the world. There would be no injustice to complain of; there would be no hate and no rivalry; there would be no industrial conflicts; but human beings would live among their fellows as they would like to be lived with. That would bring a state of blessedness to humankind.

It is fine to greet you this morning. I have not so much attempted to preach as I have tried to give you a thought which, if carried out, will, somehow I think, improve our relationships among ourselves and improve relationships throughout the world. It is good to come out and breathe the atmosphere of the mountains in your wondrous State, and it is a heartening thing to see your confident look and to realize that you are equipped and prepared to do your part in any emergency which may ever confront us. [Applause.]

PLEDGES GOVERNMENT AID TO SERVICE MEN

Speech at the United States Army Hospital, Denver, Col., Sunday, June 24, 4 p. m.

Ladies and Gentlemen, and Patients in the Hospital in Particular:

I ALWAYS welcome an opportunity to say a word of greeting on such an occasion as this. I do not think you have ever quite understood how deeply and genuinely interested the government is in the work of the hospitals which are under its care and sponsorship. Nobody can ever know all the burdens which attend the obligations of war readjustment. There come to the President all the grievances of those who think they are not becomingly treated; there come the grievances of those who think that the government is too lavish and too generous and non-efficient. There come appeals from members of families who think that their sons or husbands who have been impaired in the Federal service are badly neglected. There comes to the President a reflex of every phase of the tremendous responsibilities that follow war, and if the experience did not do anything else for me, I am very sure that I would be impelled to consecrate all my influence and all my endeavor to the end that there may never be another war in which the United States shall be involved. [Applause.] I do not think I can convey to you just what I feel; there is so much sorrow and discouragement about it all; but the government is much more sympathetic than you think, because, after all, its agents are human beings.

There are many abuses incident to the national defense. We find our hearts stirred by patriotic devotion and concern for the country, and seemingly all of us give everything we have, even life itself, to the defense of the flag and the nation; and yet some are frequently standing aside and taking advantage of the situation for their own benefit.

94

It has made me conclude that if ever there is another war and I have anything to say about it, we are going to do more in this country than merely draft the boys; we are going to draft every dollar and every resource and every activity for the national defense.

Of Interest for the Service Men

I cannot speak to you intimately about the hospitals; I only know of them from the Washington end; but I know that the head of the Veterans Bureau is a very efficient, a very sympathetic and a very zealous public official, and I know that he is surrounded by very capable advisers and assistants. I know further that the Congress which provides the money and the administrative branch of the government which sees to the expenditure of the public funds are both anxious to do everything possible for the comfort, the happiness, the rehabilitation, and the restoration of the service men of this country who were impaired by their participation in the war.

There is one thing I think you boys ought to help us to do. I speak but the truth when I say that there is none who would stint for one moment or hold back or refuse any number of dollars properly to care for the men who were really incapacitated in any degree by their war service. The government wishes to give to them every care, every consideration, and every advantage that can be given from the bounty of a great, rich Nation; but, on the other hand, you boys ought to save your government from the expense involved on account of those who take advantage of the government's generosity to live useless and selfish lives of ease. There are such, and no one need be surprised at it. It has been my fortune to live during the development and the regrettable passing of the great Grand Army of the Republic, which embraced the finest manhood of America from the 60's down to the present day. They had amongst their members those who sought to profit by the government's bounty and generosity, just as any group will have. When recently we called 5,000,000 men into the service of the Nation, they were made up of the average young American manhood, and, on the whole, they constituted a mighty fine representation of American manhood; but there were among them some who were ready to impose on the government. I know that to be the case, and I say so frankly to you; but we do not propose that that shall deter us in our effort to do, not the handsome thing, not the gracious thing, not the generous thing, but what we owe to the service men of the Republic.

Pledges Every Aid to Defenders of the Flag

I can feel, though, perhaps, I cannot adequately express, the attitude of the people of this country toward those who went forth to the World War. I know that it is one of reverence, one of gratitude; it is one of good wishes; it is one of deep and affectionate concern for the service men of this country.

I think we are doing measurably well. Like all the great problems incident to the war, the problem of the ex-service man was so deep and almost so incomprehensible to the average man and involved so much of activity and expense, that there was no one in all America who appraised it correctly. We have not as yet completed settling the contracts for war activities; we have not even approximated the adjustment of accounts and the disposition of surplus property. You would think, if you sat in Washington and were connected with the government, that the war activities were going to run on and on forever. The war brought adversity to thousands who were employed at home; it brought disaster to manufacturing industries; it brought an end to commercial enterprise; it caused an upheaval in our civic, social industrial and commercial affairs.

When you feel impatient because of the government's failure to do all that you think ought to be done, I beg to remind you that your case is only an example of human inability to grasp all the problems incident to the tremendous upheaval of the world. I say to you frankly I think we have done better in the United States than has been done anywhere else in the world. I do not know that we are remiss,—but if we are remiss today in performing properly the obligations which the nation owes to you of the service, I can pledge you one thing in the best faith in the world: We are going to keep everlastingly at it until we do the right thing in expressing to you in a practical way the gratitude and the reverent regard of the United States of America for your service to the flag. [Applause.]

LAW ENFORCEMENT DUTY OF NATION; NEITHER
PARTY *LIKELY* EVER TO URGE *REPEAL* OF
THE EIGHTEENTH AMENDMENT

Address on Law Enforcement, The Auditorium, Denver, Col.,
Monday, June 25, 12 o'clock, noon

*Governor Sweet, Mr. Mayor, Senator Phipps, My Coun-
trymen All:*

WHILE one delights in words of welcome such as we
have heard from the platform today, I may say
that they were somewhat superfluous, because the
people of Denver, with their smiling faces and kindly greetings, have expressed a welcome that no human being can
put into words. I like to come to Denver, and I believe
I may be, perhaps, a little more popular than heretofore
for I remember the last time I was here you only gave me
half of the hall [Laughter]; but you were none the less
cordial. It is a joy to breathe the atmosphere of your
wonderful city and State. I am not going to enter into
a debate with the mayor about the size of either; but
Colorado was certainly a fit State to mark the one hun-
dredth anniversary of the formation of the American Union.
Somehow I think you have been especially favored. Perhaps
it is the sparkling atmosphere, the glorious sunshine, and
the tremendously inspiring stretches which give that impression. I could not help but feel yesterday that, in some
manner, nature especially designed to boost you, because
here at the very ridge of the continent she erected her
mountains as a monument to God, a monument which no
human hand could erect, perhaps to intensify the reverence
of a religious people and increase their devotion to the
great Creator.

I wish I could have the prayer of Dean Brown in the hands of every citizen of this Republic. I wonder if the audience noted the prayer as carefully as I did. The Denver newspaper boys should see to it that it is printed in "box" so that every citizen may preserve it. [Applause.] Very often the clergy say things that might well become the most eminent statesmen of the Republic. The dean suggested for you and for me what ought to be the aspiration of every American and what ought to be in the hearts of all the people of this Republic.

There is much I should like to discuss before you today. The governor has suggested a theme to which I shall make reference before I have finished. I might speak of many questions which I fancy would be of concern to Colorado. I have been a witness to the changing interests of your State. In the East we knew of Colorado at first only as a great mining State with incalculable riches. Then we saw her developing in agriculture, and we finally learned of her aspirations in manufacturing and industrial lines, until we have now come to know the State as a very cosmopolitan western community. Therefore you are naturally deeply concerned in the various phases of governmental activity which have their influence upon the life of the Republic.

Checked Government Extravagance

I think we have been doing pretty well in America toward getting back on the right track once more. This Republic suffered with the world from the tremendous upheaval that attended the Great War. We saw the inflation of enterprises of all kinds; we saw the feverish activity of many industries; we saw take place an expansion that was beyond human appraisal; we saw the draft summon the manhood of the country, and we experienced the losses, the sufferings, and the hardships of the war. Yet from that great tumult I believe we have emerged in better condition than any other nation involved in the war, and in the resolution of America to "carry on" we are finding ourselves and gradually going forward.

I am glad to tell you that we have put an end to the extravagance which threatened the ruination of the Republic; we have called a halt to excessive expenditures which would in time have bankrupted any people on the face of the globe. We have reached a point where the National government is living within its income. [Applause.] In that respect we have brought a wholesome lesson to Denver and to the State of Colorado. [Applause.] I am going to refer to this subject in a more formal manner tomorrow, but you have been so kind I do not mind telling you about it in advance. We have so managed the business of government that we have reduced Federal expenditures, which consumed 70 per cent of all the taxes collected at the height of the war outlay, down to 40 per cent, while local and State taxing authorities, though the war has long since ended, have increased their proportion of all taxes collected from 40 per cent to 60 per cent. I say to you, my countrymen, a Republic cannot live under excessive taxation. [Applause.]

Seeking to Aid Business

There is another phase of the taxation problem which may not be lacking in interest to you of Colorado. I hope what I am about to say will not be considered as having an offensive political tinge; but, perhaps, you have not stopped to think that before the World War none of you, probably, knew that you paid a Federal tax. The Federal revenue was collected indirectly at the ports of entry and by internal taxes which did not directly affect the individual. A sufficient sum was raised in this way to carry on the operations of the Federal government, and you hardly knew that you paid a penny, except when you bought a postage stamp. Now the government is collecting in one way or another $3,000,000,000 annually.

That will serve to remind us that we ought to have appreciated the good old times when the Republican protective tariff policy filled the treasury and at the same time gave that protection to American industry which stimulated the development which has made our record a matchless one in the story of the world. [Applause.]

I do not know that I should have mentioned the Republican protective policy, though my statement, I believe, is historically correct. I may add that I have come to learn there are many protectionists in the West who do not adhere to the Republican party; and it is well that this is so, because in this great Republic of ours, the best able to buy of any nation in the world, I believe we ought to maintain a policy that will give the home market first of all to the producers within our own borders. However, that is rather aside from what I had in mind. I wanted to bring you the suggestion that, in a most conscientious manner, your government is seeking to aid business in the adjustments which necessarily have to follow the war. We are seeking to help the varied forms of industry from the depression and disaster which attended deflation.

We are succeeding in bringing down to the lowest possible limit the expenditures of the government until conditions in that respect are approximately normal once more. We are also trying to bring about a measure of cooperation between the citizenship and the government which will enable the United States of America to work in confidence that not only today but on the morrow and the day after we shall be pursuing the normal course of a progressive, fortunate people. I repeat that I believe we are better off today than any other nation in the world. I am only sorry that other nations cannot share our good fortune. We have sought to show them the way, to encourage them to take cognizance of the new order which has followed the war, and then resolutely to set to work, as humanity always must do, to recover from a great misfortune. I want America to go on, and I want your help in order to make sure that America shall go on. [Applause.]

The Multiplicity of Laws

It has been said that "of the making of books there is no end." Quite as truthfully it might be paraphrased, "of the making of laws there is no end." We Americans undoubtedly hold all records for the making of a multiplicity of laws, State and National. If we were as assiduous about obeying and enforcing obedience to them as we are in demanding and enacting them, there would be no particular occasion for me to address you today on the general subject of law enforcement. We all recognize that effective administration of the laws and the establishment in the public mind of an attitude of willing acceptance and obedience to law, are the most impressive mark of a civilized community.

Laws, of course, represent restrictions upon individual liberty, and in these very restrictions make liberty more secure. The individual surrenders something of his privilege to do as he pleases for the common good, and so organized society is possible. It is successful just about in proportion as laws are wise, as they represent deliberate and intelligent public opinion, and as they are obeyed. Civilization had to travel a long way before it came to be commonly accepted that even an unwise law ought to be enforced in orderly fashion, because such enforcement would insure its repeal or modification, also in orderly fashion, if that were found desirable.

At this point it is worth while to raise a voice in protest against the vast volume of half-baked criticism that is constantly aimed against Americans on the ground, as is alleged that they are an undisciplined and rather lawless community. The criticism, of course, arises out of the fact that during the period of a very short national life, during which the currents of human affairs and interests have moved more rapidly than in any other period of history, we have been under the necessity to establish institutions, laws, modes of administration, which would meet not only the requirements of a new community established in a new world, but would permit adaptation to rapidly changing conditions. It comes also of the very erroneous impression of many nationals that our liberty is a license, instead of guaranteed freedom under the law.

Our Problems Those of a New Country

Older countries have had the privilege of developing laws and institutions slowly, gradually, painstakingly, through multiplied centuries in which change was commonly extremely slow. America had to build on the foundation of long-established European models not always adaptable to our requirements, and therefore necessitating many experiments in modification and readaptation. Moreover, we started our experiment just at the time when the old medieval order was being changed at high speed by the processes of the industrial and social revolution which marked emergence from the later Middle Ages into the onrushing era of modern industrialism, modern science, and modern democratic procedures in government.

Accomplishment Without Parallel

The founders of our country were compelled to establish institutions here, at a time when their whole inheritance of intellectual, moral, political, and industrial traditions was being wrenched by the most amazing revolution that human society has known. In the circumstances, their achievement in laying the foundation, and our later one in building our present superstructure upon it, represent an accomplishment, I believe, without parallel. Thus viewed, I think we will find complete justification for satisfaction in our progress thus far, and confidence in an assured future.

Our problems are the problems of a relatively new country, and of a new form of political. organization, in a time of social flux. We shall not succeed if we attempt to solve them all at once; but no more shall we succeed if we assume to ignore their existence, to shut our eyes to the fact that they are before us. The very basis of our political establishment is the idea of a dual sovereignty, of the States and the Nation; the idea of concurrent authority and concurrent responsibility. That is so elemental in our system that to do away with it would amount to demolishing our whole scheme of government.

Certain functions and responsibilities have been imposed upon the National government, while others have been reserved to the States. Between these two authorities there will always be unavoidably something like a twilight zone. Personally, I have never liked that phrase. I have regarded it as a peculiarly unfortunate and misleading description. The intermediate zone which receives light from two sovereign luminaries ought to be the best, not the worst, illumined region. I believe it can be made exactly that if we will but realize the necessity for real cooperation between National and State authority, if we will only develop effective means for the exercise therein of concurrent jurisdiction.

Problem of Concurrent Jurisdiction

The problem of concurrent jurisdiction is not a new one brought to us with the eighteenth amendment. It is as old as the Federal government. It has required to be dealt with by Congress and legislatures, by executives and by courts, in a multitude of relations to commerce, finance, transportation, and indeed the whole realm of concerns in our complex society. It has demanded our attention in all the multitude of issues ranging from the regulation of trusts and transportation, and even of certain relations with foreign governments, to the proposal for a uniform statute of marriage and divorce.

There have always been those who insisted that particular policies could not be carried out because of the conflict of jurisdictions; but experience has proved that, whenever a given issue became so acute that evasion was impossible, procedures have been devised for dealing with it. Whoever will go back to the debates over the enactment of the anti-trust law, or the discussions of the interstate commerce measures, must recognize that these were but varying phases of the same general question that comes before us in connection with the enforcement of the prohibition law.

A great deal of useful accomplishment toward uniformity and clarification of State and National laws has been effected through the efforts of the American Bar Association. This, of course, has been an unofficial effort—a labor of love and patriotism—conducted by men especially qualified for its direction. It has seemed possible that something rather more formal and official might be evolved from these beginnings, which should help in perfecting the coordination. President Roosevelt recognized this possibility when he called a council of governors to consider problems then demanding harmonious and uniform treatment. Under the present administration a similar course has been adopted in bringing together the State executives for consideration of methods to give full force and effect to the concurrent authority of States and Nation under the eighteenth amendment.

We have proceeded upon the same general principle in fixing a program for the utilization of the waters of the Colorado River. Indeed I have thought such conferences contained the germ of an idea which may some day grow into a useful auxiliary to our constitutional system—a formal council of coordination, representing State and National governments, authorized to examine into particular needs in this area, to devise projects in coordinated action, and to propose them formally to the Congress and the legislatures. Without possessing any powers of legislation or of mandatory initiation, such a body might render an advisory service which, if made permanent and continuing, would conceivably be of great advantage.

Eighteenth Amendment Will Stand

But, for the present, there are immediate problems before us which can not await the possible creation of any such slow moving mechanism of philosophic consideration. The prohibition amendment to the Constitution is the basic law of the land. [Applause.] The Volstead Act, providing a code of enforcement, has been passed. I am convinced that they are a small, and a greatly mistaken, minority who believe the eighteenth amendment will ever be repealed. [Applause.] Details of enforcement policy doubtless will be changed as experience dictates. Further, I am convinced that whatever changes may be made will represent the sincere purpose of effective enforcement, rather than moderation of the general policy. [Applause.] It will be the part of wisdom to recognize the facts as they stand.

The general policy of the States to support the prohibition program, and to cooperate with the Federal government regarding it, is attested by the fact that almost unanimously the States have passed enforcement laws of their own. A difficulty, however, arises at this point. Considerable testimony comes to Washington that some States are disposed to abdicate their own police authority in this matter, and to turn over the burden of prohibition enforcement to the Federal authorities. It is a singular fact that some States which successfully enforced their own prohibition statutes before the eighteenth amendment was adopted have latterly gone backwards in this regard.

Communities in which the policy was frankly accepted as productive of highly beneficial results, and in which there was no widespread protest so long as it was merely a State concern, report that since the Federal government became in part responsible there has been a growing laxity on the part of State authorities about enforcing the law. Doubtless this is largely due to a misconceived notion, too widely entertained, that the Federal government has actually taken over the real responsibility. The fact is quite the contrary. The Federal government is not equipped with the instrumentalities to make enforcement locally effective. It does not maintain either a police or a judicial establishment adequate to or designed for such a task. If the burden of enforcement shall continue to be increasingly thrown upon the Federal government, it will be necessary, at large expense, to create a Federal police authority which in time will inevitably come to be regarded as an intrusion upon and interference with the right of local authority to manage local concerns. The possibilities of disaster in such a situation hardly need to be suggested. Yet it is something that we must recognize as among the menaces in this situation.

Law of Land Not to Be Byword

The Federal government ought to perform, in connection with the enforcement of this policy, those functions which are obviously within its proper province, such as compliance with the law in all its aspects as it relates to international commerce, the importation and exportation of liquors, the collection of Federal revenue, the prevention of smuggling, and in general the enforcement of the law within the proper realm of Federal authority. But the business of local enforcement, by States and cities, ought to be in the hands of the State and local authorities, and it should be executed in all sincerity and good faith, as other laws are presumed to be executed. [Applause.]

Determined to Do Full Duty

What I am saying must not be construed as indicating any relaxation of the National government's purpose to do its full duty in this matter. I have no doubt that if the burden is cast, in indue proportion, upon the national authority the Federal government will, not only under this administration but under whatever others may come in the future, assume and discharge the full obligation. [Applause.] But I am pointing out that this ought not to be made necessary. The National policy ought to be supported by the public opinion and the administrative machinery of the whole country. For myself, I am confident that we are passing now through the most difficult stage of this matter, and that as time passes there will be a more and more willing acceptance by authorities everywhere of the unalterable obligation of law enforcement. The country and the Nation will not permit the law of the land to be made a byword. [Applause.]

This issue is fast coming to be recognized, not as one between wets and drys, not as a question between those who believe in prohibition and those who do not, not as a contention between those who want to drink and those who do not—it is fast being raised above all that—but as one involving the great question whether the laws of this country can be and will be enforced. So far as the Federal government is concerned, and, I am very sure, also so far as concerns the very great majority of the State governments and the local governments, it will be enforced. [Applause.] A gratifying, indeed it may fairly be said an amazing, progress has been made in the last few years toward better enforcement.

It is a curious illustration of loose thinking, that some people have proposed, as a means to protecting the fullest rights of the States, that the States should abandon their part in enforcing the prohibitory policy. That means simply an invitation to the Federal government to exercise powers which should be exercised by the States. Instead of being an assertion of State rights, it is an abandonment of them; it is an abdication; it amounts to a confession by the State that it does not choose to govern itself, but prefers to turn the task, or a considerable part of it, over to the Federal authority. There could be no more complete negation of State rights. [Applause.]

Obligation of the States

The National government has been uniformly considerate of the sensibilities of the States about their rights and authorities. But when a State deliberately refuses to exercise the powers which the Constitution expressly confers on it, it obviously commits itself to a policy of nullifying State authority, the end of which we are reluctant to conjecture.

The policy of nullification has never appealed strongly to the American people. There are some historical records regarding efforts of States to nullify national policies; but the spectacle of a State nullifying its own authority, and asking the national sovereignty to take over an important part of its powers, is new. When the implications of this strange proposal are fully understood by people and parties devoted to preserving the rights of the States, the new nullificationists, I venture to say, will discover that they have perpetrated what is likely to prove one of the historic blunders in political management. [Applause.]

I am making my appeal in this matter to the broadest and best sentiments of law-abiding Americans everywhere. We must recognize that there are some people on both sides of this question in whose minds it is absolutely paramount. Some would be willing to sacrifice every other consideration of policy in order to have their own way as to this one. This constitutes one of the most demoralizing factors in the situation.

It was very generally believed that the adoption of the constitutional amendment would take the question out

108

of our politics. Thus far it has not done so, though I venture to predict that neither of the great parties will see the time, within the lives of any who are now voting citizens, when it will declare openly for the repeal of the eighteenth amendment. [Applause.] But, despite all that, the question is kept in politics because of the almost fanatical urgency of the minority of extremists on both sides. Unless, through the recognition and acceptance of the situation in its true light, through the effective enforcement of the law by all the constituted authorities, and with the acquiescence of the clearly dominant public opinion of the country, the question is definitely removed from the domain of political action, it will continue a demoralizing element in our whole public life. It will be a permanent bar to the wise determination of many issues utterly unrelated to the liquor question. It will be the means of encouraging disrespect for many laws. It will bring disrepute upon our community, and be pointed to as justifying the charge that we are a Nation of hypocrites. There can be no issue in this land paramount to that of enforcement of the law. [Applause.]

Universal and Partial Prohibition

It is easy to understand the conditions out of which much unrest has developed, but it is not easy to comprehend so much of complacency amid a developing peril. I want to give warning against that peril.

Many citizens, not teetotalers in their habits, lawfully acquired, because of financial ability to do so, stored up private stocks in anticipation of prohibition, pending the ratification of the amendment and the enactment of the regulatory law. Many others have had no scruple in seeking supplies from those who vend in defiance of the law. The latter practice is rather too costly to be indulged by the masses; so there are literally millions of Americans who resent the lawful possessions of the few, the lawless practices of a few more, and rebel against the denial to the vast majority. Universal prohibition in the United States would occasion far less discontent than partial prohibition and partial indulgence.

109

It is the partial indulgence which challenges the majesty of law, but the greater crime is the impairment of the moral fiber of the Republic. The resentful millions have the example of law defiance by those who can afford to buy, and are reckless enough to take the risk, and there is inculcated a contempt for law which may some day find expression in far more serious form.

Call for An Awakened Conscience

I do not see how any citizen who cherishes the protection of law in organized society may feel himself secure when he himself is the example of contempt for law. [Applause.] Clearly there is call for awakened conscience and awakened realization of true self-interest on the part of the few who will themselves suffer most when reverence for law is forgotten and passion is expressed in destructive lawlessness. Ours must be a law-abiding Republic, and reverence and obedience must spring from the influential and the leaders among men, as well as obedience from the humbler citizen, else the temple will collapse. [Applause.]

Whatever satisfaction there may be in indulgence, whatever objection there is to the so-called invasion of personal liberty, neither counts when the supremacy of law and the stability of our institutions are menaced. With all good intention the majority sentiment of the United States has sought by law to remove strong drink as a curse upon the American citizen, but ours is a larger problem now to remove lawless drinking as a menace to the Republic itself.

Law of the Golden Rule

There is another phase of law-observance to which reference is impelling. I am thinking of the law of the Golden Rule, a statute from the Man of Nazareth, who brought new peace and new hope to mankind, and proclaimed service to men the highest tribute to God. [Applause.]

Service is both the inspiration and the accomplishment of quite everything worth while which impels us onward and upward. With service which the Nazarene would approve are associated all our ideals and our finer aspirations. We accept the doctrine for ourselves, as we ought,

110

because we must be firmly established and healthfully and hopefully strong ourselves before we can be effectively helpful to others.

But I believe the law of service demands our larger helpfulness to the world. No, I do not mean entanglement in Old World policies or sponsorship for the adjustment of Old World controversies. I do mean the commitment of this Nation to the promotion and preservation of international peace [applause], to the judicial settlement of disputes which, unless settled, lead to added irritation, strained relations, and ultimately to war.

I would like the United States to give of her prestige, her influence, and her power to make the International Court of Justice an outstanding and universally accepted agency of judicial determination of justiciable questions and the peaceful way to international settlements. [Applause.] It is too much to say that such a court will give a guaranty against war, but it will prove the longest step toward war prevention and maintained peace since the world began. And we of America do want to prevent war. [Applause.]

Eagerness to Aid Humankind

In such a thought is concern for our own country no less than anxiety for a world which is finding readjustment difficult. I am thinking of more than our own freedom from conflict, with all its attending burdens and sorrows. I am thinking of our America having a commitment to an exalting enterprise to save us from the reaction to mere sordid existence, and to keep our hearts aglow while we serve as a vanguard in the march of civilization.

The World War was a frightful calamity, from which the earth will not have fully recovered in a century to come. Nearly five years have passed and peace is not yet secure. Our own cost was beyond an understandable appraisal, but I sometimes feel the war was worth much of its cost, because it brought an American awakening and revealed the soul of the Republic. We experienced the supreme commitment. We saw our America ready to do or die for our concept of civilization and its guaranties. [Applause.] It exalted us and made us a better, a more patriotically devoted people. I would like to go on, with soul aflame in eagerness to aid humankind, while promoting security for ourselves.

This is no under appraisal of the essentials of material existence. We may rejoice in the flood tides of material good fortune; we may becomingly boast the measureless resources of the Republic, through God's bounty in creation and man's genius in development, but we are not living the becoming life unless we are seeking to advance humankind as we achieve for ourselves. I would like the ages of envy and hate, and conquest and pillage, and armed greed and mad ambitions to be followed by understanding and peace, by the rule of law where force had reigned, by the decisions of a world court rather than the decrees of national armies, by the observance of the Golden Rule as the law of human righteousness, so that the wail of human suffering and sorrow might be lost in the glad rejoicings of the onward procession of mankind. If we observe the law of service, if we heed our finer impulses, if we keep alive the soul which we revealed in our national defense, we will add to security for ourselves, and give of our strength to this ideal world advancement. [Applause.]

CONCERN FOR THE "LITTLE FELLOW"

Speech at Greeley, Col., Monday, June 25, 2:45 p. m.

My Countrymen All:

ONE could hardly wish for a more cordial and a more gracious welcome than you have given us today. It is wholly unexpected and it makes me love all the more the memory of the great American for whom your community was named. He must have been right when he told the boys to "go west and grow up with the country."

112

I am glad to pay tribute to your community for another reason. I understand it is noted for its efforts directed to the betterment of education, notably in the training of teachers. We never took a more important step in America than when we made teaching a life profession. I remember when I was a young man every ambitious country boy and girl taught school as a mere makeshift, in order to get a little money with which to do something else. Teaching in those days was not a profession. I have heard my mother tell of teaching school when her extreme compensation was $20 a month. She was required to board herself, and it took more than a month's earnings on her part to buy a calico dress. That was the practice of the times; but nowadays teaching has become one of the greatly honored American professions, and as we have honored the profession we have made progress in education. I like to say—for it is no unseemly boast—that ours is the best common school system in the world. I know that statement is sometimes disputed; but it was my good fortune only a few years ago to encounter a commission from what was then considered to be the most efficient educational nation of Europe. That commission, however, had come to study the common school system of the United States of America.

Discusses Sugar Situation

We are making some progress at Washington toward giving fuller and more helpful recognition to education on the part of the Federal government, and we are going to have, some of these days, a Department of Education and Welfare. [Applause.] I hope that realization will come before the next Congress closes its long term. I do not want you to misunderstand me; I do not favor the Federal government taking upon itself that responsibility for education which belongs to every community in the United States, because whenever a community loses interest in and concern for its educational activities there is little to hope for in this Republic of ours.

Now let me turn your attention for a moment to another thought. I have not come to talk politics to you,

113

but, as you know, there has been considerable discussion recently as to the high cost of sugar, and a good many people have found fault with the President because he did not exercise the authority recently conferred upon him by Congress to raise or lower tariff duties to meet existing conditions. I at once caused an inquiry to be made into the sugar situation, and I became persuaded that a modification of the sugar tariffs, so far as the President had authority, would have little to do with a decrease of price to the American consumer, but might destroy the American sugar industry itself, to which the American consumer must look for stabilized prices in the future. I believe with all my heart in ample protection to the American sugar industry, because, in my opinion, American self-reliance in the production of sugar will make us free from the greed of the great sugar-producing countries of the world.

Sugar Industry in Colorado

I am proud of the great development of the sugar industry in the State of Colorado. I need not tell you, my countrymen, that the government is always concerned with the good fortune of all the people of the United States. It is not concerned merely with the good fortune of the corporate interests; it is not concerned alone with the good fortune of the captain of industry; your government is not alone concerned with the welfare of agriculture; it has at heart a deep and abiding concern for the little fellow, the one who makes up the great rank and file of American productive activity. We want him to prosper, because, unless he does, genuine good fortune cannot abide throughout the United States.

Now may I be just a little bit personal, nay, fraternal? I am glad to greet the brethren who wear the fez. We saw a lot of them in Washington recently, and it did us much good, because those who came brought to us the example of American fraternity, that fraternity which gives consideration to a brother as you would like it for yourself; and when you teach the lesson of fraternity you call upon America to play her part as a frater in the relationships of the world. I preach the gospel of individual and personal fraternity, the gospel of State fraternity, the gospel of fraternity among nations, so that we can each be helpful to the other and by our common effort do something to uplift and forward human progress throughout the world.

I am glad to greet you. It is fine of you to come to see us, and I wish for you the best ever in every righteous activity to which you may be at any time committed. Good-bye. [Applause.]

COAL STRIKE PROBLEM; AGRICULTURE AND AMER-
ICAN TAX DOLLAR ANALYZED. WOULD HAVE
UNITED STATES AID IN WORLD PEACE

Address at Cheyenne, Wyo., June 25, 5:30 p. m.

Mr. Governor and My Countrymen All:

THERE is considerable speculation sometimes as to what
the President knows. [Laughter and applause.] I
am quite ready to agree that he does not know as
much as he ought to know, and, to tell the truth, I do
not know half as much as I thought I knew when I grad-
uated from college; but I do know about "Salt Creek." I
have heard much about it; and yet I am frank to say to
you, as the governor's remarks would tend to indicate,
that neither those of us in official life who come from the
East, nor many of our citizens generally in that section
know of the wonderful West as they ought.

I was telling this afternoon of an incident which happened to me and I will relate it at my own expense. Six
years ago I was in the West participating in a political
campaign, and was riding one day from Butte, Mont., to
Pocatello, Idaho. The friend who escorted me to the train
introduced me to some gentlemen who were traveling the
same way and said I would find them interesting company.
He further said, "By the way, Senator"—I was then in the
Senate—"one of these gentlemen is the largest sheep-
raiser in Idaho or Montana.

I thought that was my chance. We sat down together,
and I said: "It is very interesting to know of your importance in the sheep-raising industry. We have the wool
king of the United States in my home county."

116

The gentleman replied: "That is very interesting. To whom do you refer?"

I answered: "Uncle David Harpster, who is recognized everywhere as the wool king of the United States and as the man who has had more to do with the fixing of the rates of the tariff on wool than any man in all the country."

He said: "That is very fine. Tell me how many sheep has your 'wool king' in Ohio?"

In truth I did not know, but, determined to make good my claim of kingship, I said: "Well, I am not exactly sure, but I know he has from 3,000 to 5,000." [*Laughter.*] I could tell in an instant that I had "slipped;" but he turned the conversation in another channel, not wishing to embarrass me. But after we had ridden along for a half hour or more we got back to the sheep question again and I said: "I meant to ask you, my friend, how many sheep have you?"

He replied, with a knowing smile on his face: "We have had rather an ill run of luck this year; the lambs have not turned out well and we have been rather discouraged. We only have 436,000."

That reminded me that I did not know how to appraise the West; but I do know how to appraise your cordial reception, your generous courtesy, and your encouraging manifestations of confidence and approval. It is a joy to greet you.

Wants States' Cooperation

I am not here on a political mission. I am doing precisely what the governor has said, namely, trying to learn more about the United States of America and seeking to have the people of the United States know more about their government. It seems to me if we can understand each other better we shall certainly get along very much better.

I liked the governor's assurance of the State's cooperation in the enforcement of the Federal law, but I want that cooperation in other directions than along prohibition lines.

I want the cooperation of Wyoming and every State in America in everything that is of common concern to all the people of this great Republic. [Applause.]

I presume there comes to you a feeling of regret on the passing of many of the characteristics of earlier days. I should like to join you in one respect. I would be sorry to see the cowboy go, but if I lived in Wyoming I could never get over having the cowgirl go if the girls who have ridden up to the platform are fair samples of them, as I presume they are. [*Laughter and applause.*]

I never stand before an audience residing distant from the seat of the Federal government, without wondering what particular phase of National affairs they would prefer to have reported. Here in Wyoming you are so varied in your employments, and contemplate such tremendous possibilities in your vast resources, that I am bound to assume your interests are more or less the same as in any sister State, proud and confident of the future. The difference, if there is any, between yours and a more populous and more largely developed State lies in the confidence with which you approach all problems. There is something in the atmosphere of the great mountain West, something in the freedom of your seemingly boundless areas, which makes you unafraid, and which develops men. In passing I want to testify to my own appreciation of what Wyoming has done towards erecting a memorial to a great character from your State known to all America. I refer to General Cody. All America lionized him and wishes to see his distinguished career properly memorialized.

Admires Spirit of West

I like the spirit of the West—the conquering spirit which makes sure of accomplishment. It has turned the unexplored, and unmeasured stretches into glittering stars in the constellation of "Old Glory," and added mightily to the strength and eminence of the Nation. More, it has proved man's capacity to strike an agreement with inexorable nature, and apply his genius to the bounteous bestowals of the Creator, and turn them into habitations and utilities in the supreme service of life.

Much of the romance of the cattle-ranging days has gone, though the literature it inspired will not be soon forgotten. Life is in large part a chronicle of supersedures, and it is not surprising that "Wild West" days should give way to the restricted practices of growing populations and regulated methods in dealing with a vast domain. But the supersedure which has written its decrees throughout the vast areas west of the Mississippi, has not robbed you of your eminence as a cattle raising State. Perhaps I ought to say, in the present day, that you still hold your eminence as a great participant in the stock-raising industry.

Slump Following World War

In that position you have been experiencing some heavy discouragements since there came the inevitable slump which followed the World War. Here, as elsewhere, you were hard hit. I congratulate you that you have escaped complete disaster, and I rejoice that the Federal government has been helpful in enabling you to avoid it.

Not alone did the government feel an obligation to come to your assistance because you had made a magnificent response to the Nation's need while engaged in a gigantic war, but a government fit to survive is always deeply concerned in the threatened destruction of any activity which is essential to the larger community life. As the government, acting for all the people, is vitally interested in that manufacturing production which makes for employment and equips the labor forces of the Nation with consuming capacity to buy from the farm, just so are the great industrial communities, and the public generally, vitally interested in the welfare of farm and ranch, whence comes the food upon which our National existence depends. This indissoluble relationship, which makes the welfare of one activity vitally necessary to the welfare of all, is always a matter of government concern. We are sometimes so eager to correct, we are sometimes so misled by that political adventure which inclines to make appeal to larger numbers, that we err in attempted remedies, and make matters worse rather than better. But I am stressing the point of good intent upon the part of the great, dependable body of men, legislators and administrators, who speak with governmental authority.

Tribute to Senator Warren

Let me say in passing that that statement will be substantiated by a very notable body of citizens who honor you with their presence today quite as much as do the members of the executive branch of the government. Senator Warren has told me that he and the members of the party which travelled with him to the great Territory of Alaska have just returned and are stopping for the night in your splendid city of Cheyenne. I know you will give them a cordial welcome. I want to express my personal pleasure in finding Senator Warren at home, and, while I am speaking in a personal vein, let me tell you of Cheyenne and Wyoming that there is no one in the United States who is more trusted or more honored than your senior Senator. [Applause.]

I am convinced that we sometimes apply remedies which it had been better never to attempt at all. Having been a witness to the life activities of a general practitioner of medicine, commonly known as a country doctor, I am a firm believer in giving nature a chance, instead of over-doctoring a sick patient. It has been my strong belief that the world, fevered by war, with nerves exhausted and disposition made irritable, needs less of experimental remedies and more of a chance to calm down, while nature takes a turn at the longed-for restoration.

World's Work Must Be Done

We have seen fevered madness turn to violent revolution, but the patient has not improved. We have seen capital so enriched in the great saturnalia of expenditure that men lost interest in the normal pursuits and the justifiable profits of righteous endeavor. We have seen workmen so liberally rewarded for a little toil that many men are striving ever to do less. Both are wrong. The world's work must be done. There is no escaping it. God willed it so. There can be no permanency to law or any system or policy which contemplates life and its luxuries without toil. The world has no use for a loafer, big or little, whether commanding capital or directing labor, and there is no place in the world that hates the loafer more than does the West. The greatest need of the world today is work, hard work, honest work, efficient work, work to make amends for war's madness, work to effect the needed restoration, and put the train of human progress on the right track once more. Nature makes her restoration through unremitting effort, and the insistent call today is for work at the table of the directory, at the superintendent's office, at the foreman's desk, at the workman's bench, on the farm or ranch, in the professional office, yea, in the pulpit, teaching God's own demand "to love mercy, do justly and walk humbly with thy God."

Conscience in Modern Industry

I do not say that work alone will effect the complete reformation, but it will aid nature in the supreme restoration. When we are again contemplating the steady flow of rewards for earnest endeavor, we may resort to legislation for such equitable adjustments as conscience and honor have not enforced.

Life in general found its reflex in your frontier life of days agone. You saw the victory to the vigorous and strong. Not every victory was just, not all of herded wealth was defensible. The rustlers who stole and rebranded are found in some form or other in every city and industrial community, and law does not always deter them. But you drove them out of Wyoming a generation ago, and they must be driven from every business community, because the outlaw is a community menace.

I would like to acclaim in the United States fewer citizens who get all they can without appraising consequences, and more citizens who strive for what they believe to be just, and find their larger reward in the respect and reverence of their fellow men.

You have seen the merchant who has chosen the policy of fair profits and just dealing grow in esteem and expanding trade in exact proportion, and write big the success which marked his career. You have seen similar results in great fields of productivity. The lowest possible margin of profit, consistent with good business, enlists the confidence and favor of the consuming army, while the gouger, the profiteer and the cheater flare in wealth for a passing day or two, and then march on, arm in arm, to oblivion or distrust. I would like the rugged justice of the frontier to become the conscience of modern industry and commerce.

Government Aid to Stockmen

My thoughts have carried me far away from the thought of your post-war depression. I meant to make proud allusion to the prompt and effective assistance the government was able to give to your stock-raisers, thus helping them and their creditors to a renewed confidence and restored stability. I know how the War Finance Corporation, reestablished and refinanced under the present administration to perform a peace service after war's inflation and the subsequent deflation, came to your rescue and effected it. I know how Congress hastened to save to you the home-market with a protective tariff. The home-market, while not always enough for a people so capable in production, is the best in the world, and we wished American producers to have the first chance in supplying it. Your cattle-raisers found new assurance, and your wool-growers were newly encouraged. Let us hope the tide has sufficiently turned to make sure of a flood of deserved prosperity.

I shall not venture to recite the further aids to agriculture, to the stock-raiser and the grain-grower, so recently enacted by Congress. The details were related by me in Kansas last week. One observation is sufficient. The American farmer is now equipped with every facility for farm financing which is available to any business in the world, and there is every confidence in an upward trend. If it fails, then the individualism which developed the mighty West and made ours the foremost Republic in the world, will be destroyed in futile plans which lead inevitably to industrial paralysis or an impotent social order.

A few years ago, one of your Wyoming statesmen made the astounding statement that your State alone contained enough coal to supply the entire land with fuel for four centuries to come. Whether the statement was extravagant or not, it was at least an intimation of your mineral resources of which the nation at large had never dreamed.

How incomprehensible, indeed, are your limitless possibilities! And you are but one of many States of seemingly incomparable material riches. Let us hope that the genius of statesmen and the common sense of business may be combined to solve the problems of transportation and distribution, so that your wealth may be made an asset to the Nation as well as the State.

Coal Problem a National One

I am always conscious while I am looking you in the face and speaking to you that I am being aided by a modern creation of science which enables me to talk to all the world, so to speak. So I wish to discuss for just a moment a national problem. It may seem a far cry to talk in Wyoming about the coal problem, but it is one of the pressing problems of the country. In New England today there is anxiety about next winter's fuel supply, traceable to the experienced hardships of last winter. That severe trial, to New England in particular, followed the coal and railway strikes, which resulted when winter came on in inadequate supplies and insufficient transportation facilities.

The government is not blind to the situation or deaf to appeals. It is doing everything possible, so far as authorized by law, to dispel public apprehension. Under the authority of an Act of Congress, the United States Coal Commission, made up of able and earnest men, has been engaged in a thorough investigation of this vital problem, and will report to the Congress next December. It is going thoroughly into the labor controversy, studying living conditions and community life in the mining regions, ascertaining facts about the inadequacies which prevent prompt distribution, inquiring into engineering problems

123

and the economic errors incident to over-development, investigating the excesses in profits reflected in inordinate charges for coal, and preparing an exhaustive report on the entire industry. It will be revealing and, we hope, remedial. We shall know the facts about a basic industry, which is a source of peril to the Nation's industrial life, and a more or less continuous threat to our domestic comfort, sometimes a menace to life and health.

It is too early to say whether the commission will suggest plans of permanent cure which the Congress will adopt. I do know that it will bring us to a new understanding of a problem which must be solved. We shall have a publicity which will make greed impossible, and point the way to solve a question which must be answered in behalf of a vital public interest.

Doubtless there will be a recommendation of vast storage during seasons of light consumption, in order to guard against the heavy demands in winter or in periods of suspended production. Probably there will be recommendations for enhanced distribution, the need for which is already proven. There may be revelations as to cost of production, which, through insistent public opinion, will destroy price-making abuses. I hope for a revelation of the economic blunder in operating mines half and quarter time, by which the higher labor costs are made necessary.

Asks Aid of the Consuming Public

Meanwhile we shall the better guard against inconvenience and hardship if the consuming public will help as best it can, without expecting the government to assume all the responsibility. If the coal-consuming public would buy coal during the periods of scant consumption, it would guard itself against price-panics and dangerous shortage when consumption is at the peak. In the hope of lowered prices, the buying is postponed, and that very postponement is contributing to advanced prices. There is need for some individual initiative and responsibility in preparing for the wintry days to come. There is a mistaken notion that somehow the government may wield a magic wand, or strike with the iron hand, and produce cheap coal. It can do neither. We can no more force the mine-worker to produce coal than we can force the farmer to grow wheat or corn, or wool. We saw that erroneous belief exploded a year ago.

Position of Mine Owners

Many mine-operators, who were as much responsible for the strike as the workmen who struck, insisted that under law-enforcement they could produce all the coal that was needed. The law-enforcement was provided but no coal was produced. There can be no coal mining in free America under the force of arms. But if we understand the situation fully, and offer justly, and the men accustomed to produce coal will not work to meet the public need, then the public will provide their successors. The common weal transcends every other interest and puts aside every obstacle. We will find the solution. I hope we shall find it without further hardships or endangered life or menaced industry; but we shall not find it in nationalizing the mines. That would be only another step toward national paralysis, which a sane America will everlastingly avoid. Nor shall we solve it by maintaining a basic industry, like that of bituminous coal production, under a plan of operation which affords the mine worker only a hundred or a hundred and fifty working days a year. The normal man, aspiring for himself and his family, cannot live that way, even though he is paid what is seemingly a generous wage, because his wage days are not ample for a life of honest industry and becoming thrift.

The American Tax-Dollar

Such a problem is very insistent. It cannot be dodged, nor solved by demagogy. It demands our best thought and all our courage. Let us hope that in the search for a

125

way to full justice in dealing with the coal problem, we may find a suggested plan for dealing with kindred problems which are ever menacing our industrial peace and hindering our full accomplishment.

Just a word in conclusion. My attention was called only yesterday to the division of the American tax-dollar. When a scientific analysis is made, it appears that, after taking from the tax dollar the amount paid to support the army and the navy and other branches of the National defense, and the amounts paid for pensions, compensation, and to fulfill the obligations which we owe to the men who gave of their strength to the National defense, after deducting all of the items relating to warfare and its varied phases, there remain but fifteen cents of the American tax-dollar to be applied to the ordinary expenditures of the government and to the promotion and furtherance of our National peace time interests. When we stop to think, my countrymen, that we are collecting $3,500,000,000 annually for the Federal government and that only $15 out of each $100 are applied to the pursuits and normal ways of peace, do you not think we in America ought to do everything we can that is in harmony with our nationalism and our ideals and traditions to wipe out the enormous expenditures for war? [Applause.]

Appeal to the West

It is largely for that reason that I am asking the people of the West to give of their influence and their force to persuade the legislative branch of the government to support the administrative branch in having our great, strong, and confident nation give of its influence and its power to make a better and more firmly established International Court of Justice, which shall serve, as courts serve in our own United States, in avoiding conflicts by the just and lawful decision of controversies. I want America free from war, but I want America to play her great part in enabling the world to free itself from war. [Applause.]

126

BANS INTERNATIONAL ENTANGLEMENTS

Speech at Laramie, Wyo., June 25, 9 p. m.

Mr. Mayor and My Countrymen All:

YOU have afforded us a very happy surprise tonight. I had not realized before that we had reached the "most exalted community on the American continent." It is a very pleasant experience.

I am afraid your mayor made one slight mistake, although I know how good his intentions were, when he referred to Laddie Boy. Laddie Boy is not with us; he is crying his eyes out at the White House in Washington because he cannot be with us. I like what the mayor said. I like dogs; I like their unfailing fidelity, and I wish we might have more of the same quality among humanity.

It is a curious thing what makes us attached to a community. I presume it is an old story with you, but I like to think of Laramie because I loved Bill Nye. I knew Mr. Nye personally; I knew how much of happiness and joy and brightness he brought into the world, and the man who can do that is a real contributor to the contentment and progress of humanity. Sometimes I think we do not have enough joyousness in our everyday affairs.

"All One American People"

I like to look at you. I have come to understand that no portion of the United States has a monopoly on good looks or good fortune or progress. I care not where you go in these United States of America, you find a forward-looking, forward-moving body of American citizens. You find it in Wyoming precisely as you find it in Colorado or Missouri or Ohio or New York or Massachusetts. We are all one American people, with one aspiration, one love of country, one pride in the Republic's accomplishments, and one love for dear "Old Glory." [Applause.]

I know, too, that Laramie is the center of learning in Wyoming. That is a fine distinction for any community.

127

Any community that adds to human knowledge and the processes of disseminating it and makes men and women —and particularly young men and women—better fitted for the problems of life, better equipped to embrace American opportunities, makes its contribution to American advancement. However, let me say to the young people present here tonight that it is of little value to become educated and equipped unless those qualifications are employed to practical advantage.

Wide Scope of American Opportunity

I do not know what directs men's activities in life into certain channels; I do not believe anyone can say; but I will tell you an old story of mine. I like it because it illustrates the character of American opportunity and gives proof of American democracy. I grew up in a village of 600 people, and, as you know, in the small town or village democracy is found in its purest form, for in such surroundings there are no social strata. The blacksmith's son, the carpenter's son, the minister's son, the doctor's son, the grocer's son, all mix on one common plane of youthful, hopeful fellowship. In the village where I was a boy, I watched grow up the classmates with whom I was associated, and later in life I became interested in looking them up to see what had become of them. What an interesting story I found it to be! One of them was Charlie, my chum, who was not striking in any way, but a bully good fellow who had the same opportunity as was enjoyed by the others. He never amounted to anything in life worth recording. Another was Keeler. If anybody had an advantage in our whole class of "stunners," as we called ourselves, it was Keeler. He was a lucky chap, because he inherited something like three thousand dollars, and three thousand dollars was a great amount of money in those days; but he followed the wrong road and achieved nothing. Another was the shoemaker's son, who had a notion that he wanted to be a geologist. He had heard a geologist lecture in the town and he started to study geology. In order to equip himself and make his own way he became a Pullman-car conductor, but, while studying geology this country boy, this shoemaker's son, became interested in the Bible and turned out to be a really great preacher. Then there was Frank who was the carpenter's son. His father loved him as any other father would love his son. You would not have thought that he had any special prospects; but Frank grew up, was aided to an education by his father, turned his education to practical use, and when he died, only a year ago and all too soon, was one of the great captains of industry in America. He was drawing a salary of $40,000 a year, and I believe earned every cent of it.

Then there was another—the grocer's son. You would never have thought he would amount to much, but his father loved him and educated him, and the grocer's son of the village of 600 is today the chairman of the Federal Reserve Board of the United States, the greatest financial institution in the world. I will not enumerate what became of the others. Some suffered disappointment; some lived lives of mediocrity.

Chance for All in This Republic

I merely point out to you that in the life of America there is opportunity for every boy and girl precisely alike, and education is the equipment that enables them to embrace opportunity. I want every boy and girl in America fitted to embrace the opportunities which may come. I hope you are fitting your growing citizenship in Wyoming to embrace to the fullest advantage what will continue to be, my countrymen, beckoning opportunities as this Republic expands and grows more active in the affairs of the world.

Speaking of the affairs of the world, let me say, in conclusion, that I do not think you would want to be citizens of a Republic professing to be lovers of humanity and believers in Christianity which was afraid to play its part in helping the advancement of humankind. So I have come West to make report as to the state of affairs in the government and at the same time to tell you that I believe with all my heart that we must play our part in seeing to it that there shall never be another destructive war, and to that end that we should take our part in international affairs without entanglement. Good-night. [Applause.]

"THE GOVERNMENT IS YOURS"

Remarks at Ogden, Utah, June 26, 8:50 a. m.

Ladies and Gentlemen, Boys and Girls:

I HARDLY knew there were so many people in the great State of Utah as I see this morning in Ogden. I do not know of a place of like size in the East where early in the morning so many would come out to extend greetings to travellers. I like to say to you, because it is in my heart to say it, that you have given us a very pleasant surprise and a very heartening manifestation of your friendly interest.

I wish I could talk to all the boys and girls, but it is not possible for me to reach all of them. Therefore, I shall ask to be excused from speaking at any length. I should like to say, however, that those of us who comprise the official party are travelling westward in order to know better our great country. We are having the very great satisfaction of a more intimate acquaintance with the people of continental United States and we are going to have a more intimate knowledge of the great Territory of Alaska, which is nearly as large as a third of the United States proper. Better, however, than the acquaintance with our material possibilities and resources is the contact with the American people themselves.

His Vision for the Future

I wish I had it in my power to bring you a little closer to those responsible for the affairs of government, because, after all, the government is yours, and if we could have a more intimate contact between the people and the government and a clear understanding of the needs of every

130

situation, we would get along very much better in this country. Nevertheless we are doing very well. I like to say to my fellow Americans that in the effort to recover from the effects of the tumult of war, which disorganized and disarranged everything, we in the United States are making the most rapid strides of any people in the world. [Applause.]

I sometimes wish that by the wave of some magic wand I could bestow something of our good fortune on the less fortunate people of the earth. We must not be too careless, however, for good fortune is sometimes a fleeting thing. I want America to hold fast to the fundamentals on which we have builded; I want America to do the things which will make certain, if possible, of continued good fortune; aye, I want America to do the things that will give these boys and girls, these splendid children of Ogden and of every other community in the land, a better country in which to live tomorrow than we know today. [Applause.]

TELLS OF PRESIDENT'S RESPONSIBILITY

Remarks at Bountiful, Utah, June 26, 11 a. m.

Ladies and Gentlemen and Particularly Young Ladies and Young Gentlemen:

I HAVE found a new slogan in your wonderful country which I am delighted to adopt, namely the one which refers to "Utah's best crop." I do not know when I have seen so many happy, smiling, sturdy children in so short a period of travel. A thousand delights have come to us while we have been more intimately acquainted with your wonderful State. I love the names of your villages; I love the prospect that greets the eye when one looks from the window of the door in the morning; I love the magic and wonderful picture that nature has painted everywhere; I love the prospect of great productivity in the fields, but I love above all else the boyhood and the girlhood of marvelous Utah. [Applause.]

Nothing can ever go wrong with a Republic in which so many healthy, happy children are developing amid the opportunities and privileges of our America. It is fine to see you. I am glad to stop and greet you, and I may say to you that your visitors are having a much better time in coming to see you than you are having in seeing them. [Applause.]

I imagine that most people think it is a very wonderful thing to be President of the United States, and it is a great distinction, but it is also a great responsibility to be the first officer of government for such a people as ours. I wish to tell you that the greatest joy, the finest compensation, and the greatest inspiration which can come to the incumbent of the presidential office are found in getting away from Washington and meeting people just as I am meeting you this morning. It is a joy to those in authority to know that there is so much happiness, and so much confidence in the future of our country. I have had my own faith renewed this morning, and I am grateful for the opportunity of greeting you as well as for your greetings to us. [Applause.]

UTAH'S RECEPTION GRATIFYING

Remarks to Assembed School Children in *Liberty* Park, Salt *Lake* City, Utah, June 26, 11:45 a. m.

Girls and Boys of Salt Lake City:

I T IS quite impossible for me to speak at length or to be heard by any considerable number of you, but I am going to tell a secret to those of you who are immediately in front of me and then you can tell the secret to your friends. I am travelling with some members of my official family, but I am sorry that Herbert Hoover, the Secretary of Commerce, is not now with us because I read in one of Mr. Hoover's official reports that Salt Lake City has a population of about 120,000. I am prepared to tell Mr. Hoover that Salt Lake City has a population, at least from appearances, of approximately 1,000,000 of the best people in the world. [Applause.]

I wish I could convey to you in some way our appreciation of the happiness you have brought to us, the cheer you have given us, and the renewed confidence you have inspired in us. It is a pleasing and a delightful experience to meet and greet you and to be met and greeted by you. You have been just the finest in the world. I speak only the truth when I say that I have always liked Utah, and I like it better than ever at this moment because of the cordiality of your greeting and the magnificent pictures of citizenship and resources which it has been our privilege today to enjoy. Good-bye. [Applause.]

WORLD WAR COST UNITED STATES $40,000,000,000;
YET TAXES AND PUBLIC INDEBTEDNESS RE-
DUCED BY BUSINESS ADMINISTRATION

Address on Taxation and Expenditure at the Tabernacle,
Salt Lake City, Utah, Tuesday Evening, June 26

Governor Mabey, Senator Smoot, My Fellow Americans All:

THE governor has been kind enough to say that some of us have won your hearts. In return I wish to say that the citizens of Salt Lake City and Utah have been winning some hearts themselves. I cannot tell you how happy you have made us. There could come to nobody in the world a more gracious, cordial, and heartening reception than you have given us in your wonderful State and beautiful city. [Applause.] I almost wish I were not President, for I should like to fling aside my manuscript and just talk to you. If I were sure that I were speaking only to you I would not make what might be termed a speech, because the governor has already made a better one than I can make. [Laughter and applause.] I congratulate Utah and I congratulate the United States of America that there are such men as he in the executive chairs of many of our commonwealths throughout the Union. [Applause.]

I was glad that Senator Smoot presented to you the Speaker of the House and two members of the Cabinet. I wish I could present to you all the members of the Cabinet. We have not only a happy and harmonious family, but we have in the Cabinet a very able family. [Applause.] I wish to take this occasion to say, because I desire you to know it, that if there has been any measure of success

134

in the present administration which appeals to your approval, the members of the Cabinet have had a very great share in bringing about that success. [Applause.]

The Power of Inspiration

I wish I could have you know how good it is to be in the land of the "empire builders." I have not the faculty of description, but there is something exalting about it; there is something that gives a new faith in life, something that gives a new confidence that one can accomplish and attain. How fortunate you are that you live here in sight of the mountains, majestic, immovable and inspiring! My mind turned to them while the governor was speaking and referring to your reverence for the Constitution, the fundamental law of the Republic. If there are those in America—and I regret to say that there are—who would like to destroy the institutions on which this Republic is builded, let them look to the mountains and see how impossible is the task which they would undertake. [Applause.]

Inspiration comes from the things the "empire builders" have wrought. We have been hearing about them and knowing about them for years and years while you have been making your superb contribution to the development of the West and the building up of a greater Republic; but I never knew before that you had in some way discovered that magic which brings a shower of beautiful roses from a wonderfully clear sky or which makes them bud and blossom on a paved pathway to express the welcome you extend to travelers within your borders. [Applause.] It has all been so beautiful that you have won our hearts, and I want you to believe that nothing in our trip across this wonderful continent will leave a sweeter or more abiding impression than has been gained in your great community today.

Problem of Taxation

My countrymen, there is a suggestion of personal tribute in choosing my topic for an address in Salt Lake City. I have so long associated Senator Smoot with great problems of taxation, and have witnessed so much of his able and faithful endeavor to enforce economy and thereby lift the burdens of taxation, that I find myself involuntarily thinking, when I come to your State, of the menace of mounting taxes and growing public indebtedness. The removal of this menace is not alone a Federal problem, for we are recording gratifying progress so far as the Nation is concerned, but the larger menace today is to be faced by municipality, county, and State. The Federal government is diligently seeking to prove itself a helpful example, but the improved order must come in the units of government into which Federal government never intrudes. There is no particular reason why I should speak of it, except that we are all concerned about general public welfare, and I have thought that possibly a recital of Federal accomplishment would serve to encourage State and local work which must be done.

A short time before I became President, a trusted but cynical old friend said to me one day that he understood I intended to make a specialty of economy in administration. I admitted my aspirations in that direction, and he replied:

Enumerates United States Loans to the Allies

"Well, that's the right idea, but don't tell anybody about it. You may think it will be appreciated, but it will not. Every time you lop somebody off the government pay roll or keep him out of a profitable piece of government business, you make him and all his friends and associates your enemies; and, on the other side, not a soul in the country will ever thank you for it. Everybody grumbles about taxes, and nobody ever demonstrates any appreciation of the man that tries to save them from taxes."

A short time before we left Washington on the present trip another friend said to me: "The administration has saved the country a good deal by reducing its expenses and cutting down the tax burden. But take my advice, and don't talk to any of your audiences about it. People always grumble about taxes, but they don't want to hear anybody talk to them on that subject."

To which I replied that I believed, in the present state of affairs, all such rules were suspended, and any public man who had anything cheerful to say on the subject of taxes and government expenses, would find plenty of audiences altogether willing to listen to him. I believe the American people are so profoundly interested in the subject of taxation and government costs nowadays, that an audience like this will even be willing to let me talk to them for a few minutes on the subject. [Applause.]

Colossal Loan to Allies

One of the financial incidents to our participation in the war was to loan a vast sum of money to our allies. I wonder how many of you ever stop to think that the $10,000,000,000 which we advanced to our allies, after our entrance into the war, was just about equal to the total cost of the Civil War to North and South together. The Civil War lasted four years and strained every nerve and resource of the Nation. Yet its actual cost to the governments of both sides was considerably less than the amount we advanced to the allied governments during the World War.

And that was only a mild beginning of our financial transactions in war. For every dollar we loaned to our allies, we spent about three more on our own account. In a little more than three years, between the day war was declared and peace was signed, we spent twice as much money out of the Public Treasury as had been spent by the National government in all of its previous history. I am not going to talk to you today about whether the money was all wisely spent. Whether it was or not, the results were worth all they cost, and a good deal more. What I propose to present to you now is some consideration of the fact that no matter how willing we were to make the sacrifice, no matter how cheerfully we incurred

137

the obligations, we had to face at the end the big and very practical reality that these obligations must be paid.

World War Cost the United States Forty Billions

You have inferred from what I said a moment ago that we spent roundly $40,000,000,000 on the World War. How many of us ever stopped to think that that was rather more than the total wealth of the Nation at the time of the Civil War? We paid out of our current taxes, while the war was going on, more than 25 per cent of its cost; that is, as much as the entire National wealth so late as the year 1820. At the beginning of August, 1919, the public debt reached the highest point in its history, $26,500,000,000. That was just about ten times the amount of the national debt at the close of the Civil War.

We are still too close to the events of the Great War to be able to realize the enormous burdens placed on our country. Quite aside from the large operations of public finance which it necessitated, private finance has been called upon from the very beginning in 1914 to make special arrangements for financing the huge foreign trade that resulted from Europe's extraordinary demands. Long before we were in the war our financial machinery had been compelled to shoulder the financing of an enormously exaggerated export trade to the warring powers. For a time Europe withdrew gold from us in great quantities, but presently it returned in yet greater, bringing to us and to the European countries the difficult problem of maintaining the exchanges and supporting the gold standard. Costs of everything rose to an artificially high basis, and in every direction expenditure was stimulated.

Altogether, the war was not only the greatest horror the world has ever known, but the greatest orgy of spending. This was inevitable, but that fact does not make the results any easier to deal with. The cost of government, of business, of every domestic establishment went up enormously. Every business man, and every householder, knows how it affected his personal concerns.

I want to suggest some of the ways in which it affected the whole business of government—government of the States, cities and the Nation,—and the expenses of every revenue-raising and spending division throughout the Nation.

Recently I have been furnished with some specific figures on the subject of the cost of government by the Bureau of the Census. I am not proposing to impose upon your patience with an elaborate presentation of figures, but I want to suggest a few that will point my observations about the enormously increased cost of government everywhere. Take the cost of State governments. I am informed that the revenues of the States in 1913 aggregated $368,000,000, and that in 1921 they had increased to $959,000,000; that is, they had increased 161 per cent, and every dollar of that increase had to come in some way or other from the public. The expenditures of the States in 1913 aggregated $383,000,000, and in 1921 they were $1,005,000,000; an increase of 163 per cent. The indebtedness of the States in 1913 amounted to $423,000,000, and in 1921 to $1,012,000,000; an increase of 139 per cent.

Cost of City Government

Turn now to the cost of city government. The Census Bureau has compiled data on the governments of 227 of the large cities. It is shown that those cities in 1913 collected $890,000,000 in all revenues, and in 1921 they collected $1,567,000,000; that is, they were compelled to take 76 per cent more in taxes in 1921 than they had taken in 1913. The same group of cities expended in 1913, $1,010,-000,000, and in 1921, $1,726,000,000—an increase of 71 per cent. The total debt of this group of cities in 1913 was $2,901,000,000, which by 1921 had risen to $4,334,-000,000—an increase of 49 per cent.

County administration appears, from the rather limited information which at this time the census authorities have been able to produce, to have shown a much larger proportionate increase in cost and tax collections than did the government of cities. It is stated that for 381 counties, distributed among 38 States, and regarded as fairly typical, the increase in receipts from principal sources of revenue increased 127 per cent from 1913 to 1922; that is, for every hundred dollars of revenue collected in 1913 $227 was collected in 1922. But that is not all. The total indebtedness of these same 381 counties increased 195 per cent in the same period; that is, for every hundred dollars of debt in 1913 they had $295 of indebtedness in 1922. Statistics were not available dealing with cities and towns of less than 30,000 population; nor with townships, school districts, drainage districts, irrigation districts, road districts, and other subdivisions which exercised the power to raise revenues and incur debts. It is well known, however, that substantially similar increases have affected all these taxing subdivisions.

Relative Income Taxes

The figures of both the Treasury and the Census Bureau, in short, make it perfectly plain that, whereas the cost of the Federal government is being steadily reduced, the cost of State and local governments is being just as steadily increased year by year. In nearly all of the States the cost of State and local governments increased from 1919 to 1922. The Treasury made up statistics on this point for one group of 10 States—Arizona, Connecticut, Michigan, Minnesota, New Hampshire, Ohio, Oregon, South Dakota, Washington, and Wisconsin. For this representative group it is shown that while Federal taxes paid by these 10 States declined from over a billion dollars in 1920 to $650,000,000 in 1922, their State and local taxes rose from $728,000,000 to $965,000,000 in the same period. In another tabulation, covering 28 States, which was the entire number for which the statistics were available, it was shown that from 1919 to 1921 there were increases in local taxes in 23 States and reductions in only 5. In spite of the enormous burden of paying for the war and paying interest on the war debt, State and local taxes in 1922 represented 60 per cent of all taxes paid.

Let me present another aspect of the same matter. We hear much about the grievous burden of the income tax, and everyone of us who pays it is able fully to sympathize with everyone else who pays it; but it is fair to consider what our income taxes would be if we lived in some of the other debt-burdened countries of the world. A married citizen of the United States, with two children and an income of $5,000, paid $68 tax on that income in 1922. If he had been a citizen of Canada he would have paid $156. If the German tax rate had been applied to his income, it would have cost him $292. If he had been a Frenchman the French rate would have required him to pay $96, and if he had been a British citizen, instead of giving up the $68 which he paid to Uncle Sam, he would have drawn his check for $320.76. The same man, with an income of $10,000 would have paid $456 income tax in the United States and $1,128.32 in England.

The great burden of the war was, of course, imposed on the National government. The Department of the Treasury states that in 1917 the Federal government's revenues were $1,044,000,000; in 1918 they were $3,925,-000,000; in 1919 they were $4,103,000,000; in 1920 they were $5,737,000,000; and in 1921 they were $4,902,000,000. For 1922 the total dropped to $3,565,000,000, and for 1923 it is estimated at $3,753,000,000. Assuming continuation of the present basis of Federal taxation, the receipts for 1924 are calculated at $3,638,000,000, and for 1925 at $3,486,000,000.

Per Capita Cost of Government

Not all of this revenue is raised by direct taxation. The Treasury estimates indicate that in 1923 only $2,925,-000,000 and in 1924 $2,850,000,000 will be produced by direct taxation; the remainder will come from various miscellaneous receipts of the government. You will, I am sure, be interested in the Treasury's statement that, whereas in 1914 the per capita cost to all the people of the Federal government was $6.97, in 1918 it reached $36.64 and in 1919 $37.91. It might reasonably have been presumed that with the war now long past taxes would have begun to fall off, but the statistics show the contrary. Instead of

141

a reduction, taxes for the fiscal year 1920 rose to $53.78 per capita, which was the peak of the war burden. Even for 1921 they only fell to $45.22. But in 1923 they will be $26.29, or considerably less than half as much as in 1920. Figures, especially the figures which come from such an authority as the Treasury Department, are conclusive arguments. These figures show that for two years after the war ended Federal taxes continued much higher than at the height of the struggle. They show that in the first two years of peace the cost of government was still continuing above the 1918 level, but that since the high point of 1920 they have been reduced more than one-half. It is a record of business administration to which the party now in control of the administration feels justified in referring with no small measure of satisfaction. [Applause.]

Settlement of the British Debt

I have observed that the cost of the war to our government was around $40,000,000,000. After paying a generous share, about 25 per cent, from current revenues collected while the war was in progress, we still had to borrow enormously. At its highest point, on August 31, 1919, the National debt was $26,596,000,000. I know you will be interested to be told that from that day, August 31, 1919, to June 30, 1923, we have reduced it to $22,400,000,000—a reduction of considerably more than a billion dollars a year. [Applause.] Moreover, we are now working under a program which involves extinguishing a half billion of the debt each year. No other country in the world has been able to make such a record.

In addition to all this, we have within the past year settled the British war debt to our government, arranged for its funding and its gradual extinction over a long period of years. In recognition of the notable service of Secretary Mellon, his associates at the Treasury, and the members of the Debt Funding Commission—one of whom is your senior Senator—and the American ambassador to Great Britain, I wish to say that the settlement of the British debt has been acclaimed all over the world as one of the most notable and successful fiscal accomplishments ever recorded. [Applause.] Not only does it insure that the regular quarterly payments which the British government will make to our Treasury will correspondingly relieve the burden upon American taxpayers, but the more important fact, in a time of widespread uncertainty and misgiving throughout the world of business everywhere, that these two great governments could get together and arrange such a settlement has been one of the most reassuring events since the armistice. [Applause.]

Too Much War Debt Cancellation Talk

There had been too much talk of possible cancellations or repudiations of the war debt. Such a program would have wrecked the entire structure of business faith and of confidence in the obligations of governments throughout the world. There was need, pressing and urgent need, for such a sign of confidence, assurance, and faith in the future as this setttlement furnished. When the British and American governments united in this pledge that their obligations would be met to the last shilling and the last dollar, there was renewed financial confidence in the world. I undertake to say that no event since the conclusion of hostilities has contributed so much to putting the world back on its way to stabilization, to confidence in its governments, and to the established conviction that our social institutions are yet secure. [Applause.]

No consideration of public finances can omit the fact that the single item of interest on the public debt exceeds $1,000,000,000 annually. For the fiscal year 1923, this item will be $1,100,000,000. Beyond this, we will reduce the public debt this year by $330,000,000, and next year by approximately $500,000,000. That is, over 35 per cent of the National revenue will this year go to paying interest or extinguishing the principal of the public debt.

I have not been able to gather conclusive statistics as to the accomplishments of States, cities, and counties, to compare with this showing of the Federal government. But with some general knowledge of the fiscal positions of States and cities in general, I feel quite safe in proffering my congratulations to any State, any city, any foreign country, which has made a better showing in the matter of reducing its public debt within the period since the war. I most earnestly regret that all have not been able to make a similar showing.

On this latter point I wish to say a word further. Taxation decidedly is a local as well as a National question. Prior to the war Federal taxation was an unimportant item; it was so small that in 1917 State and local taxes, in a group of 10 representative States, in all parts of the country, constituted 73 per cent of the entire tax burden.

The Federal tax was indirect and unfelt. Then came the enormous cost of the war, which the Federal government had to bear, and in 1918 State and local taxes constituted only 42 per cent of the entire tax burden. In 1919 they represented 44 per cent of the whole; in 1920, 41 per cent. But in 1922, the last year for which figures are available, State and local taxes were again in excess and represented 60 per cent of the entire tax burden. The States represented in this calculation are Arizona, Connecticut, Michigan, Minnesota, New Hampshire, Ohio, Oregon, South Dakota, Washington, and Wisconsin.

The Rule of Thrift

The world, its governments, its quasi-public corporations, its people, acquired the spending habit during the war to an extent not merely unprecedented, but absolutely alarming. There is but one way for the community finally to get back on its feet, and that is to go seriously about paying its debts and reducing its expenses. [Applause.] That is precisely what the world must face. The greatest and richest government must face it, and so must the humblest citizen. No habit is so easy to form, none so hard to break, as that of reckless spending. And on the other side, none is more certain to contribute to security and happiness, than the habit of thrift, of savings, of careful management in all business concerns, of balanced budgets and living within incomes. [Applause.] If I could urge upon the American people a single rule applicable to every one of them as individuals, and to every political or corporate unit among them, it would be to learn to spend somewhat less than their income all the time. If you have debts, reduce them as rapidly as you can; if you are one of the fortunate few who have no debts, make it a rule to save something every year. Keep your eye everlastingly on those who administer your governmental units for you; your town, your county, your State, your National government. Make them understand that you are applying the rule of thrift and savings in your personal affairs, and require them to apply it in their management of your public affairs. [Prolonged applause.] If they fail, find other public servants who will succeed. If they succeed, give them such encouragement and inspiration as will be represented by a full measure of hearty appreciation for their efforts. [Applause.]

Careful Scrutiny of Estimates

This brings me to a brief reference to what has proven so helpful to the Federal government in effecting the approach to the expenditures of normal times. For the first time in our history we have the National Budget, under which there is an effective scrutiny of estimates for public expenditure. More, we have coordinated government activities in making the expenditures which Congress authorizes.

It seems now unbelievable that we should have been willing to go for a century and a third without this helpful agency of business administration. But we did, and only now have we come to an appraisal of the cost of this great neglect.

It has been no easy task to establish the Budget and make sure of its acceptance. Out of long time practices the varied and many government departments felt themselves independent institutions, instead of factors in the great machinery of government administration. They often got all they could from Congress, and made it a point to expend all they got.

Accomplishments of Budget System

Under the Budget plan we were able to reverse the policy and awaken a spirit of economy and efficiency in the public service. We not only insisted that requests for appropriations should stand the minutest inquiry, but after reduced appropriations were granted, we insisted on expending less than the appropriations. There was no proposal to diminish government activities required by law or demanded by public need, but there was first the commitment to efficiency and then commendable strife for economy.

We effaced the inexcusable and very costly impression that government departments must expend all their appropriations, that no available cash should return to the Treasury. And we sought to inspire as well as exact, in the practices of economy.

One illustration will not be amiss. On June 8, 1921, before the budget was in operation, word came to me that the business head of one of our institutions, far from Washington, was puzzling how to expend $42,000 which he had in excess of actual needs. Ordinarily such a matter would never reach the Chief Executive; but this one did, quite by accident, and I wired a warning, and followed it with a letter reciting the need of retrenchment everywhere, and expressed the hope that every government official with spending authority would join in reducing the government outlay. The appeal was effective, and this one government agent not only saved most of his available $42,000 for that fiscal year, but in 1922 he saved $81,000 more. He proved what could be done, and we are seeking to do it everywhere under the government.

Do not imagine it has all been easy. It is very popular to expend, and there are ruffled feelings in every case of denial. But there are gratifying results in firm resolution and the insistent application of business methods.

More Popular to Spend Than Deny

The Budget Director is the agent of the President, and he speaks on the authority of the government's Chief Executive. One day last winter the director came to me in great anxiety, telling me that a department chief would not sanction an $8,000,000 cut in his estimates. At that time we were seeking to prevent a threatened excess of expenditures over receipts amounting to $800,000,000 for the next fiscal year, and every estimate was being cut to the very bone.

I sent for the department head, and he was still insistent in his opposition to the reduced estimate. I called for a conference of the department experts, and the budget experts, and told them that if they could not agree, I would decide. They conferred, and instead of returning to me for decision, the estimate was cut more than $12,000,000. [Applause.] The point is that we have introduced business methods in government, and, instead of operating blindly and to suit individual departments which had never visualized the government as a whole, and felt no concern about the raising of funds, we are scrutinizing, justifying, coordinating, and not only halting mounting costs, but making long strides in reducing the cost of government activities.

The Government Living Within Income

Perhaps the budget system would not accomplish so much for taxing and spending divisions smaller than the State, but a resolute commitment to strike at all extravagance and expend public funds as one would for himself in his personal and business affairs will accomplish wonders.

A man ought to live within his income, so should a Nation, and your Federal government does so today. [Applause.]

It is largely unmindfulness that piles up the burden. Able and honorable men often press for a Federal expenditure to be made in their own community or in other ways helpful to their own interests which they would strongly oppose if they were not directly concerned. That is true of Federal appropriation as well as municipal, county, and State expenditure, and I know of no remedy unless public officials are brought to understand the menace in excessive tax burdens and indebtedness, beyond extinguishment except in drastic action, and resolve to employ practicable business methods in government everywhere, and resist the assault of the spenders.

Danger of Governmental Extravagance

It is too early to know whether there is a Republic of ancient times with which appropriately to parallel our own. We know of their rise and fall, and we may learn lessons from their failures. A simple-living, thrifty people, with simple, honest, and just government never failed to grow in influence and power. [Applause.] The coming of extravagance and profligacy in private life, and wastefulness and excesses in public life ever proclaimed the failures which history has recorded.

I would not urge a stingy, skimpy, hoarding life on the part of individuals, or an inadequate program of government. The latter must always rise to deliberate public demand. But private life and public practices are inseparably associated.

I would have our government adequate in every locality and in every activity, and public sentiment will demand it and secure it, and require no more, if we may have the simple and thrifty life which makes the healthful Nation.

Pays Tribute to the American Legion

These reflections, my countrymen, are not conceived in doubt or pessimism. We have so nobly begun, we are so boundless in resources, we have wrought so notably in our short national existence, that I wish these United States to go on securely. I would like developing dangers noted and appraised and intelligently and patriotically guarded against. A nation of inconsiderate spenders is never secure. We wish our United States everlastingly secure. [Applause.]

War brought us the lesson that we had not been so American in spirit as we had honestly pretended. Some of our adopted citizenship wore the habiliments of America, but were not consecrated in soul. Some to whom we have given all the advantages of American citizenship would destroy the very institutions under which they have accepted our hospitality. Hence our commitment to the necessary Americanization which we too long neglected. The American *Legion*, baptized anew in the supreme test on foreign battle fields, is playing its splendid part. Those who bore war's burdens at home have joined, and all America must fully participate. It is not enough to enlist the sincere allegiance of those who come to accept our citizenship; we must make sure for ourselves, for all of us, that we cling to the fundamentals, to the practices which enabled us to build so successfully, and avoid the errors which tend to impair our vigor and becloud our future. [Applause.]

Soul of America Committed to an Ideal

Just a word in conclusion, my countrymen. There grew out of the war another advantage which was worth its enormous cost; it revealed the soul of America and it committed us to an ideal. When we found our country actually endangered there was nothing we could not accomplish with the American soul aflame. Then came the armistice and the post-war adjustment. I think the greatest misfortune that could come to America would be to have her drift back into the rut of a more or less selfish existence. I want America to have something of a spiritual ideal. [Applause.] It is for that very reason, apart from the selfish advantage which attends, that I am seeking a way to commit the public sentiment of America in favor of our participation in an International Court of Justice. [Applause.]

149

When you stop to think that, when divided up, 85 per cent of the American tax-dollar, 85 per cent of the enormous public fund of which I have been speaking, goes to pay the expenses and obligations of war and only 15 per cent to the promotion of the ideals and practices of peace, do you not think we ought to play our part, my countrymen, in helping the world to abolish war? [Great applause and cheers.] There come to the President, I think, impressions that cannot come to all of you in quite the same way. Into the Executive Office there flow the griefs and the dissatisfaction of the country; there are encountered the problems incident to the proper, deserved, and obligated care which the country wants to give the men who became impaired in its service; there come to the government echoes of all the sorrows inseparable from the aftermath of war. There come to the Executive the questions growing out of the problem of expenditures; aye, more, there come to the Executive echoes and reflexes of the problems and the hopelessness of the situation of other nations of the world. There came to me one day a very personal experience. I stood on a pier at Hoboken, N. J., and I saw five thousand coffined dead brought back from the battlefields of Europe. You will never know what an impression such a scene makes until you look upon it yourself.

Ambition to Aid All Mankind

I do not preach a pacifist policy. I would not want the boys and girls of Utah to grow up thinking that their first obligation is not to their country and its defense in time of peril, or when its honor is at stake; I would never preach that; but I want the boys and girls of Utah, as I wish the boys and girls of Ohio and Indiana and every other State in the Union, to grow up believing that their government has reached a point when in expressing the aspirations of the American people we will give of our influence and our strength and our power to help the world do those things which will render war less likely to occur among the nations of the earth. [Great applause.]

150

I do not say that an International Court of Justice will abolish war. I do say that an International Court of Justice is the longest and most practicable step in that direction taken thus far in the history of the world. The nations of Europe have established such a Court and we ought to be adherents thereto, not at the expense of surrendering anything that we cherish in our National life or assuming a single obligation that might come from entanglement in European affairs. Oh, my countrymen, I should like to be able to say, with your united backing and the consent of the United States Senate, that America is ready to play her part in lifting international relationships to a little higher plane; so that we may put an end to the things that bow humanity in grief and impose burdens on the treasuries of nations which they can ill afford. Let us have a new hope and a new promise, and let us be in a position to say to our children and their children that life is not encouraged for the purpose of sacrifice but for that greater accomplishment which is becoming in the eyes of God Almighty. [Great applause.]

ACHIEVEMENTS OF THE PIONEERS

Speech at Toquerville, Utah, June 27, 11 a. m.

Ladies and Gentlemen:

IT IS a very great pleasure to be able to stand here and greet you this beautiful morning. It may be true that no President has ever before come to Zion Park, but when they find out about this section as I have done, they will all be coming. [Applause.] We have had a wonderful ride this morning, and during its course I have been thinking of some of the compensations of life. You live here beyond the reach of the railroads, in God's great open country, far away from some of the much-prized contacts of more fully developed communities; but you have that tremendous satisfaction which comes from having turned your energy to the recovery of the wilderness and making the land productive by your efforts. Surely God must have had some intent when He created this great wilderness country which you have reclaimed, and He must have expected such a result from you, for God never does anything without some design.

Work of Vast and Lasting Importance

I should like for a moment to pay my reverent respects to the pioneers who are gathered here. The work of the pioneer is of vast importance, and high tribute should be paid to the men and women who, taking with them their all and leaving behind the comforts and refinements of civilization, have advanced into the wilderness and given of their energy and courage to bring a new land to fruitfulness. Our people have been and are a wonderful race, but no part of our citizenship has been more brave, has accepted hardships with less complaint, or done more toward the making of the Republic than the pioneers. You of the pioneer group must surely find your compensation when you think of the results you have achieved.

Constitute Finest American Citizenry

What a blessed thing is the consciousness of having made a habitation for such a wonderful group of men and women and boys and girls as I see before me this morning! There is no place in America where a finer citizenship can be found than that which is made up of the pioneer company of Americans that I see here. [Applause.] Someone told me that when we came in here we would be in a region where conditions made life difficult and arduous; but here I find this splendid gathering which would delight anybody. I tell you it makes me happy this morning that I can have the privilege of being President of such a Republic as ours.

It is a great joy to see you; to be able to greet you, and to find you happy and contented in the work you are doing in building this great empire. I wish you every success, every happiness, and every good fortune in the world. [Applause.]

SHOULD STRIVE FOR THE COMMON GOOD

Speech at Cedar City, Utah, June 27, 8:30 p. m.

Ladies and Gentlemen:

IF IT were not so late I should like to wait for a few moments, because the man who operates the voice amplifying device has not as yet returned from the trip to Zion Park, and I wanted you to see one of the marvels of modern science as exhibited in the amplifying of public speech. It is not very often that those so far from the larger centers have such an opportunity, and I thought you would enjoy the experience. A speaker talking before one of these devices (indicating) can have his voice carried from this platform to the farther edge of your city and can be heard distinctly. However, it is not in operation for the moment.

I will take the opportunity to say how pleasing it is to us to be so cordially greeted by so large a representation of the citizenship of southern Utah. We have had a very wonderful day—wonderful in many ways. We have come to have a new love for the beautiful; we have found a new charm in the marvelous works of nature; we have seen exhibited the results of her convulsive moods and then, in the canyons and gorges and other aspects of Utah's magnificent scenery, we have seen the effect of her relentless force operating throughout the ages. With it all, I think we have come to have, perhaps, even a greater reverence for the Creator, a new wonderment at His purposes, and a new curiosity to know when we ourselves are going fully to understand those purposes. It has been an enthralling day.

Pride in Accomplishment Impels Progress

One of the things that has interested me most has been to see how men and women will toil with all their might and with all their hopes on a little strip of land, seeking to make Mother Nature yield to their designs. I

153

have come to the conclusion that it is due to something more than the mere ambition to subsist and make a home. I believe the more impelling purpose must be an inherent one in man to have something he can call his own, a place where he can see the results of his handiwork. [Applause.] After all, that is about the greatest inspiration there is in life. It so happens that we have too little of such inspiration in the great working centers of population, but out here in the great valleys a man turns his hand to toil, sometimes successfully, sometimes with disappointment, and yet always he has time to appraise the thing that he has done and to find a pride in his work. If I were going to give a message to the boys and girls who are listening to me at this moment, I would tell them always to have a pride in what they undertake to do in life, for pride in accomplishment always impels humanity onward.

Oh, it has been good to see you, and I wish I could leave with you an adequate impression of the happy and wonderful day we have had. It is good to come so far from the great centers and find this distinctly American population working hopefully and confidently in the making of a greater America. [Applause.] You are doing your part handsomely, and I offer you my congratulations and pay you my tribute. I cannot tell you how proud I am as President of the United States that you are carrying forward your splendid work. [Applause.]

"You Are Citizens of the Greatest Republic in World"

You live in a wonderful State, and the people of Utah are truly "empire builders." Senator Smoot was telling me today that the resources of Utah are so great and her industries so varied that although a wall were built around the State, shutting it off from the world, yet her people could live within and for themselves alone. But you do not want to do that. You are citizens of the greatest Republic in the world, and the Republic wants you to be a part of it.

I like to tell you, for I believe it with all my heart, that all of the Republic is concerned in the common welfare of America. It is impossible to have a great country where one section prospers at the expense of another; we can not have a fortunate country where one class of its citizenship is doing well while another is suffering. We can only have a happy, contented, and thriving people when the common weal is in fact the common weal and everybody is a participant in the common good fortune. I wish you your share of the common good fortune of the United States of America. [Applause.] I wish you every good that can come to you. If I am the first President to visit your section, I am going to give some of my successors such an impression of you that they likewise will want to come. I am sure they will enjoy their visit, as we have done today.

I thank you all for your cordial greeting and this manifestation of your interest and friendship. It is, I can assure you, more than cordially reciprocated. [Applause.]

Tells of Covered Wagons of the Past

[At this point President Harding's attention was called to the fact that there were present a number of the original pioneers of Iron County; whereupon he further said:]

I am glad to salute the pioneers, and I should like to shake hands with each one of them, as I should like to shake hands with all who are present, if time permitted. To the pioneers let me say that they make a strong appeal to me. I know something of the type of men who make successful pioneers. I saw them go out from my own community in Ohio to build up the wonderful West, particularly that portion embraced within the States of Missouri, Iowa, Kansas, and Nebraska. I saw some of them, possessing a little material store in life, cut adrift from everything, build their covered wagons, place all their belongings therein, as well as their families, and start westward with the "Star of Empire," to build a new empire of the West. It took courage, and only the fit survived and made a success of it. I know the sturdy stuff of which the pioneers were made. I pay you pioneers of this section my greatest respects for the foundation which you laid in building this magnificent community of southern Utah. Now I should like to meet the pioneers.

BELONG TO RACE OF "EMPIRE BUILDERS"

Remarks at Brigham, Utah, June 28, 7:45 a. m.

Ladies and Gentlemen:

THIS is the first time I have ventured to come out to say good morning in a dressing gown, but I know the men will understand the circumstances and the ladies will forgive me. I understood, however, that you were good enough to come down to greet us, and, though I have been sleeping rather late because of strenuous days, I could not go through your little city without saying "how do you do." It is fine to see you on this splendid, bright, and beautiful morning.

I believe you must belong to the race of "empire builders," because you have in your faces those evidences of strength, determination, cheer and devotion which characterized them. I am delighted to come out to greet you on behalf of Mrs. Harding as well as for myself. [Applause.]

RECLAMATION BENEFIT TO REPUBLIC; AID FOR
AMERICAN SUGAR INDUSTRY; HE WOULD
OUTLAW ARMED CONFLICT

Address at Pocatello, Idaho, Thursday, June 28, 11:15 a. m.

Governor Moore, Ladies and Gentlemen, Fellow Americans All:

IT IS a great privilege to stand before such a gathering of fellow Americans. We have been entranced by the wonders of nature, the magnificence of your mountains, the indescribable stretches of valleys which you have made to blossom, and the hills eternal. All through this splendid country we have been engrossed, enthralled, delighted, and entertained, but, after all, there is nothing to compare with the view which a body of your citizenship affords. [Applause.] I do not say that because it may be especially pleasing to you; I say it because it is a delight to me. Somehow you have a wholesomeness and a heartiness, and you afford the inspiration that comes from a distinctly 100 per cent American audience.

It has been a wonderful experience to travel in the West. I have been here before, but without deriving, perhaps, the same pleasure, and I am sure not with the same appreciation. I came to Pocatello some six years ago and not half so many of you came to see me at that time. [Laughter.] So I assume that your presence today may be considered as a tribute to those who are in authority in our government. It is a fine thing for those who represent the government to get into more intimate contact with this wonderful land of ours. What a pity it is that the city of Washington, beautiful as the capital of your Republic is, knows only the atmosphere of official life, and what a pleasure it is to enjoy the inspiration and broadening influence of a visit to this wonderful western land, no longer a frontier, but a most important part of the great Republic!

We had a tremendously interesting experience yesterday. Perhaps we came in more intimate contact than at any other place with the work of determined and resolute men engaged in turning the waste places into gardens. There came to me the suggestion of a rather intimate relationship between the processes of turning waste lands into fertile fields and gardens by the application of the water stored up in the mountain gulches and springs and the making of a great Republic. Here lies a tremendous valley needing only the touch of water to make it blossom like a garden, and by man's genius the water is applied and we see the magnificent transformation. I wonder sometimes if there is not a parallel in the life of the Republic. We have the great waste stretches in American life that need only the irrigating touch of American patriotism from the heart of the mountains, which represent our underlying foundations. When you irrigate the waste places, you add greatly to the resources and the advancement of the Republic.

Pledges Aid to the Sugar Industry

Then there comes another impression from this western trip. I have been speaking of some of the problems of government, and the experiences of yesterday and today have all the more impressed me with the importance of one problem for which we must find a solution. I refer to the problem of transportation. No matter how liberally and bountifully you produce, unless you can find the transportation necessary for the delivery of your excess to the consuming world elsewhere, you have worked in vain. If you will stop to think you will realize that the first transaction in human relationships required some sort of transportation for the delivery of the exchanged products. Here in the wonderful West you have the problem of transportation. I am glad to note that some practical methods of your own are being applied. I have been noting the development of the sugar industry in Colorado, Idaho and Utah. I can well understand how the one-time inordinate cost of sugar, because of transportation costs, led you to the development of that industry out here in the Rocky Mountain region; and, so long as I am President, every influence is going to be given to the maintenance of the American sugar industry, so that we may be self-reliant. [Applause.]

We rode yesterday over a new railroad and occupied the first passenger train to use its rails. That road has been built down into the southern section of Utah in order to deliver the iron ore to the mills at Provo. That is another manifestation of the application of man's genius in providing his own necessities within a given area and thus removing another difficulty of transportation. The same suggestion applies to the woolen mills. It is of great advantage in this resourceful land of ours to develop industries which will to some extent remove the problems of transportation. When we speak of transportation, my countrymen, we find ourselves more closely drawn to what is termed the "national viewpoint." We cannot live in America by entertaining only a local or sectional viewpoint. We could not have government aid in the building of necessary improved roads if Congress had only a narrow sectional viewpoint. You could not have the government aiding your irrigation projects, as I think it ought to aid and will aid them, if Congress did not have a National viewpoint. We must always be thinking of the concerns of our common country, and I like to see the manifestations of national interest everywhere which have come to me on this trip across the continent.

Rights and Obligations of Rail Workers

Let me speak for a moment to the men in overalls on my left, who have come out here and given me a most pleasing welcome. I never boast about it, but I used to play in the band myself and I know what it is to leave the bench and take up a horn and toot it. I rejoice in

159

the welcome which has come from the railroad men; but I want to say to you on this side that the boys on my left are just as much concerned with transportation as are you. It is the most important function in American life, because without transportation there is no inspiration to production. The most important thing about transportation in this country is its dependable continuity. I would not say anything to the men on my left that I would not be equally ready to say to those on my right; but I speak the truth when I tell you that I think the men who are engaged in transportation in this country ought to be the best paid men in any employment in America, and they ought to toil under the most fortunate working conditions.

Compensation for Honest Work

When I step on a railroad train I want to know that the man who has made the track has put his heart and soul into a perfect work; I want to know that the man who has constructed the car in which I ride has produced a perfect piece of American mechanism; I want the man who inspects the wheels to have made a perfect inspection, and I want the man who sits in the locomotive cab to have a steady eye, a clear brain, a brave heart, and a cool head at all times, because upon his judgment and the activities of every man coordinated in the railroad service depend the lives of those who ride on the American railways. I speak only the truth when I say that such men ought to be the best compensated in any public service. I speak another truth when I say to them that they have not any right under any conditions to bring about a suspension of that public service. [Applause.]

I do not mean to say that the government will ever require you to work against your will; that cannot be done in free America, for men may only be required to work as they choose to work; but when they enter a public service employment upon which the welfare of the country depends, they ought to enter into some sort of arrangement whereby service will not be suspended because of any

160

grievance until there has been a hearing and the justice of the cause has been determined. We have all the same interest in this America of ours, and you are just as much concerned in the continuity of transportation as are the people on my right who are dependent upon it. Do you not see, my countrymen, that in this marvelous land of ours our interests are mutual, and every great decision, no matter whether it affects employment in connection with transportation, or production, or irrigation, or what-not, must always take into consideration the common good rather than the particular good of any individual or group or section?

Pledges Just Treatment for the Indians

I am reminded of another matter. I notice on my right some Indian maidens, and I do not think there is a more appropriate place in the country for me to say a word about our Indian citizenship and population. The United States wants to treat the Indians just as it treats everybody else in America. They have been our wards, to a certain extent, but the government has tried to bring them into the assumption of responsibility on their own account and to equip them to embrace our ideas of civilization, as civilization has been forced upon them. I do not believe there would be any Indian problem if the question to be considered were one between the government and the Indians alone. The Indian problem arises because of citizens quite apart from the government who have been preying upon the Indians in their era of good fortune.

The Indians have given wonderful service. I hold in my hand some figures which were prepared for my benefit on this occasion which are so interesting that I want to make a reference to them. During the World War, 12,000 of our Indians gave of their service in the khaki uniform, and distinguished themselves in battle quite as notably as any other class of our citizenship. [Applause.] They came back not only with the joy of having been of service to the Republic, but with a fine record for conduct. Those who had command of them say that they never complained; that they were easily disciplined; that they were without fear, and they were always ready to face death. They brought home with them, best of all, not only a number of distinguished service medals but eleven croix de guerre. Furthermore, while these numerous sons of the Indian tribes were at the front, the Indians at home subscribed $25,000,000 to the government's war fund. That was a manifestation of interest on the part of the Indians which deserves our highest commendation. [Applause.]

I wish that the Western citizenship which comes in contact with the Indians would join in our efforts to make them ready to embrace the opportunities of American citizenship. The government is doing its full part. We have established 224 schools for Indian children, and 35,000 of them are in attendance at such schools. The Christian churches are maintaining 81 sectarian educational institutions among them, with missionary teachers, and the government employs 150 physicians and operates 78 hospitals for the Indians. We are doing these things with a great deal of success, but that is no more than the Republic owes to the Indians. I rejoice to say that, in addition to doing these things, we have brought about a condition under which the Indian is no longer disappearing, but is growing in numbers, as well as in equipment to take advantage of the opportunities afforded by American life. [Applause.]

Principles Which Guide Humankind

The governor spoke of your rugged, unfailing reverence for the fundamentals of the American system of government, and I should like to dwell on that theme for a moment, because here in America, under the Constitution which I believe to have been inspired, we Americans in less than a century and a half have builded the most wonderful Republic on the face of the earth. It is only 147 years since the signing of the Declaration of Independence and only about 135 years since the making of the Constitution. In that short period we Americans have developed an empire to the amazement and wonderment of the earth. It is inconceivable to me that this matchless American accomplishment could have been founded upon false principles. We laid the eternal foundation of civil rights, and then the capstone of human rights, and then we erected the third, namely, that of religious liberty. Civil liberty, human liberty, and religious liberty are the foundations on which we have builded this Republic. God grant that nothing shall turn us away from any of these fundamentals. [Applause.] We can have no free Republic without all of them. I want this Republic of ours to continue to live and march in the vanguard of nations.

Opportunities of Youth

There stand before me a number of little girls. I cannot tell from their garb or their smiling faces or their conduct whether one is the daughter of a working man and another the daughter of a banker. They are all fine examples of American opportunity. Every boy and girl in America have the right to aspire, and under the Constitution opportunity beckons to them all precisely alike. There is an obligation of government to equip these boys and girls so that they may better embrace American opportunity. There is the obligation to maintain equality of opportunity and to equip the growing citizenship of the Republic to embrace it. If we shall only do that I know, my countrymen, we shall go on to greater numbers and greater achievement which we cannot even approximately estimate from our appraisals of America today. We are boundless in our material possibilities, and I know that, if we only keep the faith and maintain the institutions of the fathers, we shall finally have a Republic that no human being today is able to forecast. I hope in the growth of numbers and the widening of our influence, we shall adhere to those principles which have made us what we are and that we may continue a happy, hopeful and confident people; otherwise, we shall not be able to play our part in the leadership of the great human procession.

Cherishes American Aloofness from Intrigue

The governor made allusion to my efforts for the encouragement of the peace of the world. I had not intended to speak on that topic; but let me say that I cherish American aloofness and American independence from the intrigues and the conspiracies of the Old World as much as any citizen in all the land. We have, however, witnessed the spectacle of a tremendous world upheaval which ought never to have occurred. We have seen millions of human lives sacrificed and billions of wealth expended. The cost in life and treasure has been so great that we shall not recover in two centuries to come. We have seen our own sons sacrificed in that great conflict, and sorrow and bereavement brought to homes everywhere throughout the Republic. I do not know that there will ever come a time in human affairs when men will be so actuated by conscience that there will be no more armed conflict; but I do believe that the great American people, who have learned to progress without the conflicts of force, ought to give of their influence in directing the world to a plane where war cannot occur. [Applause.]

I sometimes wonder if your western communities are like those in which I grew up. I remember when I was a boy we had a trial before the justice's court nearly every day in the week. There never was a Saturday in our village without a dozen street fights; it was a dull day without that number of conflicts occurring. It seemed to be the accepted thing that many disputes had to be settled by resort to fisticuffs. When I went to the county seat town as a young man I remember we appraised the lawyers by the number of cases they had on the court docket. We were then getting out of the fighting period and having our disputes settled in court. Nowadays we have so far progressed that we largely appraise a lawyer by the number of cases he does not have on the court docket, it being the theory that the best lawyer keeps his client out of court. That much progress has been made.

Declares Arbitration Has Its Perils

Among nations it has been the practice to resort to arms for the settlement of disputes.

We have long been advocates of arbitration in America and we still adhere to that theory; but arbitration, my countrymen, has its perils. I am beginning to think that

164

I would join the labor forces of the country in opposition to arbitration. In any arbitration we are bound to accept an umpire, either chosen by lot or chosen by some disinterested power, and I do not mind saying to you I would a thousand times rather trust a decision, in which America is interested, to an international court of justice, with judges of high standing, than to any arbitration tribunal that has ever been created. [Applause.]

There is already established a court of justice. It is not precisely to our liking, but I think, so long as we are moving in the direction of the possible settlement of justiciable disputes, that this Republic of ours ought to give its influence and its power to the support of an international court, seeking to make it conform to American ideals so far as we can, and then hoping to go on progressively until the nations see the wisdom of leaving their disputes to peaceful settlement rather than to the arbitrament of arms.

Government Ready to Help Its People

My countrymen, as President, I have come to have a much more intimate knowledge of the cost of war. There has come to me the expression of the sorrows incident to war; there has come to my notice the unspeakable cost of war; there comes to me day by day the call of the service men who were impaired in the defense of the Nation. When I consider these things and stop to think that out of every dollar you pay in taxes to the Federal government 85 cents goes to pay for the cost of war, past or present, and only 15 cents to the employments of peace, I think that, if we are going to come up to God's highest ideal of humanity, we should do all in our power to wipe out every possibility in the future of a conflict of arms and devote our energies, our attention, our best thought, and all we have to those highest accomplishments which come to the victories of peace. [Applause.]

It is fine to have greeted you, and I thank you from the bottom of my heart. I wish you the best ever, and I am pleased to say to you that if there is at any time, from the viewpoint of the Nation, anything it can do to further the development of your splendid State, the government is in the most hearty sympathy with you and ready to help you. [Applause.]

Before the presentation of the horseshoe, I wish you to know some of the members of my official family. You are very much interested here in the work of the Interior Department. I have the pleasure of presenting to you the Secretary of the Interior, Doctor Hubert Work. [Applause.]

Then I know there is another member of the Cabinet in whom you are greatly interested, and it is my pleasure to present to you a really great Secretary of Agriculture, Mr. Henry C. Wallace. [Applause.]

I should like also to present the Speaker of the House but I am informed that he is not at present in the car.

PRIDE IN INDIVIDUAL EFFORT ESSENTIAL

Remarks in Acknowledgment of Gift of Horseshoe Presented by Mr. Thomas Adkins, at Pocatello, Idaho, June 23, 11:55 a. m.

My Countrymen:

I WANT to address you again in order to make acknowledgment of the gift which has been presented to me.

Mr. Adkins, I am exceedingly grateful for this testimonial. I will, in conformity with your admonition, carry it further than was originally intended by those who drove the wagons and met their unfortunate fate. There is something else about it that I treasure even more. It is not alone the kind wishes of the blacksmith; it is not alone that it is a symbol of good fortune, but I like to possess it as a mark of the handicraft of an American mechanic whose numbers, alas, are growing far too few. In our modern life we are not developing the great mechanic as we once did. I can remember when the blacksmith was the most notable citizen in all the community. Everybody turned to him for assistance; not a few turned to him for advice; all of his friends turned to him for the neighborhood gossip, and he was a great factor in the community. I think the most interesting man I have ever known in all my life was Chandler Smith, a village blacksmith, who shod the horses, sharpened the plowshares, reset the wagon tires, and then when he had no special and urgent repair work to do turned his attention to building wagons and buggies, and he made better ones than any modern commercial manufacturer ever turned out. They were really great men, Mr. Adkins, who carried on the trades in the earlier and pioneer days, and I hope, sir, that you are preserving their type in this western country.

I had no intention of speaking so long, but if there is one thing needed to bring us back to the industrial heights in America it is to have men who work at the bench or elsewhere put more soul in their work. [Applause.] I know that Mr. Adkins has put his soul into the making of this horseshoe. Let me say that the greatest compensation in life is the pride in the things you have been able to do. [Applause.] That is what makes the waste places turn into gardens. If we can only have a great industrial army in America with pride in the work to be performed, each man eager to do his work better than everybody else, I am sure about the future of industrial America. I thank you, Mr. Adkins, and I also thank you, Governor Hawley.

WESTERN MARCH OF CIVILIZATION

Speech at Blackfoot, Idaho, June 28, 2:30 p. m.

Ladies and Gentlemen: --------

YOU have done us very great honor and given us very great pleasure in coming out in such great numbers to extend us your cordial greeting while we are traveling across your State. I am afraid I cannot convey an adequate understanding of the pleasure it is to one who is in authority to come into direct contact with the American people as it is my good fortune to come in contact with them while on this journey across the continent. It makes me more pleased than ever to hold a position of great responsibility in the Republic, and I speak truly when I say that it makes me more anxious than ever to serve my countrymen faithfully and well.

We have been noticing how the determination and courage of American manhood and womanhood have been turning the wild, waste places into gardens and habitations. As we were coming up the valley this morning I was thinking of an incident that occurred only a little while ago. Among my callers at the White House, one day, was a group of Indians. With them was a fine old chief bearing his bow and arrows that had been his weapons throughout his active life. He stopped and shook hands with me, and in his few words said: "Me give white chief," and he handed me the bow and arrows, by means of which he had procured game and made his way through life. There was a suggestion of tears in his eyes, and I asked him the reason. He replied: "Me no need any more; me get food like white man." That was rather a pathetic incident, but, on the whole, rather a pleasing one, because it indicated that in the westward march of civilization even the representatives of old Indian life have come to embrace that which we look upon as the accepted habit of humanity and have come to participate with us in the great western development.

Space and Distance No Longer Barriers

One word more: I want you to know, my countrymen, that, though you live in a region that is seemingly far West to those whose homes are in the East, nevertheless, you are in very close contact with your government; you are, in fact, quite as close to the heart of the Republic as you ever need to be. Distances no longer are barriers. I spoke in Kansas City some nights ago, and was given assurance that every word uttered by me was heard by friends in the city of New York. How wonderful that is! There will come a day, undoubtedly, when we may speak across the continent and be heard as plainly as I am now heard by those who are in this audience. I remember that about a year and a half ago I spoke on the occasion of the burial of the Unknown Soldier, when the tribute of the Nation was paid to the war dead. At the same time an audience was gathered in San Francisco to listen to the address which I then delivered in Washington, D. C. I have photographs of the gathering. A lady who was present afterwards told me that she kept looking at the floral decorations around the entrance to the stage as though she expected me to appear.

It is a great pleasure to greet you, and I wish you all the best fortune in the world.

OPPOSES MONOPOLIES AND SPECIAL PRIVILEGES IN NATURAL RESOURCES; COOPERATION BETWEEN CONSUMERS

Address at Idaho Falls, Idaho, June 28, 3:30 p. m.

Governor Moore, Ladies and Gentlemen, My Country-men All:

YOUR governor embarrassed me a little when he referred to Idaho as the greatest State in the Union, because, as you know, there are 48 States. [Applause.] If, however, I were to judge by this assemblage today, I should be ready to make a guess that Idaho is the most populous State in the Union. [Applause.] What a splendid manifestation this gathering is of the wonderful development of your magnificent State! I never dreamed of seeing one-tenth as many people today. You have given us a most delightful and heartening surprise.

In the course of our travels today your governor told me about the pioneers of this section who had the courage of heart and the foresight to open up this great section to settlement and development. I wish they could all return here today and see what wonders their beginning hath wrought. You yourselves are the finest manifestation of the development and expansion of the American Republic. I think I speak truly and without disparagement to any other section of America when I say that you represent the most typical and wholesome American development in all the land. [Applause.] You have sprung from those who subscribed early to the tenets of American faith, and you have grown in that faith and practiced it until you have made what was once a frontier a part

170

of the Republic, so marked by advancement, so ample in progress, so wholesome in every reflection of civic and material activity that I can really see little difference between Ohio or Indiana or Illinois and Idaho. You are all a part—and a magnificent part—of this great Republic of ours; and I want you to believe that it is just as much pleasure and quite as much satisfaction for the President to see you as it is for you to see the President. [Applause.]

Believes in Gospel of Understanding

I like to come to your great State and to other American commonwealths for another reason: I am a great believer in the gospel of understanding. I like to bring the government closer to you, and I like to bring you closer to the government, because, if the government can understand you and you can understand the government, we are going to have teamwork and better cooperation. I think the government ought to know your problems, and I think you ought to know the government's difficulties in dealing with those problems. I know it is an inspiration and a help to me to see for myself the possibilities of development through government aid, and I want you to believe that the Federal government is just as deeply interested and as anxious to aid in working out your problems as you are in having them worked out. You must not, however, expect the government to do everything; you must play your part with that resolution and deter-mination which characterized the pioneers when they entered upon the great work of preparing this land for settlement and development. I think, perhaps, we have come to expect rather too much at the hands of the Federal government. If there is one place in America where that ought not to be so it is in the wonderful West, for the magic development of the West has come because of the efforts of sturdy manhood and womanhood who were eager to do for themselves. The problem of the government is to maintain such conditions as will make possible your continued progress.

171

I will take this opportunity to allude to another matter of which the governor spoke. He referred to the fact that this is preeminently a seed section. Have you stopped to think what a wonderful tribute that is to your excellence? When men plant seed they choose the best there is. I can remember distinctly how my grandfather picked out the seed corn for the next year. He selected the very choicest and best developed ears and preserved them carefully for the next year's planting. So when other sections of the United States turn to Idaho Falls and vicinity for their seed, whether potatoes, peas, or what not, they are paying you the finest tribute that can come to the excellence of your products and the possibilities which you yourselves have developed. It is a great thing to raise good seed, and, if I may make the application, you are raising the finest boyhood and girlhood in all the country. [Applause.]

We have come to Idaho today in the course of what perhaps may be regarded as the most extended tour for inspection of National concerns that it has ever been the privilege of an American President to make. Including a trans-continental tour, a visit to Alaska, and a return to the Capital by way of our great Pacific States, the Panama Canal, and Porto Rico, it will enable us to consider first hand a series of National interests extending from Arctic to tropics, from Atlantic to Pacific. They embrace a range so wide and varied that we may fairly doubt if any other government is called upon to deal with a comparable array of interests, involving the welfare of so great a community.

Idaho Truly Imperial Commonwealth

It is true that the present tour is being devoted largely to the newer, the less developed portions of our National domain; but these are the parts of our country in which very largely the future of our country lies. The character of our institutions, the society we shall develop, our relations with the rest of the world, must be largely determined by the direction which development in these newer parts of our country shall take.

172

In Idaho we all recognize one of those truly imperial commonwealths, yet to a great extent in the making, which we look upon as store-houses of opportunity and resources. Yesterday we visited a great wonderland in a remote section of Utah; a region of surpassing riches, yet almost unknown to our country outside the State of Utah. It was a wonderful experience for all of us, a reminder such as I wish might be brought home to every American, impressing us with a new conception of the immensity of America's estate and opportunities. Your Idaho is another such community, boasting an unexampled wealth in everything that a great people may require. Your magnificent West needs only more of population, more of capital, to support the wonderful enterprise and initiative of its people, who have carried its development so far in so short a time.

Development of Natural Resources

When I said a moment ago that the character of our institutions and the kind of society we shall develop in this Republic, are bound to be determined largely by these newer regions, I had in mind a particular phase of the industrial and commercial problems about which I wish to speak briefly. From the beginning of western development it has been the ambition of these communities to secure the widest diversification of industry, to become so far as possible self-contained and self-supporting. So you have wrought in your mines, your forests, your fields; you have introduced new and varied forms of agriculture; you have established manufactures that a generation ago would have been deemed impossible here. You recognized early, what we of the East now are coming to realize, the necessity to build up such self-contained societies of widely varied interests and occupations, because in a country of our "magnificent distances" we cannot always place so great a reliance upon transportation in our exchange of products as we have committed ourselves to in the past. In the long run we shall have a more homogeneous, closely knit, and self-reliant Nation as we shall the more nearly

173

approach the idea of self-sufficient communities in all parts of the country.

So I want to report to you of the West the conviction of the administration that the time has come to adopt a broad policy of encouraging the utilization and development of your resources, human and material. That conservation which would lock up such riches as these, and raise barriers against their development when the Nation needs them, is not true conservation; it is rather the policy of the miser who hoards his wealth with no conception of making it serviceable to himself or to the society which enabled him to possess it. We will always oppose monopolies and special privileges in natural resources. We are committed to the program of making these resources serve the man of moderate means, the home-builder, the worker, the producer. Within these limitations upon free opportunity, we must cling to policies which shall envisage the fullest, the broadest, the most generous and intelligent utilization of these tremendous possibilities.

Problem of Consumer and Producer

One of the most engrossing problems of our time, confronting all countries and all societies, is the exorbitant cost of living. We realize that the real producer, under our elaborate and costly system of distribution, is not permitted a fair share of his product for his own use and enjoyment. We have become convinced that somehow our system of distribution has grown too cumbersome, too costly, too complex, too indirect, too unrelated to the interests of real producer and legitimate consumer. We must find methods to take up as much as possible of the slack in the long line between producer and consumer; to give the producer a better share in that which he furnishes to the community, and to enable the consumer to meet his requirements at reasonable cost.

To this end many experiments have been made in cooperative production, transportation, distribution, and purchasing. To a great extent, such experiments have proceeded from the enterprise and initiative of the western

174

people, to whom these problems have presented themselves with especial insistence. But for the spirit of cooperation, the willingness to be mutually helpful, the determination to give first place to the interest of the community, you could not have made your West what it is. Working cooperations on a great scale, practical in operation and adequate to cope with our problems can never be possible except where there is this spirit, determination, and purpose. It is because the West has led so far in devising such workable programs that I have thought to say a few words along this line today.

Developments of the last generation have brought the instrumentalities of transportation, of finance, of corporate organization and operation into a closer harmony with the true public interest than ever before. Government has sought to make itself helpful, to point the way, to remove ancient barriers of custom or tradition, and to curb the excessive demands of privilege, in order to cheapen for the great public many of the services which formerly were dominated by private interests and operated with too exclusive a consideration for private profit. Anything tending to break down personal initiative, to destroy enterprise and ambition, must not enter into any program which can hope for the approval of the American people. Ours is an individualistic society, and we want it to remain so. We want this Republic to remain always the land of opportunity wherein every man's abilities and usefulness shall measure his personal advancement and prosperity. The kind of a program to encourage cooperation and coordination which I have in mind, would not interfere with the freedom of proper opportunity; rather, it would enhance the individual's chance to better his individual fortune.

Systems of Credit and Finance

The need of this time is to shorten the bridge between producer and consumer, and to reduce the toll that must be paid for passing over it. We all know a good deal about the various cooperative societies, associations and corporations which have undertaken, in many cases with notable success, to improve the position of the agricultural producers. Such organizations have been successful in all parts of this country, and in many parts of the Old World. They have already done a great work and taught us many valuable lessons. Where there are obstacles, imposed by unfortunate statutes or public policies, in the way of expanding such activities as these, they might well be gradually removed through measures of helpfulness and encouragement.

On the whole, I think the agricultural community has been more alive to the promotion of its interests along these lines than has the urban community. The farmers have seen where their interest lay, and have been more prompt and energetic in adopting effective measures to promote them, than the people of the city and town have been. There is need to have working and practical cooperative associations of producers in the country, and at the same time to have equally effective cooperations among the consuming communities of the cities and towns; and, finally, to link these two sets of cooperators together in a coordination for mutual advantage to both. I believe it is possible, and altogether desirable, that systems of credit and finance should be developed, under public auspices, to encourage both these kinds of cooperation, and to draw them together into a harmonious working scheme of widespread distribution at the lowest possible expense.

The Revolutionship of Incomes

We have in recent years given much attention to developing a system of agricultural finance, particularly adapted to the needs of Americon farm producers. Some critics have indeed protested that it was class legislation. Perhaps it was; but, as I suggested in discussing the problems of agriculture in Kansas the other day, it was in the interest of a vitally important section of the community which has heretofore had altogether too little consideration. Not only have I no apology for what has been done in the interest of the agricultural community; not only do I regard it as one of the monumental achievements

176

of the last generation in developing our country's institutions; but I venture to suggest that we might with profit to the whole people consider the possibility of effecting an analogous organization to promote and encourage, through measures of credit and finance, a proper organization of the consuming community in both cities and country.

I have not attempted to work out even an outline, much less the details, of such a system; but I believe it is possible, feasible, and certain to command the sympathy of men and momen who have the true interest of the country at heart. I hope to be able, as the result of studies and investigations, to recommend for the consideration of the Congress measures which shall represent a beginning along this line. It is a big and pregnant subject to which no thinking man or woman can deny the fullest and most careful consideration. My thought is that government should give the largest encouragement, consistent with sound economics and proper government functions, to every effort of the people to help themselves in dealing with the high cost of living and the relationship of incomes to our household budgets.

Cooperation Among Consumers

I have wondered if it were not possible, for example, that a scheme of cooperation among consumers, financed in part at least through a carefully organized and supervised adaptation of the principles of the savings bank or the building and loan society, might be made to serve a splendidly useful purpose in this department of our economic life. I think this would be preferable to having limited sections of the community undertaking to establish financial independence and economic solidarity, as some of them have lately been doing. The development of such a general program into a sound working business scheme would doubtless be found chiefly an affair of the State governments, but one in which the jointure of State and National authorities might prove practicable and even necessary.

I bring this suggestion to you, not as a wrought-out proposal of a policy, but as the suggestion of a direction which might be given to activities of this kind. I believe the suggestion is worthy of careful examination and consideration. I am convinced that its discussion would be fruitful of good results, and a reminder to some who are disposed to take unreasonable toll from both the consuming and the producing public, that this public has the right, the power, and the ability to devise means to protect itself.

Sympathizes with American Farmers

The aim and object of our every policy must be the establishment and maintenance of an independent and self-respecting, reliant and industrious, intelligent and self-helpful American citizenship. We must seek to encourage thrift, to promote saving, to make the American home the headquarters of an ever-broadening culture, a larger understanding of the complex problems of our times, and of a determined aspiration for the fullest measure of economic and social justice.

I am aware, my countrymen, of the hardships which have come to the American farmer since the war. I can understand and sympathize with his dissatisfaction and unrest; but I beg to remind you that unfortunate conditions have not come to the American farmer alone. They have come as well to those engaged in other forms of industry and to financial institutions; they have been one of the inevitable reflexes of the aftermath of the World War.

While I wish the processes of correction had not been so slow; I know that the government has been acting in the utmost sympathy toward those who found themselves in distress and with every desire to be helpful in every consistent way within the law. I know that we have provided the most generous, the most liberal, and the most ample financial accommodations for the American farmer that may be had by any enterprise or by any farming population anywhere in the world. I do not say that the steps taken by the government will cure all the ills of agriculture in the United States; but I have every confidence that the sturdy citizenship, the unalterable purpose, and the intelligence which characterize the American farmer will work out an early solution of present problems and difficulties.

Let me say in passing that there used to be an impression that a man could be a farmer when he could not be anything else. There never was a more mistaken notion. I am just as convinced as that I stand here that it takes more intelligence to be a good farmer than it does to pursue any other occupation. [Applause.] I do not say that because yours is a farming community. I know a little something about farming myself, and I know that a "wooden-head" cannot be a successful farmer.

The Science of Modern Farming

I will cite an instance: The present head of the Federal Reserve Board, Mr. Crissinger, is one of the best farmers in America. On a certain occasion I rode with him to one of his farms in Marion County, Ohio. His next-door neighbor, who had a field of corn adjoining, with only a fence between, was showing corn about eight inches high, while Mr. Crissinger's corn was the height of a man's thighs. The neighboring farmer asked Mr. Crissinger: "What is the matter with my corn? My land is the same as yours; I prepare it and plant the seed in the same way that you do; I use the same fertilizer; but I do not get the corn." Mr. Crissinger replied: "Do you ever stop to think how you cultivate?" His neighbor answered: "No; but I plow and remove the weeds." "Yes," said Mr. Crissinger, "but you are cultivating so deep that you are tearing the roots from the soil, and corn will not grow under such conditions." That was a simple reason; but the incident showed that Mr. Crissinger was an intelligent

179

farmer, while his neighbor did not know enough to be a good farmer. It takes the finest minds in the world to understand the intricacies and difficulties, and the science of modern farming.

Agriculture is the most independent occupation in the world. The day will come, if it is not here now, when those engaged in agriculture will constitute what may be called "the aristocracy of America." I have stated a thousand times—and pretty soon I am going to realize my desire—that I want a finer farm than the small one I now possess; and then I want to remain on that farm in the self-reliance that comes to every farmer, and I intend to attach to the fence a little sign reading: "This is the farm of W. G. H. Everyone who does not agree with me may drive on, or jump into the river." [*Laughter and applause.*]

Farming an Independent Pursuit

Sometimes farming is not as prosperous as commercial and industrial pursuits; but, I repeat, it is the most independent occupation in which men may engage. The people of America rely upon the farmer for their food, and, therefore, agriculture is our basic industry. I wish you the best good fortune that can come to you. You have been kind to come here to greet us. You have given us a new pride in America; you have given us new assurance that you will continue to play your part in the development of the Republic.

Before leaving the train for the automobile drive, I wish to take the opportunity of presenting to you some of the officers of the government who are in our party, because they want to know you and I want you to know them. First I present to you the Secretary of the Interior, Dr. Hubert Work. [Applause.]

I next present the Secretary of Agriculture, Mr. Henry C. Wallace. [Applause.]

I also desire to have you know the "boss" of the House of Representatives, Mr. Frederick H. Gillett, Speaker of the House. [Applause.]

HAS PRAISE FOR THE BOY SCOUTS

Remarks at Idaho Falls, Idaho, June 28, 4 p. m., on Presenting to Troop 6, Boy Scouts of Rigby, a Streamer for Having Obtained the Largest Increase of Membership

Scouts of Rigby:

IT GIVES me very great pleasure to be able personally to attach to your banner this tribute to your excellence and your unusual record in increasing your membership. It is always a splendid thing to receive any testimonial of excellence; and it is a joy to me to have the opportunity of presenting to you a mark of distinction for your efforts in building up the great organization of the Boy Scouts of America. I know of no organization in all the land which gives finer promise of a wholly patriotic American future.

GOVERNMENT AIDED LIVESTOCK INDUSTRY

Speech at Dubois, Idaho, June 28, 8:25 p. m.

Ladies and Gentlemen:

IT IS good of you to extend this greeting to us. We have had a wonderful day in your State, and I think we have seen more people than any of us believed lived in the State of Idaho, great and important as it is.

I realize that in reaching this point we have come to what is practically the center of the livestock industry. I myself think that raising livestock is one of the romantic occupations of life. I know it is a very important one not alone to you in your State, but to all the United States. The government has known something of the difficulties through which the industry has been passing. It was hit pretty hard by the slump which came after the World War and the general tumult which followed and dislocated the usual order of things. I am very happy to say to you that I know the government, through the operations of the War Finance Corporation, has been helpful to you in saving the industry. I know something about the activities of that corporation and how, when it was reestablished by Congress, it came to the assistance of an industry greatly in need of help. I hope you are well on the way to a complete recovery.

Federal Aid to Stock Raisers

In addition to the assistance which the government provided through the instrumentality of the War Finance Corporation, recent legislation, enacted only in March last, designed to provide better financial facilities to agriculture in general, has especially made provision for the financial relief of the stock-raising industry. We have come to know how long a period is required to mature livestock for the market. Your turnover requires time, while in other industries the turnover is quick, and you were entitled to the government's assistance in a great emergency because you were put out of balance by the government's necessary activities in war. I do not know the industry as, perhaps, I ought to know it; but it seems to me it must be an appealing one, and, as I gaze out upon this wonderful stretch of country, bounded by mountain ranges, I can well fancy that it is an ideal place in which to follow such an occupation.

Ought Not Have Envy in America

It is a very great pleasure to see you. You will not, I am sure, think I am saying it just because it is you when I tell you that one can nowhere in America see a more hardy, a more confident, and a more impressive manhood and womanhood than we are seeing in this marvelous western section. [Applause.] Impressed as we are by the manhood and womanhood of this great region, we are still more impressed by its promising childhood. Never

182

in my life have I seen so many beautiful, healthy, sturdy children. They have brought joy to the heart of every one of our party during our travels. I do not know just what the secret is; but I suspect that, after parenthood, wonderful climate, glorious air, golden sunshine, and majestic surroundings all must contribute to the happy result. I will not say that I am envious of you because of the free and open life you lead, for we ought not to have any envy in America. It requires all kinds of conditions in various States and all manner of varied industries and pursuits to make a great Republic such as ours, but in contributing to its grandeur you are playing your wonderful part.

I like to tell you, because I speak with authority, that you are just as close to your government as though you lived in Washington itself. The Federal government is concerned with the welfare of all the people of this great Union. Sometimes there is ill fortune in one section and sometimes in another. It is then not always easy to adjust conditions, and it is not always precisely the function of government to make the adjustment, but those responsible for the government do seek to correct conditions so that the intelligent, self-reliant citizens of this great country may make the adjustments for themselves.

Privilege to Be an American

I think it is a great privilege to be an American. I have come to a new understanding of the vastness and greatness of the American Union. Unless one moves about he always has the same horizon. I have known people who never left their native communities and who, consequently, knew nothing of the world except for the information gained from literature. It is a great thing to see for oneself. I have heretofore, as a private citizen, visited the West, but one sees the country a little differently when he travels in an official capacity. I might have gone through here a thousand times as an individual, and you would not have come to the station to see me. [Laughter and applause.] You come now because I am your President; and I like you for that, because respect for those who are in authority is becoming the citizenship of our Republic. Yet those in authority are like you in every way; they are no bigger; they are no better; but you clothe them with the authority of law and make them responsible for public affairs.

I repeat it is a pleasure to see you. It heartens us and makes us prouder than ever of our country; it makes us rejoice all the more that this wonderful trip across the continent has been undertaken, because we shall return to Washington feeling that we know you better, and I hope, too, that you will know us better. Good-bye, and good luck.

TEACHING IS GREATEST OCCUPATION; WESTERN CITIZENSHIP AND CHARACTER; STOCK-RAIS- ING INDUSTRY SUPPORTED

Speech at Dillon, Montana,
June 29, 7 a. m.

Governor Dixon, Fellow Citizens of Montana, and Students of the Normal School in Particular:

THE Governor has paid a tribute to American woman-hood, and I heartily endorse that tribute, for no utter-ance of that character could be too strong to suit me. I am glad we were asked to come out early in the morning to greet each other. In the first place, we saw the sun bestow the glory of the morning light upon the wonderful mountains, and it was a fine thing for those who do not often have that pleasure to enjoy amongst these magnifi-cent surroundings. We have been able to see something of your wonderful country in the matchless hopefulness of the morning. One of the splendid things about your section of the country is that it is now only in the morning of life, and, for that matter, this great Republic of ours is merely in the morning of its life. Out here everything is fresh and has the savor of the morning, betokening cheer, fresh determination and new hope. It is a great pleasure to be here.

I hope the editor of the "Tribune" is in this audience. I wish to tell him how fine and thoughtful I think he is for sending me the little special edition of the "Tribune" to inform me about Dillon and your wonderful county. Since I have read what was contained in that special edition, I am still more glad than ever to have the privilege of coming to Dillon. I wish to pay my tribute to your county as being

185

one of the rarest in America, and I want to proclaim you to America as an example. I refer to the fact that you have neither bonded nor floating indebtedness. That is one of the finest things that may be said of a community, and, if you will only cling to that policy, you will be the happiest, most fortunate, and, I am sure, the most progressive people in America, and you will always be astounded at the public improvements which you will be able to provide. I was speaking in Salt Lake City the other night about the menace of growing public indebtedness in this country. It is a joy to come to a community that will not locally tolerate such a thing. It is also a joy to know that you are one of the centers in which education is being promoted.

Recalls Career as Teacher

I should like to tell the young ladies that I myself taught school for one year, and it was the hardest work I ever did in my life. [Laughter.] I taught a country school under the old-fashioned methods when the curriculum embraced everything from the A B C's to algebra and general history. I am sure that sometimes the teacher did not know as much about algebra as he ought; but, even with this wide variety of studies carried on in the little country school in which I taught, I had the ambition to teach the pupils something more than what they could acquire in the books. I remember that one day, there being ten minutes before dismissal time, I called the attention of the pupils to an instruction in letter-writing. As you know, people need advice in regard to letter-writing and some people, it may be said, need to be advised against writing. [Laughter.]

I placed upon the blackboard my conception of the best letter form, and then I asked my pupils to write me a letter on their slates. One boy demurred, and I was called upon to punish him because he had refused to accept the discipline of the teacher. On the Monday following I received a notice from the directors that I was expected to teach reading, writing and arithmetic and to stick to them, and if I taught anything more I need not expect my pay. That was a prevailing country view of education among some people in central Ohio no longer ago than 1882. We have progressed wonderfully since then, and you in the West, perhaps, have progressed more than we have in the Central States. Teaching is the greatest occupation in the world—I should say the greatest profession, but I use the word "occupation" because I said a moment ago that teaching was the hardest work I have ever known.

High Character Is Essential

It is a curious trend in American life that parenthood is inclined to transfer many of the obligations of the home to the public school. Therefore, you teachers and prospective teachers will have thrust upon your shoulders some of the character-building in America that I think ought to be carried on in the American home. When you think of the responsibility of character-making, you can then appraise the influence you are going to have in the Republic. We cannot have a great Nation, my countrymen, unless its citizenship is made up of men and women of a high character. I can appraise any community by the character of its people. The reason you are such a wonderful, surprising, and admirable West is because of the character of your citizenship. I like to say that I have never seen a more wholesome, one hundred per cent American citizenship than I have seen in the Western States. [Applause.]

Speaking of education, I myself am being educated just now. There is no education in the world comparable to that of travel. I thought I knew something of this land of ours. I had been across the continent two or three times, across the Atlantic two or three times, and out into the crossroads of the Pacific; so I thought I had some concept of the measure of America's physical greatness, but on this journey across the continent, there have come new revelations, new understandings, and, especially helpful, a new appraisal of the spirit and the determination of the American people. It is good to come into this understanding. I wish I could bring it to you. I wish I could bring to you a better understanding of the East, from which section many of you, no doubt, have come. What a joy it has been everywhere to meet people and have them tell me "I am from Ohio!" Only those who come from Ohio, of course, tell me that; many others have come from various other States, but they have all assisted in building up this great empire. In this contact, we, as American citizens, have come to know each other better.

I am sure I have come to know better the possibilities, the aspirations, and the capabilities of our wonderful country. Nobody can come to a full measure of appreciation of its material greatness. Adventurous navigators who discovered some of the islands on the Eastern coast four hundred years ago, stood only at the gateway to America, and yet they thought they had discovered the richest country in the world. They had; but they only knew of the gateway; they never dreamed of the possibilities of American development. Then, the colonists spread westward, and later when the Republic was established and we became a nation, the Star of Empire continued its westward march until now we have come, not to a full development by any means, but to a condition where all of our continental territory proper enjoys Statehood, and each State has become a friendly rival of the others. You are making remarkable strides in the creation of materially the richest and, I believe, spiritually the best Republic on the face of the earth.

"We Are One Common Country"

I congratulate you, my countrymen, that you live in a land which is the first of the great nations of the earth to have anything like a recovery from the woes, disasters and tumult of the World War. We have not completely gotten on the right track as yet, but we have come the nearest to it of any of the great nations. War and its intoxications, insanities, and extravagances put the world completely out of plumb. You in this section of the country suffered bitterly from it; but our people everywhere suffered from it. Commerce, finance, manufacturing industry in many sections of America, and notably stock-raising, all suffered very grievously indeed, especially when the period of deflation came.

I want you to know that the government was brought into a pretty intimate understanding of the suffering of the stock-raising industry, particularly in the West, and I rejoice that the government was able to be of some assistance in helping the stock-raising industry to weather the great storm. I know of the effective action taken by the War Finance Corporation. I hope that the aid which has been extended has enabled you to see a more promising future ahead. The Congress has recently enacted legislation which is going to enable the farmer, whether grain-grower, hay-producer, or stock-raiser, better to finance himself in the future. He will have the financial advantages that are available to any other industry in America or to any agricultural people in the world.

Wishes Public Men Could Travel More

Always remember, my countrymen, that the government is just as deeply concerned about your fortunes in Montana as it is in the fortunes of the people of Ohio, or Pennsylvania or New York. We are one common country, where the fortunes of each are dependent upon the fortunes of all. We cannot have one prosperous community while another is suffering. Our interests are mutual and reach throughout the Republic. In this common interest and common purpose and common pride we are sure to go on building up a greater Republic, and in that great work I know you of Montana will play your part.

I am glad to have an opportunity of knowing you. I should like you to know me as your President, for, if we can only understand each other, I know we shall get along to the very best advantage. It is your business to have your government understand you, and it is my business to come and get acquainted with you. I wish all men in public life could do a little more of what is sometimes called "junketing."

I am going to Alaska to learn more about that Territory, and I am immensely in earnest about it. We have in Alaska a domain as large as one-third of continental United States, and yet we are allowing it to lie undeveloped and even to go backward. That is something that the public has not known. How many people do you think in the East know that your county is as large as two of the New England States? We in America ought to know each other better. We ought to know each other's aspirations and difficulties so that we may be helpful one to another. In any event I want your help, my countrymen, in making ours a stable Republic. I want your help in holding fast to the fundamentals on which Americans have builded; I want your help in making a community not content, but gratified with the things which are achieved, so that we shall go on to greater accomplishment.

I thank you for coming out to greet us this morning. Mrs. Harding would have been pleased to have offered a smile of greeting to you, but accepting this endless western hospitality involves, a rather strenuous program; as you know she is not strong, and we were kept up last night until nearly midnight. So she did not feel equal to getting out at this hour. I am glad that I did, for it has been a great pleasure to meet and greet you all. [Applause.]

GOVERNMENT WILL NEVER FAIL

Remarks on Arriving at Butte, Mont.,
Friday, June 29, 10:25 a. m.

Ladies and Gentlemen, Fellow Americans All:

YOU have given us a most delightful greeting on our arrival in your wonderful city. There are many phases of your welcome. I find my heart especially touched to see the veterans of the Grand Army bearing the colors of the Union which they helped to save in order to make a greater

Nation. I see so many children bearing flags and so many men in the habiliments of workmen at their employment that it all looks good to me. I have been following the comments of the press. It has been uniformly courteous. It has made frequent allusion to the favor the President does when he calls upon you. Do not accept such a statement as the literal truth, for you are doing the President a very great favor when you greet him as you do. It is a privilege to me to visit you, to know you more intimately, and to become better acquainted with this wonderful country of ours. [Applause.] Frankly, I find myself exalted, lifted up and more thoroughly consecrated in heart to the service of the Nation because of the better knowledge I am acquiring of our people and our vast domain.

Enjoyed Hospitality of West

I am not, I understand, formally to address you this morning. I merely wish to say for Mrs. Harding and myself and for the members of our party, that we have enjoyed a hospitality in the West that cannot be excelled anywhere in the world. A wholesome people, living a wholesome life, have given a wholesome and wholehearted expression of welcome in the greetings which they have extended to us. It has all been so happy and so delightful that I have done nothing in all my life that has given me so much satisfaction as the trip I am now making across the continent and to Alaska. It is a joy to greet you; it is a pleasure to receive your greetings. It is good to know you; it is good to see you and to realize at first hand the reserve power which lies in the citizenship of the Republic.

I wish you the best ever in all your righteous employments, and I hope your government will never fail in meeting your highest and best expectations. [Applause.]

191

SERVICE THE GREATEST THING IN *LIFE*

Remarks at the Ball Park, Butte, Mont., Friday, June 29,
12:45 p. m., on Presenting to the Boy Scout Executive
of Montana and Five Boy Scouts of America
Medals for Heroism

Scouts:

I DO not know of anything on our western journey that
has afforded me greater pleasure than this ceremony.
The greatest thing in life is to be of service, and the
superlative degree of service is rendering help in the hour
of need. I know how a great trial appeals to the latent
manhood of every one of us. I know that somewhere
inherent in this nature of ours is strength to respond to
a call at the moment of urgent need. I rejoice to look
upon you as fine examples of young American manhood
who have met great responsibility and performed distinguished service. It is a fine index to the part which you
will play in the life before you. I am proud of you as
commander-in-chief of the Boy Scout organization; I am
proud of you as President of the Republic, because you
are a fine example and inspiration to all your fellows
throughout the length and breadth of the land.

[Thereupon President Harding, with appropriate remarks to each, pinned the medals on the coats of the scout
executive and boy scouts. After this ceremony the President spoke as follows:]

Ladies and Gentlemen:

I quite despair of making myself heard at so great
a distance from this splendid audience, but I cannot let
the occasion pass without giving some expression of my
appreciation to you for the cordiality, the heartiness and the
generosity of your very fine greeting today. I am glad
you came out to participate in the little ceremony which
we have just concluded. It has been a great pleasure to

bestow these medals, which bear the tribute of your city and of the great Boy Scout organization, to these boys who have been of signal service to their fellows. It is a great thing to emphasize the world's appreciation of service, and I am glad that I happened to be in the city of Butte at the opportune moment to present to these boys this testimonial and expression of appreciation.

I have a very great regard for the Boy Scouts and the Girl Scouts and all the young manhood and young womanhood of America. They constitute our greatest and richest possession, and I have come to the conclusion that we see the finest examples of each in the wonderful West.

It is too warm to keep you standing, and it is too difficult to be heard without the modern amplifying appliances. I know that the people on the stand do not hear my voice at all; so I will ask those who are immediately in front of me to convey to them for me an expression of the gratitude we feel for the courtesy and kindness you have shown us while visiting your great city. It is a joy to come here. We shall go away with the most agreeable memories and I know that we shall go with a feeling that you are a little closer to the government than when we came. I also hope you will feel we are a little closer to you. It is a pleasure to know you and it is a pleasure to work with you in making ours the best government on earth under which to live. Good-bye. [Applause.]

COOPERATION OF BUSINESS AND *LABOR* ASSISTED BY GOVERNMENTAL AGENCIES RESTORES PROSPERITY TO THE NATION

Address Prepared for Delivery on National Business Conditions at Butte, Mont., June 29

Fellow Americans All:

IN BUTTE, the Copper Capital of all Creation, I want to discuss briefly some business problems of our government and our country. It is an appropriate place for such an address, inasmuch as Butte's specialty is providing one of the most essential materials for the most modern of industries—electrical construction. One is tempted to dwell here upon the romance of Butte and the marvels of electrical development; but those temptations must be dismissed for today with merely an acknowledgment of the Nation's and the world's debt to the great Butte industry, and a word of congratulation on the improved status of the industry after the depression which followed the war.

It is one of the strange anomalies of our after-war disorganization, that the industries on which we had to lean most heavily for necessaries of war, and which at the time seemed most certain of great profits, were in so many cases hardest hit in the process of economic readjustment. Agriculture was one, and copper another, which had this experience. The livestock business, so vitally important to Montana as a producer and to the whole con-

NOTE: This address was prepared by President Harding for delivery at Butte, but, owing to a change in the arrangements and consequent lack of time, it was not formally delivered. It was, however, released for publication, and was printed in the press throughout the country.

194

suming population of the Nation, was among the chief sufferers.

Every Effort Made to Aid Industry

The administration and the Congress have made every effort to aid in rehabilitating this industry, and are glad of assurances that the condition is improving. I should like to talk to a Montana audience about the things we have been doing in this behalf; but that subject was dealt with the other day at Hutchinson, and on this occasion I desire to address myself to a somewhat broader consideration of business problems in general, and the relations between the American business community and the American government.

The theme is so vast, so fascinating, so instinct with vital elements in the wonder-story of American development that it would be easier to imagine oneself dealing with it as author of a volume or editor of an entire library, rather than within the compass of a platform address. But, as it does not seem practicable to administer a quarto volume to one's audience, or to bombard it with a library of economic information, I shall adopt the only feasible alternative, and talk to you very simply about some of the problems which confront our business community in these unprecedented times.

A Plain Statement of the Facts

I am going to omit the obvious prefatory remarks about the demoralized condition in which the world of business, finance, agriculture, commerce, found itself at the end of the war. Sometimes I suspect we are all given to thinking too much about those things, and too little about the progress we have made toward better and sounder conditions. Two years ago we made a careful census of unemployment in the United States, and found 4,500,000 or 5,000,000 workers without jobs. That was bad; but since then matters have been reversed, and if nowadays we are disposed to worry about the problem of employment, we have to consider ways and means to fill a half-million or a million jobs which want workers and cannot find them. That is the simplest picture of the industrial evolution of the last two years. That is the bed-rock foundation on which American business and American administration have erected their confidence that this people will not be led into the paths of devious experimentation, the mazes of untried economic theory, the labyrinths of doctrinnaire altruism. Of course, we are all altruists; but Americans have always taken their altruism with the salt of practicality and a firm conviction about the uplifting influence of three square meals a day.

High Tribute to American Labor

Right here I wish to pay tribute to the business men of America, to labor, both organized and unorganized, and to my associates in the administration. It was the fine cooperation of business and labor, assisted by the agencies of government, that made possible this marvelous rehabilitation of business. I do not purpose at this time to discuss the responsibilities for those unfortunate policies which brought a fever of inflation, quickly followed by depression and devastation, into the Amercan market-place in the two years succeeding the armistice. I propose to tell about conditions as they were found when the present administration assumed its responsibilities, and how they were dealt with.

Inflation and extravagance had continued unchecked for a time following the cessation of hostilities, to be succeeded suddenly by drastic deflation. Excesses of production and expenditure were suddenly followed by impossible restrictions upon both. Disaster fell upon business, and unemployment was widespread.

Gloomy Outlook in Spring of 1921

Early in the spring of 1921 it was realized by those in responsible places that, unless measures of amelioration were adopted and business were given some ground for hope, the winter of 1921-22 would be marked by privation and suffering, extending to millions of people, on a scale unprecedented in the history of our fortunate people. In the then existing temper of people everywhere, overwrought and exasperated at contemplating an enormous sacrifice barren of results for good, these conditions involved a menace to society. Europe was torn with distractions and revolutions, distressed with the fear of further wars, and burdened with debt. A small but highly vocal and reckless minority of extremists sought to draw our own country into the maelstrom of social disorganization. Earnest men in Europe were solemnly discussing whether civilization would survive, and thoughtful people everywhere recognized that if America should be swept into the vortex the disaster would be irreparable.

Anxious Hours for Federal Officials

I shall not tell you about the many anxious hours that the Cabinet and other officials devoted to these conditions. You have no concern about the worries of men who had sought your commission to high responsibilities; you *are* interested in what they did, and the results they achieved.

Looking forward to the prospect of a winter of acute distress, many sincere people pleaded that the government provide unemployment doles from the public Treasury. That policy had been adopted in many European countries, with results which did not commend themselves. It was not a policy the American people and government wished to inaugurate of it could be avoided. We believed it could and should be avoided. We based our belief on certain convictions about that unique combination of altruism and common sense, of generosity and hard-headedness, which has always been characteristic of Americans.

Practical Efforts Put Forth

So, while making preliminary plans for an appeal to the public to help itself, the government proceeded to do everything in its power to better conditions. At this time, I will only take a moment to remind you of a few of these measures. The policy of public finance which had kept the hand of government in the tills of the bankers, filching away from them the resources which business so desperately needed, was reversed. Business was given a tardy

197

chance to get the money it needed. A series of reductions in the Federal reserve discount rate was inaugurated. Sagacious, experienced, and sometimes extremely unpopular gentlemen, were set at work pruning down the personnel and the expenditures of the government. The Budget System was inaugurated, introducing business methods into dark corners of administration that had never been thus illuminated. Measures were adopted to lighten the taxation load and distribute it more equitably. Preliminary conversations were opened with the great nations, looking to an international conference for reduction of armaments and removal of some menacing causes of war. The Federal Farm *Loan* Board, which was practically out of business for want of funds, was provided with them in order that it might resume making loans to farmers; and the War Finance Corporation was recalled from a state of suspended animation, given a credit of a half-billion dollars, and sent out to relieve the agricultural community.

"Mobilized Under the Banner of Altruism"

Of all these things, and of others which I will not stop to enumerate, I wish merely to remind you, as a preliminary to the story of how labor and capital, business and finance, trade and industry were finally mobilized under the banner of practical altruism in the great effort to relieve unemployment and fend off the dangers in its wake. We made summons to the whole community to take itself by its economic boot-straps and lift itself out of the slough of despondency in which it was fast miring down. A National conference on unemployment was called to meet in Washington, September 21, 1921. Representatives of the great industries, of organized labor, of transportation, of civic and commercial bodies, were brought together and the situation was frankly placed before them. The need to find more jobs, by giving part-time work and similar arrangements to make existing jobs go as far as possible, was frankly stated. The whole business field was surveyed to determine where more employment could be found, and to get man and job together. Appeal was made to every employer to find work for just as many people as possible. Municipalities were pledged to take up and press public improvement works. Every employing interest, from the village home owner who had in mind to paint his fence "some of these days," to the greatest of industries, was appealed to "do it now." The needs of the country in many directions were surveyed and pictured forth, to convince employers that by getting busy at once they would serve their own advantage and make a great contribution to human welfare.

Accumulated Deficits in Equipment

It was found that there were great accumulated deficits in housing, in railroad equipment, in road building and other public improvements, and the appeal to put people at work in these directions met with instant and generous response. Emergency committees were established all over the country, by industries and municipalities, to help organize. Labor, both organized and unorganized, made an immediate and splendid response to the proposal that wherever possible work be so distributed that a larger number of people should be given a share of it and thus made self-supporting. In short, labor and capital, employers and employees, management and workers, united in a common effort which proved to be one of the finest demonstrations of applied altruism and intelligent unselfishness that has ever been accomplished on a like scale. The conference lasted several weeks, and, even before it had concluded, its results were becoming manifest in a general improvement of conditions.

Then, a rather strange thing happened. As I have described this effort, it might readily be regarded as rather artificial, as representing a hunt for tasks and operations which were not very obviously justified by business circumstances. Well, I will be honest about that; the effort *did* partake of that very character. It was an emergency measure. But no sooner had it begun to produce results, than its artificial character began to disappear, and to be replaced by a quality of genuineness in the demand for

199

labor, which caused some observers to believe that the crisis had never been very serious; but they were mistaken. They merely failed to recognize the industrial and psychological factors which go to make up prosperity. Every time a worker was transferred from idleness to earning, he became a consumer on a larger scale. As soon as he began earning, he began to spend; another worker had to be set at some other task to supply his wants. To put it briefly, we had pieced together the links in a chain of economic causes and effects, which drew the country back on the road toward employment and prosperity.

Triumph of Individualistic Methods

Closely related to this effort, was our conference on the national housing situation. In some ways I feel that this presented the most effective demonstration of how superior are the individualistic methods of our country to the paternalistic procedures of some others. Just as some people had advocated unemployment doles, so others urged government and municipal house-building to meet the housing shortage. It was calculated that during the war a deficiency of a million homes had accumulated. Much the same thing had happened in every country. Some countries tried housebuilding by the government. The results were no more fortunate than were the results of unemployment doles. They included great extravagances, construction of houses not adapted to their purposes, corruption in government administration, and profiteering by contractors.

Our own policy was to encourage the people to help themselves. The housing conference found that prices of both materials and labor were too high, money was scarce, and bad practices of both labor and builders had contributed well nigh to stop building. Yet the country needed the buildings, and labor needed the work.

The conference brought the country opportunity to recognize these factors. One of the early results was a united move among the producers of building materials, to bring down their prices to a level at which buying would be possible and activity might be resumed. I recall receiving a letter from a convention of building material producers, telling me of drastic all-round reductions in prices. That effort was typical of many others; and the aggregate effect was an enormous increase in building.

Results of Sense and Sanity

Looking back a scant two years from our present pinnacle of prosperity and industrial activity to the time when we were put to such shifts as these, it is not easy to realize how far we have gone. Whatever has been accomplished was made possible by the fact that we started with a firm confidence in the genius of American communities in the capacity of our people to take care of themselves, if they were given a fair chance, in their aspiration for individualistic freedom in preference to mass control. We thought we knew the American people, and I take some pride in telling you that we guessed correctly. For myself, I think the National mobilization, voluntarily accomplished, was no less an accomplishment than the great cooperation to win the war. It did not have the inspiration of martial glory or emotional appeal. It was brought about by a summons to sense and sanity. The method was well nigh unique among the procedures adopted by nations in that after-war crisis. Some of them, let me remind you, concluded that civilization was already a derelict, and proceeded to scrap its institutions and substitute new and strange experiments. Some entered upon the way of communistic organization, or disorganization; some plunged into socialistic projects which increased taxation and encouraged the tendency to pauperize the people. Some entered upon inflation and currency debasing, ruining their money systems in order to produce a momentary but dishonest impression of prosperity through the progressive repudiation of debts. Yet others committed themselves to the lamentable assumption that the cure for the disorders of peace was more war.

Safe and Sane Methods Adopted

It is not necessary to remind you of the disastrous results. One need not recount the misfortunes that have

201

followed upon the collapse of social organization and industrial capacity in some countries; or upon the wreck of financial systems and the destruction of investments in others; or the industrial paralysis that in some places has followed direct contributions from the State treasury. Nor need I remind you of the distress which has befallen those countries which adopted the prescription of more war as a panacea for the evils of peace.

We have little occasion to regret that our own country disappointed those who wished us to engage in similar bizarre programs. If our procedures have been rather plain and old-fashioned, they have yet produced results that justify pride and require no apologies. If we are accused of getting nowhere in particular, we may very well reply that, at any rate, we have been able to stay right here, that we regard it as a good place to stay, and that day by day we have been getting better and better. I am disposed freely to admit that some other folks have had more excitement than we have had; but a good many people in this world would be glad to exchange their stock of excitement for a modest share in our American accumulation of simple contentment and dinner-table necessaries.

Confidence in Democratic Institutions

Some well-meaning but unduly agitated people have feared lest under stress of these post-war times our democratic institutions might prove inadequate. Permit me to say that I never felt more cheerful about that particular matter than right now. My confidence is based on the things I have been learning about the capacity of the American community to take care of itself. Almost any nation, under the strain of war's necessities, can pull itself together for the common defense. We have seen that demonstrated in the universal effort which inspired heroism wherever men came into conflict. But the problems of peace, of industry, of production and distribution are really more complex than those of war. Here in the United States we have recognized that we should get on best if we summoned the entire community to full participation in dealing with our difficulties.

There never was so frank and confident an appeal to a great people to apply their soundest sense, to cling to tried and tested methods, to avoid extremes and experiments, as was made during the trying period I have been discussing. All groups, classes, interests and sections were brought into a splendid cooperation to prevent disaster. The captains of industry counselled with the leaders of labor, the men of finance, the chiefs of business, and the agents of the State, seeking only the public good through a mutual subordination of selfish aims and narrow purposes. There was mutual concession and toleration; universal recognition of the higher duty.

Fruits of Unity and Cooperation

Instead of strikes, riots, sabotage and preachments of revolution, we reaped a harvest of understanding, of established respect among groups, of enhanced regard for each others viewpoints. It was a splendid advance toward the highest possibilities of democracy as a working program, an industrial as well as a political system.

Such is the interpretation we offer to you, of the great American cooperation to conserve the fruits of peace and the fortunes of our beloved country. It is not presented to you as the accomplishment of a particular administration or the justification of any party's claims upon the public confidence. Rather, it is placed before you as testimony to the supreme sense and sound genius of a Nation which could make its cooperations extend to a continent, and its altruisms embrace an hundred million of humanity. That is what the American people have done in the last two years. No other people have had the good fortune to parallel the achievement. No other look out today upon so clear a horizon; and I venture to say that we stand only in the doorway of the new era. Thus convinced, I know that you will permit me to add just one word for the pride, the satisfaction, and the gratitude which the National administration feels in having been able to contribute something of suggestion, leadership, and direction, to this accomplishment. We will not claim much, for the great end could have been attained only through the complete unity, in spirit, purpose and patriotism, of the whole American Nation.

ALL CITIZENS NEAR TO GOVERNMENT

Remarks at Boulder, Mont., June 29, 3:05 p. m.

Ladies and Gentlemen of Boulder:

IT IS very gratifying to Mrs. Harding and to me to have you come to the station to extend to us such a generous and warm-hearted greeting, which is but typical of the welcome accorded us throughout our long journey across the continent. It is a source of pleasure, as well as profit, to those in authority to come in intimate contact with such great bodies of American citizens as it has been our privilege to meet on this trip. You are far removed from the seat of government, but I want you to know that you are just as close to the Federal government as though you lived in Maryland or Virginia, because the eyes of the government are constantly looking in all directions, hoping to make everybody in America fortunate and, through the good fortune of our people, to promote the welfare and glory of the Republic. The government is deeply interested in your well-being, but you must not expect the government to do for you what you ought to do for yourselves.

I do not believe in paternalism; I love to preach the gospel of individualism; but the government does seek to make opportunity equal for everybody in this land, and, better still, it strives in every way to prepare the boys and girls of America to embrace that opportunity.

You live in a favored section. I am not going to be envious of you, for envy ill becomes any of us; but I can understand how you take pride in your homes and how you rejoice in the gifts of Providence to your locality. I believe also that I can understand the reason for the clear complexions which I observe on every hand, and I can understand why your boys and girls are so healthy and promising. They are growing up under the most favorable conditions to be found anywhere in the world.

I thank you for coming to greet us. Such greetings add vastly to our pleasure and to our ability to be of service, because they enable us to know and understand you better, and, perhaps, make it possible for you to know and understand us better, and, with mutual understanding, we shall all get along more happily together. Good luck to you all in every way; and good-bye. [Applause.]

NATION GRATEFUL TO ITS VETERANS

Remarks at United States Veterans' Hospital,
Helena, Mont., June 29, 5:15' p. m.

Ladies and Gentlemen, Personnel, and Patients of the Hospital:

I HAVE not come to deliver an address; I have only come to offer my greetings, and I shall do so in this hall because I can say more in a few words to you at one time than I could hope to say by greeting each one of you personally.

I need not tell you that I speak for the government when I say that we are all deeply concerned in the welfare of the service men. I hope the ambulatory patients will soon be back to their homes and actively engaged in the pursuits of life as they were before the war. The war brought a tremendous burden to the country, but none of the incidents of the war carried the sorrow, the anxiety, and the concern that have been felt for those of you who were impaired in the service. Men can be and have been sacrificed in war, and the sorrow may be healed, but when men are incapacitated and impaired in health the heartstrings are touched in a more poignant manner. I am in a position to know the facts, and I speak only the truth when I say to you that the government wants to do everything in its power to put you boys on your feet again and make you, if possible, as you were before you went into the service. If we cannot do that, we want to be of help in making you as useful as you can be made in the years of life you have before you, which I hope may be many.

Tremendous Burdens Brought by War

Men, though it has been said that republics are not grateful, ours is a grateful Republic. Of course the burdens of war have brought tremendous responsibilities and anxieties; but I come from the capital; I know the heart of Congress, and I know the purpose of the administrative branch of the government. You may sometimes think that you are not accorded all the consideration which you may believe to be your due, but I can assure you that in the mind and heart of the government you and your welfare are matters of deep concern.

Let me turn to those on my left and say that you who are representing the government in seeking to relieve the service men are doing a magnificent work. You are giving expression in a practical way to that which is in the heart and conscience of the people of America. I know your work is marked by kindness and every consideration, and I doubt not that it is made more efficient by the talent and the character which I know you to possess.

It is a great pleasure to greet you all. Everywhere in America one may encounter just such a scene as this. On last Sunday I spoke to the boys in the Denver hospital, where they were much more numerous than they are here. Great numbers of them there are still on their cots, unable to be about. Mrs. Harding frequently visits the boys at Walter Reed and other hospitals in the vicinity of Washington. We try, whenever we can and opportunity is afforded, to give you that reassurance which comes from the heart. We not only wish you well, but we shall do everything in the world to make amends for the draft which the government made upon you. It is a pleasure to greet you, and I shall be glad to grasp the hand of each one of you. [Applause.]

SOCIAL VISION BROADENED BY WAR; ADVANCE-MENT OF WOMEN IN INDUSTRY; EQUAL JUS-TICE TO CAPITAL AND LABOR

Address on Social Justice, Women and Labor, Shriners' Hall, Helena, Mont., June 29, 8 p. m.

Governor Dixon, Ladies and Gentlemen, My Country-men All:

GOVERNOR DIXON has spoken very truly and rather modestly of the manner in which Montana today has given welcome to the official visiting party. Your cordiality in Montana is so spontaneous and wholesome, and springs up so generously everywhere in the State, that I cannot find words to speak the appreciation and gratitude which are in my heart.

The governor said you were honored by a visit from the President. Referring to the official position, that is not unbecomingly said, but I should like to say to you in return that the President has been honored by you and has been largely benefited by his visit, for I shall return to Washington knowing more of this America of ours.

The pastor prayed to God Almighty that we might be able to realize the wonderful extent of this land. Nobody in America does realize it now, and only God in His infinite wisdom knows what the future holds in store if we will only maintain the foundations on which our fathers builded and continue on with the same resolute purpose and devotion which have made us what we are. America is a wonderful country; Montana is a wonderful State. I wonder if you yourselves know how big you are. You have counties

207

larger than entire States in the East, and I may add that you have the finest manhood and womanhood and the most inspiring childhood in all the world. [Applause.]

Marvelous Progress of the Nation

It has been said that crops depend upon soil and climate. It is conceivable to me that the human race may be affected by the same conditions. Certainly you have wrought marvels. How matchless, my countrymen, is American development! One of the newspapers today— I do not recall which one—carried a little chronological recital which interested me greatly. It brought to my mind the fact that Montana is still young; indeed, I myself am older than your State, and I claim something of youth. Our Republic itself is only about a century and a third old. The other day at the White House it was my pleasure to present, on behalf of the Roosevelt Memorial Association, a medal to the granddaughter of Alexander Hamilton, one of the greatest of the foundation stones of the Republic. Think of there only being three generations between the time when the immortal fathers erected this Republic and the present day! How marvelously and how mightily we have wrought! And no man can venture to guess as to the possibilities of the future.

I am rejoiced to pay this visit to the Temple of Algeria Shrine. The Montana Shriners came to Washington only a few weeks ago and along with them came a great many other Shriners; in fact, in Washington for a week we were all Shriners; there was nothing else to be. [Laughter.] I should like to say to the Shriners of Montana, as I should like to say to the Shriners in every other State in the Union, that their pilgrimage to the National capital gave the country a new concept of American fraternity and American fraternal ideals, and gave to the American people a new impression of their value. I was proud of the Shriners and delighted with the lesson they taught, because, men and women of Montana, we need more of fraternity in Montana; we need more of fraternity in the United States

208

of America, and we need more of fraternity and of the brotherhood of man throughout the world today. [Applause.]

Great Lessons of the World War

My countrymen, one of the greatest lessons which the World War taught to society was a realization of its stupendous producing capacity under modern organization. When the war started many of us, probably most of us, believed it could not last very long because we could not conceive that it could be economically and industrially supported for a long time. We had been taught to believe that as a whole the community annually consumed pretty nearly all that it produced, and that in order to maintain this ratio it was necessary to keep all the producers steadily at work. We were convinced that when the most efficient producers were taken by millions away from the fields, the shops, the mines, and the offices, and set at the business of armed destruction, they would very presently pull down upon themselves the whole fabric of our complex industrial system, and that the war would be smothered in the ruins. This view was the basis of what became almost an obsession with many people, indeed with most of the best informed people, during the early stages of the war. It was commonly and freely said that economic exhaustion would compel an end to the struggle before a year, and a much more popular limitation was six months.

Conflict Grew in Extent and Fury

The event showed how very little we understood either the tremendous producing capacity of the community as a whole or the strength and solidity of our industrial structure. When the first year of the war had passed, the world was just beginning to realize that in all probability the struggle was only in its larger beginning. Millions of men had been called from the fields, and yet still other men were being trained to bear arms. At the end of two years the war was greater than ever, and after three years it had still further expanded until it actually involved, whether as combatants or as the sources of supply for the combatants, the whole world. The industrial, the agricultural, the financial, the social, and spiritual forces of the world were mobilized at last for the great final test of strength. In the end that test was both military and economic. Victory rested upon the banners which were borne by the side that represented the greatest number of soldiers, of ships, of guns; which represented the greatest capacity to bring together, control, and fabricate the necessaries of war and to maintain great civil populations behind the lines.

Became a War of Conscription

It became very early a war of conscription. Governments conscripted their men for service in the field; patriotism and public opinion conscripted everybody else for work at home. A new system of division and dilution of labor was introduced through which men and women, boys and girls, old men and old women—millions of people who under the old order of peace days had been rejected from the realm of skilled production, were quickly trained to the most intricate and technical tasks. So, in the midst of the most destructive storm that mankind had ever invoked upon itself, there was presented the marvelous phenomena of a world producing at a greater rate than it had ever done before.

How was this gigantic industrial phenomenon wrought? By putting everybody at work; by inducing everybody to work to the limit of strength and capacity; by paying the workers at rates which enlisted their utmost eagerness to produce to the limit. Yes, if you please, by letting labor and capital and management all engage more or less in profiteering at the expense of society as a whole. Unheard-of wages were paid to people who in other times would have been considered quite incapable of earning them, but who, under the stimulus of the emergency, became effective and absolutely necessary factors in the industrial organization. Particularly was this true of the women, young and old, who took up tasks in the shop, the field, the transportation systems, and behind the lines of combatants, such as had never before been assigned to them. And the women made good so emphatically, so impressively, that as today we look over the whole field of the world mobilization and the world conflict we realize that something very much like a revolution was effected in the varied relationships of the industrial community.

Universal Draft In Time of War

Viewed in the retrospect we see more clearly than ever the sordid side of war. I have said before, and I choose to repeat it very deliberately now, that if war must come again—God grant that it shall not!—then we must draft all of the Nation in "carrying on." [Applause.] It is not enough to draft the young manhood. It is not enough to accept the voluntary service of both women and men whose patriotic devotion impels their enlistment. It will be righteous and just, it will be more effective in war and marked by less regret in the aftermath, if we draft all of capital, all of industry, all of agriculture, all of commerce, all of talent and capacity and energy of every description to make the supreme united and unselfish fight for the National triumph. [Applause.] When we do that there will be less of war. When we do that the contest will be aglow with unsullied patriotism, untouched by profiteering in any service.

Of course, we are striving to bring about such conditions of foreign relations and so fashion our policies that we may never again be involved in war. If we are committed to universal service—that is, the universal commitment of every American resource and activity—without compensation except the consciousness of service and the exaltation of victory, we will be slower to make war and more swift in bringing it to a triumphant close. Let us never again make draft on our manhood without as exacting a draft on all we possess in the making of the industrial, financial, commercial, and spiritual life of the Republic. [Applause.]

Women First Line of Industrial Reserves

If we had been in a state of mind to philosophize about it all, I think we might have recognized that women have been for a long time preparing themselves for this tremen-

211

dous incursion into the field of industrial production. For a long time before the war began there had been evidence of a reaction among the women against the old ideals of the Victorian period. For three or four decades, the more venturesome women had been timidly breaking away from the old-fashioned home and its old-fashioned ideals. Even those who viewed the new-woman movement with greatest misgiving and least approval had already been compelled to recognize that a new and revolutionary idea was taking possession of them. We might iterate and reiterate, and theorize and dogmatize, upon the old thesis that the place for woman was in the home; but we will have to admit that despite all our preachments, all our urgings, all our misgivings, woman was not staying there. She was teaching in the schools, she was accounting for perhaps a majority of the graduates from the high schools, and a big and increasing minority of the student community in the colleges and universities. She was practicing law and medicine, preaching sermons, working in the shops, the offices, the factories; she was, in short, becoming a competitor with her brother in almost all the departments of productive effort and activity.

Realization Came to All Suddenly

Then came the war, and all at once even the most dubious among us realized that the women, everywhere, constituted the first line of industrial reserves upon which society must fall back in its great crisis. They volunteered for every service in which they could be useful, and at once established their right to a new and more important industrial status. They built ships, they operated munition factories, they learned to perform the heaviest and most difficult tasks; they tilled the fields, filled the offices, largely conducted the hospitals, and even served as most useful auxiliaries to forces on the battlefield. Not as a boon, but as a duty, full partnership in the conduct of political affairs was conferred upon them.

All this has inevitably worked a profound change in the relation of woman to the social and political organization. We may approve it or disapprove it, we may view

212

it with satisfaction or with misgiving, but the fact is before us that woman has taken a new place in the community. And just as her participation in the industrial sphere expands, so her relations to the home and its interest are necessarily contracted. Whether we account it wise or otherwise, we must recognize that the tendency is to take the modern mother more and more away from the control, the training, the intellectual guidance and spiritual direction of her children. The day nursery and after that the kindergarten begin to care for her children in the earliest years; after that come the public school, the high school, the college and the university, taking over from her more and more of the responsibility and influence over the children. We may entertain the old-fashioned prejudices against this development—and personally I do—but we are compelled to recognize that under modern conditions a large and increasing proportion of women are bound to be at the same time mothers in the home and industrial producers or professional workers outside the home, or else they must be denied the service and responsibility of motherhood.

Sacred Duties of Motherhood

Frankly, I am one of those old-fashioned individuals who would be glad if the way could be found to maintain the traditional relations of father, mother, children, and home. But very plainly these relations are in process of a great modification. The most we can 'do is to readapt to the greatest possible extent our conditions of industry and of living so as to enable the mothers to make the utmost of their lessened opportunity for shaping the lives and minds of their children. We must hope, and we must make it possible, that mothers will not assume, when their babes of yesterday become the schoolboys and schoolgirls of today, that the responsibility of the mother is ended, and that the teacher, the school authorities, the college, the State, will henceforth assume it. Rather, we must recognize that no other influence can possibly be substituted for that of motherhood; and we must make it possible for

213

the mothers to cooperate with these social institutions of the new order, to give the children so far as possible the privileges of a home atmosphere which will supplement the advantages of mere education and training. It must be made possible for the mothers to familiarize themselves with the problems of the people, the school superintendents, the college authorities, the health and sanitation officials. In short, the mothers must be placed in such position that despite their obligations outside the home they shall not have to surrender their domestic responsibility. Rather, means must be found to enable them, through the varied instrumentalities which society affords, to equip themselves for the better discharge of their responsibility toward the children of the land.

Opportunity for Great Service

Through such effort as this there will be opportunity for a great service. Those mothers who have the advantage of the best material and intellectual opportunities will, if they make the most of these advantages, help greatly to improve the conditions of children that come from families and homes less fortunately situated. They will be able to help in lifting up the poorer, the less fortunate children, to a higher level. The mother who tirelessly seeks rightly to train her own children, to instill into them that indefinable essence which we know as good breeding, will be performing this service not alone for her own children, but in only less measure for the children who come from homes less blessed with the finer things of life. Herein is the supreme advantage of the public-school system. I have never been able to find much satisfaction in the good fortune of families who, when they are able to do so, prefer to take their children out of the public schools and give them the doubtful advantage of more exclusive educational methods. I think we should cling to the democracy of the public schools. [Applause.]

More Religion Needed in Daily Lives

The teacher, and the authorities back of her, must be equally ready to cooperate with the home and the

214

mother. In the home must still be performed the duty of instilling into the child those fundamental concepts of religion and of faith which are essential to rightly shaping the character of citizens, and therefore of the Nation. It would be an irreparable mistake if in surrendering to society a larger responsibility for the child's intellectual and physical well being, we should forget the necessity for proper religious training. That duty must be performed in the home; it will always be peculiarly the duty of a mother. We need more of religion, my countrymen, in our daily lives. [Applause.]

Mankind never has stood more in need than it does now of the consolations and reassurances which are derived from a firm religious faith. We are living in a time of many uncertainties, of weakened faith in the efficiency of institutions, of industrial systems, of economic hypotheses, of dictum and dogma in whatever sphere. Yet we all know that there are certain fundamental truths of life and duty and destiny which will stand eternal through the evolution and the revolution of systems and societies founded by mankind. There must be no mistake whereby we shall confuse the things which are of eternity with those which are of time. We must not let our engrossment with the things of matter and of mind distract us from a proper concern for those which are of the spirit and the soul.

Sound Bodies for Our Children

It must be kept ever in mind that the higher and finer attributes of humanity will rarely be developed from a human seedling planted in a soil adapted chiefly to the production of that which is selfish and sordid, in which it will be forced by special circumstances to struggle unduly for the bare continuance of existence. We will not grow strong minds in unsound bodies, nor may we hope that illuminated souls will often seek habitation in human frames weakened and tortured by disease and malnutrition. To an astounding and alarming certainty it has been demonstrated that a large proportion of school children, and even of adults, suffer from undernourishment. I may congratu-

215

late you that there is little of it in the West. Certainly we have seen none of it in your State. Perhaps it is true that as to most of the adults the fault is of the individual rather than society. Whether that be true or not we can at least agree that the children are not to be blamed for their share in such misfortunes. If society has permitted the development of a system under which the citizens of tomorrow suffer these deprivations today, then the obligation is surely upon society to right the wrong and to insure justice to the children who are not responsible for being here.

Help for Parents Essential

But we can not expect to bring full justice, full equality of circumstances and opportunity to the children, unless we shall make it possible for the parents. We are all too much given, I suspect, to a rather unthinking admiration for our highly mechanized social system under which we have so abundantly produced wealth and the possibilities of comfort and culture. We have not thought enough about the evils attendant upon the great inequities which mark the distribution of our stupendous product. But we are coming into a time when more and more we are giving thought to these things. Our satisfaction in the material achievements of our industrial age is being qualified as it never was before by our questionings along these lines. We are thinking of the weaker links in the social chain. We believe the equality of opportunity must be attended by a fitness to embrace it.

Great Broadening of Social Vision

Here, again, the war was responsible for a great broadening of our social vision. It made its demand upon the highest and the lowest, the proudest and the humblest. It demanded a sacrifice that was just as great in the case of the poor man as the rich man. What was more, it brought a realization of the fact that men and women were of real service to the community just in proportion as they were capable of producing the things that were needed. So the workers, the builders, the producers attained a new sense of their dignity and importance. Contemplating its supreme crisis, the community was willing to render to those who were capable of serving it effectively in this juncture, a greater share of their product than they had formerly been accustomed to receive. Wages, the world over, went to new high levels; salaries and fixed incomes shrank to lower levels of actual exchange value. There was a leveling up from the lower strata and downward from the higher. On the whole, despite many instances of injustice and of maladjustment in this process, its results marked a long advance on the road to equity and justice among all elements of the community. A few years of civilization's desperate grapple with destiny brought to the working masses of the world an aggregate betterment of conditions, a general improvement of circumstances and opportunity, which otherwise would have been possible only through the slow processes of generations.

Rights of Capital and Labor Equal

We know now that the advances which were thus effected in the direction of social justice and economic equality will not be relinquished without determined opposition. There were those who, regarding the injustices of the old order as inevitable, mistakenly assumed that by a simple process which they called the "deflation of labor" the old relationships would presently be restored. They insisted that "wages must come down"; some of them went so far as to sound the slogan that "organized labor must be crushed." These had forgotten the lesson in organization, in cooperation, in community of sacrifice, by which civilization had been able to rescue itself. They had forgotten that the right of organization, and of cooperative dealings, is not any longer the special prerogative of management and of capital. The right of men, and brains, and skill, and brawn, to organize, to bargain through organizations, to select their own leaders and spokesmen, is no whit less absolute than is the right of management

217

and of capital to form and work through those great concentrations of interests which we call corporations.

Labor as the Builder of Capital

Labor, indeed, is fast becoming one of the great builders of capital. Whether it concentrates its savings by depositing them in its own banks, of which the number is rapidly increasing, or pools them with the general savings of society by making its deposits in other banks, the result is the same. Labor is more and more coming to be the financier and backer of its own employment. We shall not go back to the time when considerable elements in the community were wont to assume that a sharp line of demarcation should be drawn between labor and capital. Labor is becoming more and more a capitalist on its own account, and capital is more and more discovering that it must work, must contribute, must give us, through some superiority of method and management, a justification for its existence as a sort of separate estate. Those to whom the management and investment of capital is intrusted must recognize, as I know most of them already do, that the right of organization and the title to those special efficiencies which come to organization are not the exclusive prerogative of capital. They are equally the prerogative of labor.

Attitude of Administration

I am quite aware that there were some who imagined, before the present administration was voted into responsibility, that it was going at least to acquiesce in, if not definitely sympathize with, projects for the deflation of labor and the overthrow of labor organizations. Before this time these have come to realize their error. Nothing has been farther from the purpose of the present administration than any thought of destroying the right of either labor or capital to organize, and each to deal in its organized capacity.

We have recognized that there are evils and abuses on both sides of the almost imaginary line which now is presumed to separate labor and capital. We have wished and sought to minimize these abuses, through better organizations and better understanding, without destroying organizations or the right to form them. We have not wished to compel men to work when they did not want to work; we have not wished to compel employers to keep men at work under conditions which were impossible; but we have earnestly sought to lessen the occasions for conflict between the two parties. We have tried to bring to both of them a realization that both owed in this connection an obligation to the great public interest which is always the great sufferer by reason of their conflict. [Applause.]

Nation Saved from Extremists

In this connection let me say quite frankly that I know there were some elements which hoped for a great and decisive conflict between organized employment and organized labor, and that those elements were not all on either side of the imaginary dividing line. On the capital side of the line were those who hoped that the administration would lend itself to their program of breaking down organized labor and sending it back to the era of individual bargaining for the individual job. On the labor side of the line were those who hoped, by exorbitant demands and an attitude of uncompromising insistence, to force the nationalization of some of our most important industries and services. Between these two extreme groups, confident we had behind us the overwhelming public opinion of the Nation, we have tried to hold the scales even; to prevent on the one side the destruction of organized labor, and on the other side to frustrate those programs which looked to the ultimate destruction of private capital and the nationalization of all the instrumentalities of production. [Applause.]

How well have we succeeded? At least, we have saved the Nation from the extremists of both sides. Those who were sure that our salvation lay in the destruction of organized labor and the precipitate reduction of wages have found that the National administration was not disposed to acquiesce in their program. For many months past they have noted that the demand for labor was greater than the supply; that, instead of millions of men out of jobs, there were tens of thousands of jobs without workers; that, instead of a sharp and progressive reduction of labor's wage, there has been now for a long time a steady, continuing, persistent increase in that wage. On the other side, those who would have been glad to drive the country into an industrial crisis through the stoppage of production, and to force the nationalization or communization of industry, have been equally disappointed in the outcome.

I believe our policy, and its results, have reflected the sound judgment of the overwhelming majority of the American people. [Applause.] I believe this people is firmly and finally committed to the ideal of preserving the fullest rights of private initiative and private enterprise, together with the right of organization on both sides of the line between capital and labor, and always consistent with the right of the public to be served efficiently and at a reasonable cost.

Safely Through a Trying Period

We have come thus far, and thus fortunately, through the most difficult period of reconstruction that we have ever known. We have been sheltered against the world storm of tendency to social revolution. The best test of policy is by results. By that test, we ask no more than a fair and reasoned verdict on our program. We ask that its results be compared with the showing, in these after-war years, that can be presented by any other country on the face of the earth. We ask that you examine the contrast, thoughtfully and seriously, between the general state of the public weal in this country and in others. For our vindication, we point to a great nation, its credit preserved, its industries crowded to the point of capacity production, its people employed, its wage scales high beyond all comparison with any other in the world, its banking system standing as the final bulwark of sound money and the gold

220

standard, and its average level of comfort and prosperity unexampled among the races of men.

Russia's "Mad Experiment"

If I could make the fortunate picture stand out by offering contrast, I would speak of Russia and the colossal failure of its mad experiment. The dissatisfied working forces of America, where there are such, and the parlor theorists who have yet to create a single thing useful to aspiring human kind, will find there less of freedom, much less of reward, and little of hope in much proclaimed emancipation. Royal absolutism has been destroyed, only to be superseded by what appears to be despotism in the name of democracy. To a limited few of democracy's advocates has come vast power. Perhaps wealth attends. Undoubtedly a new Russia is in the making, and there is no doubt the present sponsorship will survive. I do not believe *Lenin* and *Trotzky* will be superseded until they have lived the span of life; but I do believe that, in the return to sanity, new constitutional methods will be provided in the present demoralized land of Russia.

America's Duty to "Protect and Preserve"

Apart from the tragedy of it all, I am glad Russia is making the experiment. If 20 centuries of the Christian era and its great story of human progress, and the countless centuries before the light of Christianity flamed have been lived and recorded upon mistaken theories of a righteous social order, then everything is wrong. Christianity is a failure, and all of civilization is a failure. I think Russia is going to rivet anew our belief in established social order. Meanwhile we know ours is the best the world has revealed, and I preach the gospel of holding fast to that which has proven good, ever trying in good conscience to make it better, and consider and treat as an enemy every man who chooses our land as a haven in which to assail the very institutions which shelter him. [Applause.]

There are two phases of the commitment of the great human family. It is of little use to advance unless we

221

hold to the advanced position. It is useless to construct unless we preserve. In the recognized test which our civilization is now undergoing America's supreme task is one of preservation. I call upon America to protect and preserve. [Applause.]

Prosperity Here to Stay

In conclusion, my countrymen, let me venture a guess as to that which is uppermost in your hearts. I know of your natural aspirations, and I have been talking to you of the social order which has come about in the process of our development. What brought the early discoverers to the shores of America? It was the search for wealth and better conditions. What caused men and women from the East to settle in the West? It was the search for wealth and better conditions. This impelling force has swept completely across the continent until we have our American development of today. Before the World War plunged us into the great tumult, we were living under fortunate conditions and were probably the happiest people the world has ever known. But the war brought reverses. It demoralized business; it upset accepted practices; it strained finances; it dislocated material industry; it brought disaster to agriculture. All the world has been endeavoring to find a solution for the problems which arose in the aftermath of war. Your government has been doing everything that it knows how to do within the Constitution and within consistent and reasonable limits to be of aid in bringing about complete restoration. I believe we have done better than any other people in the world; I believe we are getting squarely on the right track again, and I believe that the recovery which industry has experienced is going to spread throughout the land and become permanent so that prosperity and good fortune will prevail throughout the Republic. [Applause.] I hope with all my heart that you in this great State of Montana will share it fully in every way.

I think I know another thing that is in your hearts. A man confident in his possessions, sure of his way, assured by experience that if he only has the opportunity he can achieve and go forward, only asks for conditions under which he may peacefully work out his own salvation; and I know there is in the heart of all America the prayer that never again shall this Republic become involved in war. [Applause.] I would not come to you and suggest even the possibility of the genius and conscience of man devising a means whereby war shall never again occur, but I do come to you, my countrymen, and say, with all the sincerity of my being, that I think this great, free, and fortunate land of America ought to give of its influence, its strength and its power—that it ought to do everything that a great Nation can do—to make sure that war shall never again occur. [Applause.]

The World Court Proposal

It was that impelling thought that led me to do a rather unusual thing in the history of America. As you know, under the Constitution the President has the authority to conduct our foreign affairs. He can negotiate treaties; he can make covenants; but they never can become binding until sanctioned by two-thirds of the Senate. It has been the custom for the President to negotiate treaties and conventions with foreign governments and then go to the Senate for their approval. Knowing of the establishment of an International Court of Justice to which the disputes of a justiciable character of the various nations could be taken, noting the success and high character of the Court, and believing that the World Court was a long step in the direction of ironing out the difficulties that lead to conflict, I reversed the order, and, instead of committing America to an adherence to the protocol under which the Court was established, I asked the Senate first to give me its consent and approval to a movement looking to America's participation in the World Court. Could anything be fairer or better than that? I could not accomplish anything under the Constitution without the consent and approval of the Senate, and the Senate could not do anything without the cooperation of the Executive. I believe in teamwork at

223

all times and under all conditions, and so I have asked the Senate's approval to the initiation of negotiations looking to our adherence to the World Court without surrendering anything of the independence of the United States and without entangling us in any of the affairs of the Old World in which we are not interested, but, rather, that we may stand before the world as a great, free people believing in the peaceful adjustment of international disputes which do not involve the honor of nations. I want you of Montana; you who believe in even-handed justice, you who crave peace and have peace in your hearts, to give of your influence in order that this Nation may play its becoming part in the world and lend its power to the establishment of such institutions as will in the future prevent the sacrifice of your sons and daughters and your material fortunes and enable America to realize the fulfillment of God's highest intent for those whom He created in His own image and whom He expected to go forward in the light of an everlasting peace. [Applause.]

INSPIRED BY YELLOWSTONE PARK

Speech at Livingston, Mont., Sunday, July 1, 9:15 p. m.

Mr. Mayor, My Countrymen All:

IT IS a very great pleasure to be greeted so cordially by so many of you on this Sabbath evening. We have been spending two wonderful days in your vicinity; and we spent this Sabbath day, I believe, quite as close to God Almighty as though we worshipped in temples erected by man, for we spent the day amidst the grandeur, the majesty, and the inspirations of the great Yellowstone National Park. I hope, aye, I believe, that every one of our party finds himself this Sabbath evening with a greater reverence for the Creator and a deeper desire to be worthy of God's best intent.

224

The Yellowstone Park is a wonderful place. It is a great possession for you of Montana and the other States which have territory therein; it is a great possession for those who live nearby; it is a great possession for the United States of America. I have been marvelling at our experiences of the last two days. During that time we have seen literally a fine cross-section of the citizenship of our land. I believe that during my brief sojourn in the Park I have greeted personally travellers from every State in the American Union, and, in addition to that, I have had the privilege of greeting citizens of England, of Canada, and of Cuba. Manifestly all the country is beginning to turn its face toward the Yellowstone National Park, and I am glad of it, for there is nothing more helpful, nothing more uplifting, nothing that gives one a greater realization of the wonders of creation than a visit to that great national institution.

Lesson in the Wild Life

I have gathered some interesting impressions from my sojourn in the park, and I wonder if similar impressions have come to you who live nearby. For instance, because of the protection of wild life in the park, there has been created amongst the wild creatures there an air and feeling of confidence which causes them to experience a sense of security. We saw it everywhere; and as I watched the wild life of the park today, unconcerned and unmindful of the human beings about them, manifesting their confidence in the security of the situation, I thought how helpful it would be to human kind if we could have a like confidence in one another in all the relations of life.

There was another incident that appealed strongly to me. As we were nearing the end of our trip this afternoon, and were coming down one of the long grades, our car suddenly approached a mother grouse and a group of little grouse chicks. The excellent driver of the car brought it to too sudden a halt, but he did it out of regard for that young wild life which was not capable of knowing the danger or protecting itself. The driver did not want to destroy one of those little grouse chicks, not much bigger

225

than a hickory nut—I do not know whether or not you are familiar with hickory nuts in this section [*Laughter*]— and I liked him for what he did. He exhibited one of the finest impulses that animate the heart of man, namely, to spare innocent, defenseless life. The old mother grouse seemed not to know or care, because she did not realize the danger, but our driver did. I should like to see that example more frequently followed in our relationships with one another. Those who know, those who are strong, those who are in a position to command ought always to be ready to protect the weak, the helpless, and those who do not know. I am sure that if we will more faithfully carry out that principle, we shall be even a better people than we are. [*Applause.*]

"Seeing America First"

If you have been observing our travels you have noted that it is not customary for me to deliver addresses on the Sabbath. I believe in keeping the day holy. I believe, my countrymen, in a religious America, for I know that we shall be a better people as we become a more moral and pious people. I think, however, it will not be unseemly if I say on this occasion, since you are so deeply interested in the National Park, that I should like to have brought to the attention of all America what a wonder State you are and what a wonder spot the park is. I have crossed the Atlantic three times with very great satisfaction, and I have learned valuable lessons from observation in the Old World; it has been my fortune to travel part way across the Pacific; but, knowing the Yellowstone Park as I now do, I have no hesitancy in saying to everybody in America, "you ought to make it a point to see the Yellowstone National Park before you venture beyond the borders of the United States." [*Applause.*] I know of nothing to compare with it anywhere in the world, and I am glad we are making of it such a success as a National playground.

In addition to being able to visit the park it is good to have the privilege of coming to this wonder section of our country. You of Montana live in a vast and wonderful State. I hope you will never allow it to become too common to you. Not so very long ago I heard the pastor of a Washington church deliver a sermon in which he admonished his congregation never to allow the uncommon things to become common. If I could convey his thought to you, I would urge you never to allow the grandeur of the mountains and the majesty of this great western country to become so common to you that you will lose the ability to appraise the value of their inspiration and worth. You live in a wonderland, indeed, and we who have come from sections further east have been marvelling and indulging in the most extravagant comment of admiration and approval.

The Gospel of Understanding

I speak the plain truth when I say to you that I am rejoiced that I have come to know better your State and the people of your State. It is a fine thing, my countrymen, to know each other better. I love to preach the gospel of understanding. I want you to understand your government, and I think your government ought to understand you. If we can only have understanding in the world and, with that understanding, the practice of the Golden Rule, we shall not only be a peaceful people among ourselves, but we shall always remain at peace with the nations of the earth.

Again let me thank you for the cordiality of this surprising greeting tonight, and accept my very best wishes for a happy and a fortunate future.

I said a few moments ago that I wanted you to know your government better; so if you will permit me, I will present to you two or three members of the official party; but first of all I should like to present Mrs. Harding to this wonderful group of people of Montana. [Applause.]

Next I wish to present to you a Cabinet official in whom I know you are very greatly interested, and who is, I am happy to say, a very excellent official, the Secretary of the Interior, Dr. Hubert Work. [Applause.]

I introduce to you another Federal official in whom, I am sure, you are greatly interested, and who is also a very excellent one, the Secretary of Agriculture, Mr. Henry C. Wallace. [Applause.]

I know you have heard about another public officer. Some years ago he was called the "czar" or "despot" of the House. Such a title is no longer applicable, but one of the foremost officials of the Federal government is the gentleman who presides over the House of Representatives, and I take pleasure in presenting to you the Speaker of that body, Mr. Frederick H. Gillett, of Massachusetts. [Applause.]

Now I hope you know us better, as we feel that we know you somewhat better. I thank you again for coming to the station to give us this kindly greeting. [Applause.]

AMERICA'S VAST RESOURCES REVEALED

Speech at St. Maries, Idaho, July 2, 11:15 a. m.

Ladies and Gentlemen:

I WISH to take this opportunity to say to you how pleasing it is to have your cordial greetings. You are not greatly different from other people in this wonderland of the West, for everybody has been so cordial and kindly that our trip has been made a very happy one, and we have been heartened in the work which we have to do. I asked a gentleman a little while ago the population of St. Maries. He did not seem to know. I know now; I should say it must have a population of about 20,000. [Laughter and applause.]

We have had a magnificent journey across the continent, and I shall never cease to be grateful to you of the wonderful West who have removed the barriers of the mountains and made of this continent just one common country so that we may all be in communication with one another and have common interests and common purposes.

A little while ago I was contemplating the magnificent right of way of the railway and the work that was in progress thereon, and there came to me a new appraisal of the dignity of labor. A large group of men, a short distance back, were working on the right of way improving the condition of the rails and the roadbed over which passengers and commerce move. The men engaged in that arduous toil are none the less contributors to the country's progress; they are no less builders of the Empire than were the heroes who came out here, blazed the trails, found the passes, and opened up the vast domain of the West. Everyone who adds to the efficiency of lines of communication is a contributor to the making of this wonderful empire of ours.

God's Purpose Unfolding

Out here you literally live in a great empire of freedom and strength and cheer and hope. I cannot imagine a finer place in the world in which to live, although, of course, I think all America is fine and is all wonderful. We are varied; we are measureless in our stretches; we are boundless in our possibilities and resources, and we are different, too, in many ways, in our conceptions of daily life. At one time the great rivers separated us and the mountains were barriers; but now we are just one common people and one common country, with a common purpose, a common pride, and, I hope, all rejoicing Americans. I know you are splendid Americans out here. I do not know whether it is fair for the President to say quite all that he thinks; but somehow or other you have, perhaps, the most promising boyhood and girlhood and the most wonderful babyhood in the land. Surely in this climate, in this atmosphere, in this matchless freedom of yours, you must develop the finest specimens of men and women. Then, you have in addition the inheritance of the pioneers who gave this empire to the Republic; and it is a great inheritance, my countrymen; it is a fine thing of which to boast.

It is very helpful to us to be able to come and see you. It is an inspiration to those who live in the East to come in contact with the majesty and the endless stretches of nature's wonder creation. Sometimes I like to reflect on what God Almighty intended by it all. Surely there must have been a purpose, and I am confident that He endowed man with the genius to ascertain that purpose and to turn all of these resources to practical use. In harnessing the streams, watering the waste places, and conquering the wilds, you are succeeding, I am sure, in the great work planned by the Creator. It must be a great satisfaction—and, after all, that is the chief compensation in life—to see what has been accomplished by you and the pioneers who preceded you.

I realize that the men who made the trail westward were all, perhaps, animated by the desire to find new wealth. That seems to be the great inspiration for the forward movement of man throughout the world, and such a motive is not amiss. The only thing wrong about it is when wealth is unfairly acquired at the expense of one's fellows. That is where government seeks to step in. The government wants to provide equality of opportunity and just relationships amongst men. It is just as deeply interested in doing that in northern Idaho as it is in southern Illinois, or eastern Tennessee, or wherever the American flag flies. It is a pleasure to see you, and I beg to extend to you the most cordial good wishes that can come from the human heart.

Progress in Government

I have been thinking this morning how wonderfully we have progressed from the original idea of government. In the first years of our existence we were merely a confederation of States, each of which was largely a government within itself. We endeavor now to preserve certain sovereign rights in the States, but every year we find we are drifting more and more to the National idea. I do not know whether or not you have any government-aid roads in this section; but everywhere throughout this country where conditions make such improvements impossible at your own expense, the government is taking from its treasury and contributing to the improvements which are essential to your welfare, and then, out of the increase of your wealth and good fortune, comes the compensation to the remainder of the people who live in the East and other sections.

OVERWHELMED WITH HOSPITALITY

Remarks at Banquet of Columbia Basin Irrigation League, Davenport Hotel, Spokane, Wash., July 2, 7:55 p. m.

Mr. Chairman, Ladies and Gentlemen:

I HAVE come into the banquet hall at this hour merely to greet you, for I am compelled to leave in a few moments to keep another engagement.

In the bounteousness of your hospitality you almost overwhelm even the President, who is accustomed to the strenuous life; so that it is difficult for him to keep all the engagements which are proposed for him.

We have had a most delightful afternoon in your city; it has been pleasant in every way. I think I can subscribe to the sentiment of the coach driver, who was somewhat famous in Yellowstone Park, and who, while standing one day at Inspiration Point listening to the comments of the various visitors, said: "Well, I have been driving a coach here for 27 years, and I have not heard anybody 'kick' yet." [Laughter.]

There is nothing in your program to which one can take exception. There is nothing lacking in your courteous and considerate hospitality. I can understand why you are a great and growing community, and it is a joy to be in your midst.

I know you do not want me to be late for my public engagement. Perhaps, some of you yourselves are going there. So, if you will pardon me, I will do no more than thank you for this splendid manifestation of your thoughtfulness and courtesy.

GOVERNMENT'S PART IN DEVELOPMENT OF IRRI-
GATION AND UTILIZATION OF WATER POWER
IN WESTERN STATES

Address on Development, Reclamation and Water Utilization at the State Armory, Spokane, Wash.,
July 2, 8:30 p. m.

Governor Hart, Mr. Mayor, My Countrymen All:

THERE have been some misgivings as to the purpose
of our official tour across the continent; but in simple
truth we are not engaged in a political pilgrimage;
we are really traveling across the country in order to know
better our own America and then to learn more about a
vast Territory which belongs to us and lies beyond, a Territory in which you of the Northwest are particularly interested, in which all of the United States must be interested,
and which has measureless possibilities of contributing to
the greatness and the material and spiritual wealth of this
Republic of ours.

Very naturally and altogether appropriately, when the
President travels people want him to stop and give an
account of his stewardship. It is a very useful thing for
the President to do so; nay, more, it is a delightful thing
for the President to do so, because I cannot tell you how
we have been cheered and heartened by the cordiality of
the warm-hearted hospitality which has been extended to
us. Those whom we have met everywhere during the
course of our journey have been generous in their greetings; but none have been more generous, none more cordial,
none more wholesome than you who live in this great
empire of the Northwest. You are really a wonderful

232

people, and I am glad you are a most important part of the United States of America.

Government Expenses Cut

I think it is altogether becoming when the President travels and stops to make report that he should say something about the business affairs of the government. It is quite the custom at public meetings for the presiding officer or the toastmaster to read the telegrams, and I am going to read you a telegram tonight which I think will be interesting to you. It reached me only today and came from the Director of the Budget, who is the President's official agent in conducting the business affairs of the government. I have this message from General Lord:

"The budget for the fiscal year ending June 30, 1923, has been balanced, with a surplus of receipts over expenditures amounting to $309,657,000." [Applause.]

When I tell you that in the making of the budget we began with an apprehended deficit of $800,000,000, you will understand how far we have gone toward making our receipts cover our expenditures. General Lord continues:

"On the same comparable basis, total expenditures for 1923"—

That is the fiscal year which ended on June 30th, day before yesterday—

"are $263,033,233 less than for 1922; and the expenditures for 1923 of departments and establishments engaged with the ordinary business of the government are $294,265,813 less than the expenditures for 1922." [Applause.]

Expenses that Cannot Be Reduced

The significance of these figures is very striking to me. It will be noted that General Lord states that the expenditures for the ordinary business affairs of the government were $294,000,000 less than for the preceding year. Mark you, there are some expenditures of government which no business genius can reduce. We pay, for instance, $1,000,000,000 a year interest on the public debt, and the

233

only way we can reduce the interest account is by reducing the principal. We must wipe out the debt before that expenditure can be obliterated. Then, there are expenditures incident to war and the obligations which follow war which no genius of government or financial management can greatly reduce. Among these are the expenditures required to care for the veterans of the wars of the past and to provide compensation for the impaired veterans of the World War. The sums required for those purposes run well toward another billion dollars. The point is that the United States of America is the one outstanding government in all the world which has made such progress since the upheaval of the World War that we have more than balanced our budget. We are living within our income; we have put an end to the excess of expenditures, and we are getting upon the right track ready to go forward again. [Applause.]

Marvels of Geography

Doubtless, my countrymen, one who comes from so far east as Ohio, is bound to be regarded when he comes among you of the farthest Northwest as at least an Easterner; he may reasonably expect to be confused with the Yankees of "Way Down East"; and, I suppose, need not be surprised if he is looked upon almost as an oriental. This is a big country, and our notions of latitude and longitude are largely comparative. I may say in passing that I have come to a new realization of the importance of the study of geography in the public schools. I have friends in the southern corner of Texas who speak of the panhandle area of that State as "Up North." I have heard folks in Maine talk about the journalistic marvels of Winstead, Conn., as among the wonders of the great and bounding West.

Matters move rapidly in our times and country. Having always lived in Ohio, my recollection stretches from the time when we were regarded as living "way out West," to the period when we began to be considered by real western people as effete easterners. But, whether I am viewed from New England as a westerner, or, from the Pacific Slope as a slow-going coach from down East, I find satisfaction in the fact that whoever looks at this country of ours from all directions is bound to recognize it as the biggest thing anywhere and to thrill with pride in being a citizen of it. More than that, he is bound to realize that it is the best country in the world in which to live, in which to contend, to aspire, to acquire, and to know the triumphs of righteous citizenship.

Conservation, Reclamation, Development

It has been in my mind, during these days of travel in the West, to express on some appropriate occasion a few views regarding those problems which we summon to our minds under the headings of conservation, reclamation and development. Nowadays, I think there is disposition to change the order of terms, and mention development first. Not that we are any less devoted to conservation; but there is increasing realization that in our National development we have reached the time when wise programs for development in all parts of our domain must be encouraged. Our higher aspirations as citizens always lead along lines of development.

Traveling about this country, and somewhat also in other countries, I have been constantly impressed that wise development of natural resources does not often result in their disastrous diminution. Rather, it seems as a rule to result in a growing, an expanding, an increasing supply and variety of the very riches upon which we make drafts. Europe has sustained great and growing populations for many centuries, yet I am assured that its agricultural areas are producing more per acre today than ever before.

Examples in the Orient

China and Japan have been for centuries classed as over-populated; yet their populations go on increasing, and their standards of living improving. India has been afflicted with periodic famine for thousands of years, attributed primarily to excess of population in certain parts. Yet the population has gone right on increasing; and in modern

235

times, when the rate of increase has been greatest, the liability to famine has been least. The Island of Java, which is a good deal smaller than Iowa, was rated when it had about 11,000,000 inhabitants, as one of the most densely populated areas of the world. Now it has around 40,000,000, and they are better off than their ancestors ever were. Such instances might be multiplied indefinitely, to prove that development, far from exhausting resources, commonly means their multiplication. When our own country had 3,000,000 people, they were all poor; now that it has 110,000,000, they are the richest in the world.

Illustration in Ohio

An interesting illustration of this fact is found in the history of my own State. The early settlements in Ohio were made in what was known as the Connecticut or Western Reserve. Men from the East located there, and, as has been done too frequently in some sections of the West, they imposed upon the land; they drew excessively upon its resources, and largely decreased its productivity; so that fifty years ago the farmers of the Western Reserve began leaving that section to seek the more fertile lands of the West. However, the development of urban populations in great cities such as Cleveland brought the farmer back to the Western Reserve. He applied his genius to make the land again fertile; and now the Western Reserve blossoms as it never blossomed before, and land that was deserted 50 years ago is now bringing a higher price than has ever been known in that section.

Confidence in the Future

From all this you will gather, and quite correctly, that I do not fear that present development is liable to impoverish us in the future. The precise contrary, according to every historical analogy, is what will take place. You all remember that a quarter century ago so wise a man as James J. Hill was warning us that within fifteen years this country would have to import wheat! Twice that period has passed, our population has grown enormously,

236

and yet today we are producing a greater surplus of wheat than any other country in the world. Our difficulty is not to find wheat for ourselves but to find other countries that will buy it from us at prices for which the American farmer can afford to raise it.

In 1896 Mr. Bryan eloquently assured us that gold could no longer serve as the world's money standard because there could not possibly be enough of it produced. Before the echoes of his oratory had died away, science had perfected new processes of gold extraction, and in a few years another group of earnest people were just as solemnly warning us that we could not go on using gold as our money standard, because it was getting too common. Fortunately for us, we did not get unduly excited about either prediction, and today we find that almost everybody agrees that to get back on the gold basis is one of the world's greatest needs.

Wise Development the Solution

So, contemplating the certainty that another century will give us a population of probably 300,000,000 one is forced to conclude that a wise development of resources is the only policy to which we dare commit ourselves. There was a time when the public domain was thought of as a treasure house of potential wealth to be locked up against the day when we should need it. It was assumed that by locking it up we should make it surely available whenever it was required. As a matter of fact, that would prevent it from being ready when needed. Development must be gradual; a business of the decades and the centuries. It should, indeed, be given wise direction and supervision. The opportunities of the newer country should be so administered as to insure their equitable distribution in future. We have done with the era of thoughtless and reckless exploitation of our domain. There will not again come a time when imperial estates will be distributed with lavish hands to enterprising gentlemen whose only claim is that they would like to own them. We have curbed greed in the United States of America, and are exalting justice. [Applause.]

Land of Homes and Freedom

We want the West to be a land of homes and of the freest opportunity for the establishment of families possessing independent means of livelihood. It is recognized that the very different conditions of the plains and mountain areas compel many modifications of the policies that have served so well in other parts of the country. Those modifications are being wrought out gradually, with a view to promoting here that wide diversification of industries and occupations which is invited by your variety of resources, and which is the ideal state of a modern society. It is not desirable that the West should fall into the hands of bonanza corporations, seeking to exploit it for the profit of stockholders who live somewhere else. [Applause.] But, on the other hand, it is worth while to emphasize that many of the most valued resources of the West are of such character, and their development must be on such a scale, that they can only be made available under concentrated management and by the use of capital in large units. We must enforce measures which will give capital and management attractive returns, but which will always keep in sight the primary purpose of dealing out justice, even-handed opportunity, and an absolutely fair interest in the product of human industry, effort and intelligence.

Increased by Utilization

I spoke a moment ago of the fact that as a rule the utilization of nature's resources commonly results in their increase rather than their diminution. That is peculiarly true of one especially valuable resource of your mountain west: I mean the water. The flow of a great river that runs away to the sea without being utilized for power or for irrigation is wasted forever. It is like the newspaper column which carries no advertising; the opportunity is gone when the edition is issued. To prevent the development of such a river is not to save it for the benefit of a distant future. If it is to be of service tomorrow, it must be harnessed today.

Our whole view of the relation of water to western development has changed much in the last generation. Only a few years since these waters were looked upon as potentially useful merely for irrigation and agriculture. In that era we entered upon a great program of irrigation enterprise when we had as yet but a vague notion about the dual purpose that your water resources ought to serve. But now we know that the same water can in most cases be utilized both for power and irrigation. Thus great power development will mark the sites of industrial centers, adjacent to which will grow up rich areas of intensive agricultural production. The industrial populations will provide markets, without impossible transportation expenditure, for the products of the soil; and in turn the people on the soil will afford markets for the products of industry.

Transportation and Population

Transportation will be increased and cheapened through electrification of the railways; and, in the light of what we now know about all aspects of this subject, we may confidently look forward to a generation in which the young and vigorous commonwealths of the West will boast as great a population as the entire Nation numbers today, capable of living for the greater part within themselves, representing the widest variety of occupations and interests, and having problems of transportation largely solved for them because they will be so nearly self-sufficient and self-contained.

I digress at this point to remark how wonderful and how feasible and practicable and economical is the electrification of our railways. We rode today over many miles of electrified railway, and our train slipped along with the greatest comfort and steadiness. I sat for a while in the motor cab, and I derived inspiration from the fact that as we were coasting down-grade for twenty miles, while our train was being steadied by the process of driving the motors in the opposite direction, there was being stored up energy to pull another train upgrade. I venture the prediction, my countrymen, that the ultimate solution of the transportation problem is going to lie in the supersedure of the steam locomotive by the electric locomotive, not only in the West, where you have an abundance of power, but in the East, where power can be obtained at the mouth of the mine, and thereby save the transportation charges on coal for the different railway stretches of the country. We are in an era of great possibilities. [Applause.] The experience today was my first on a great train electrically driven and it was the most delightful ride I have ever known in my life.

"Wonderland of the West"

It is doubtful if there is in the world such a region of varied opportunity and universal wealth, as this mountain empire of yours. I have been quoted in the press as referring to this region as "the wonderland of the West." I am glad to repeat the expression, for I am being constantly impressed with the wonders of the great West. It is an inspiration to look upon you and to breathe the atmosphere in which you live. [Applause.] I quite understand that my statement as to the varied opportunities and universal wealth of the West would have sounded foolish to the men and women who two generations ago toiled across plains and over mountain trails as pioneers of the new domain. They came from the East; they had been raised in the belief that here was the great American desert; and their early visions of an inhospitable land, whose possibilities they could not possibly understand, was not calculated greatly to change that impression. But today we know differently. We know of your stores of coal and iron, copper and phosphates, potash and silver, gold and zinc and lead, along with all the other minerals and metals that latter-day industry has found so necessary. We know the richness of your plains and valleys, and we know how to bring the water from your mountain heights to make them blossom as the rose and groan with plenty. We know of your fruits and forests, your cereals, your vegetables and livestock. We know that here is the land of all lands to challenge and fascinate such a race as you have planted here. Your country presents its invitation and its opportunity to whoever is capable of a contribution to human well-being; to science, to industry, to the masters of metallurgy, of the electrical arts, of agriculture. Your story, varied and colorful, will grip the interest of those who will write, in history and literature, the story of this Nation; and the scenic splendors of your hundred Switzerlands will burn its inspiration into the soul of American art. [Applause.]

Wonders Wrought by Irrigation

Western people have had reasons to complain that there is not always a sympathetic or understanding attitude in some other parts of the country, toward the irrigation development that the West must have. The people of the Inland Empire might well remind their critics that during the uncounted centuries when the greatest civilizations had their seat on the Euphrates and the Nile, they were nurtured by an agriculture which depended on irrigation; on conserving and utilizing the waters of a few great streams. If we could know all the truth, it is probable we would learn that one of the first real impulses to developing civilization was given by those who discovered the possibility of irrigation as a means to agricultural production. The archaelogists who dig into the remains of cities so old that their very names have been lost, are constantly coming back to us with accounts of early irrigation works, constructed so long before our era that we can only vaguely conjecture their antiquity. Even today there are regions in India where crops are produced by carrying in skins water from the streams and putting it on the higher ground. It was thus that men got their earliest ideas of engineering science and systematized agriculture.

Our irrigation program is after all only a proposal to repeat, on the scale of modern engineering operations, the works by which primitive man learned to subjugate the earth and make it serve the needs of a developing social order. Ancient Egypt, which originated the civilization of which we are the direct inheritors, was little more than a strip of land ten miles wide and three hundred miles long, which would have been a desert had not the Nile's waters been conserved and utilized each season following the annual floods. The Columbia river basin, alone, under the program of development on which your Inland Empire is bent, will be made the seat of a greater, incomparably richer and more varied empire of industry and agriculture than was the Egypt which served as granary for imperial Rome. Not once, but a hundred times over, will we reproduce here in the plains and mountains and valleys of our West the wealth and productivity which enabled the Pharoahs to build monuments for the wonder of all time. But the monuments to our achievement will bear inscriptions telling, not of the slavery and sufferings of generations which gave their lives to perpetuate the glory of a tyrant; our inscriptions will tell of great, free States made up of contented, cultured and Christian homes. [Applause.]

Government's Desire to Aid

I am sure you are interested in what the Federal government can do to help solve the problems on which your future so largely depends. As we have gone onward in reclamation, there has been impatience that we could not proceed faster. There have been disappointments in the progress of work involving intricate and diversified engineering and hesitant financing. But I have been heartened by the convincing evidences I have already seen of the wonderful results where water meets the land.

.The government is interested to aid your efforts, from the standpoint of adding to the National wealth, by the transmutation of arid spaces into fertile fields. It is interested also in the protection of the National finances, so that money advanced to prosper this work may not be dissipated in doubtful projects or jeopardized in experiments. We must look for plans that are safe; plans so

242

conceived that they will not unduly burden the settler in the days when he is reducing the land to production; plans that will be reasonably broad, and that will not commit the government to unwise or unseasonable expenditures.

Investment that Will Return

I have been pleased to commend the subject of extended reclamation to the consideration of the Congress, mindful of the fact that reclamation from the National viewpoint must be considered as an investment of funds which will at length be returned to the government. The government's part is to supply expert engineering service, to advance finances for enterprises too vast for private capital, and to supervise and safeguard the work so that the balance of fair dealing may be maintained between government and settler, until the dream of an enlarged West comes true. [Applause.]

I have seen the statement that if the projects under investigation by the Reclamation Service be finally approved and completed, an area of cultivable land will be added equal to one of our largest agricultural States. A proposal to create the equivalent of a new State is something to challenge the conquering spirit of America. We know that the task one day will be done. It is for us a question of method; of proceeding with such business judgment, and on such sound principles, that the future may look back and say that it was well done. Of all these problems we are particularly reminded in this region, because the Columbia conveys to the mind significant suggestions; for her no one could be indifferent or fail to appreciate the splendid picture that lies behind the curtain of the mountains.

Food for Soil, Power for Cities

It is a matter all the more compelling, because the same waters which bring wealth to the soil, also pulsate with power for your cities, your railroads, and your industries. The use of the streams for power is inevitably tied in with reclamation. One purpose supplements the other in fulfilling the destiny of the waters as they flow on their

243

way to the sea. And there are yet other uses for your waters. We must see that the navigable waterways are maintained; and here again we find that the benevolence of the Creator has provided means to advance the projects of man. Frequently it is possible to improve navigation as an incident to developing power and irrigation works. Moreover, we want the flow of the streams for these great purposes, National purposes all, conserved. In other lands has been taught the lesson of waste that followed denuding the forested slopes, and permitted erosion to end its work in flood and devastation. We in America must not be so thoughtless or profligate. We must have a policy of reforestation that will preserve the National interest, and at the same time permit use of the timber as it is needed. [Applause.]

First Concern Is for America

So we see how the discussion of reclamation naturally leads on to that of water-power; and then to the maintained navigability of streams which carry commerce; and on again to the need of saving, while utilizing, our forests. It is a many-sided problem, in essence a problem of protecting the common good. The government comes in, neither as an interloper nor as a benevolent carry-all, but in its legitimate relation, under the Constitution, to these truly National concerns which touch so intimately the people of this Inland Empire, of the Pacific Coast, of the West, and of the entire United States. [Applause.]

I tell you, my countrymen, prosperity to one section alone or to one interest alone cannot be of permanent good. To be of value, prosperity must radiate throughout the United States of America. [Applause.]

Just a word in conclusion. I have said repeatedly that I am on no crusade. I have no especial project or policy to lay before the American people. From time to time I have been reporting on the affairs of government and saying, quite apart from the partisan viewpoint, some of the things which I think we in America ought to do. It has always been my judgment, my countrymen, that our first concern should relate to our own good fortune. We must have a materially fortunate and prosperous people before we can spiritually aspire. I want America to be a fortunate country. That is why we have been striving so assiduously to bring down the cost of government in order to relieve the burdens on the American people. I want America to be producing abundantly, and I rejoice that apparently not only is everybody who chooses to work employed throughout the United States but that there are thousands of jobs calling for men at this time.

We have made a tremendous advance in America in recovering from the war; but I am afraid, my countrymen, we are losing a little of the spirit that impelled us onward and upward to the Nation's consecration to the National defense. During the perils of the war we were all alert and united in our interest for our common country. We ought to be just as interested and just as much spiritually inspired in times of peace. When we come to appraise, as I have been called upon to do, nay, as you have been called upon to do from the viewpoint of your own homes, the consequences of war, I know that I speak what is in your hearts when I tell you that we never want the United States of America involved in another war. [Great applause.]

World Court of Justice

We have come to a period in civilization when we find a richer satisfaction in the triumphs of peace. There are agents and instrumentalities for the prevention of war. I was not a supporter of the League of Nations proposal; I do not believe that America ever will be; but there are international agencies for the promotion of peace. Perhaps, I should better express it if I should say there are international agencies which tend to prevent the irrita-

245

tions and grievances which lead to war. There has been established in the Old World an International Court of Justice before which nations may take their justiciable disputes for settlement. It is a court of very high order; and America, without any adhesion to the protocol establishing it, has a judge on the bench of that international court. It is an instrumentality infinitely better calculated to adjust disputes than any agency ever before set up in the world, and I believe with all my heart that America, without surrendering any of its independence, without becoming entangled in the affairs of the Old World, without jeopardizing its interests in any way, can subscribe to the International Court of Justice and give of its power and influence to make it a great agency for the furtherance of peace in the world. [Applause.]

Peace, the Almighty's Intent

I have asked the Senate for its assent to a negotiation looking to our adherence to this Court. I want from you that irresistible expression of the conscience of this Republic which will lead the Senate to say: "Aye; aye!' we, too, favor this step in the interest of peace among the nations of the world." I can assure you, my countrymen, there will be no entanglement; there will be no surrender of anything we cherish; but it will be an expression of that conscience and that aspiration which I know are in every American heart, and will enable the energies, the force, the thought, the brain, and the will-power of America to be devoted to those activities which make for the triumphs of peaceful life, rather than impose the dangers, the liabilities, aye, the immeasurable cost of war. I do not believe, my countrymen, we are living up to the highest intent of God, the Creator, unless we give of our influence and power to the furtherance of peace among nations and confidence and brotherhood among men. [Great applause.]

BELIEVES OUR SCHOOLS BEST IN WORLD

Speech to Normal School Students at Cheney, Wash.,
July 2, 11:40 p. m.

Young Ladies and Young Gentlemen:

IT IS a very great pleasure to see you. I have come to the conclusion that those who are equipping themselves to become teachers are the earliest risers and the latest to bed of anybody I know. [Laughter.] A few mornings ago I was asked to get up at 6:30 to greet a number of prospective teachers who were attending a State Normal School, and I thought anybody who was willing to get up at that early hour to greet us ought to be accommodated. Then I was asked to greet you at 11:30 p. m. when most old people have gone to bed, and I said again that anybody willing to stay up that late ought to be gratified.

How fine a work are you engaged in who are preparing yourselves to teach! I know something of the work you are undertaking, for I myself at one time happened to teach school, and I never did such hard work in my life. Of course, I taught under different conditions than you will encounter. It was so long ago that I hesitate to name the date, but it was more than forty years ago. It was in one of the country schools where everything from the A B C's to algebra was taught, and the pupils ranged from five and a half to seventeen years of age. I was not seventeen myself at the time. I think it does not obtain now, but in those days it was the fashion to "run the teacher out." I had three big boys in my school all of whom were older than I. Their first names were Frank, Jesse and James and they called themselves Frank and Jesse James. Some of you will remember the romance and the terror of the James brothers in those days, and you can understand what I was up against; but it was a fine experience. It is said that nowadays one has to be a

247

school teacher in order to be worth while in America, and, consequently, I think I see before me a fine prospective crop for the future. [Applause.]

Commends America's Educational System

Education is a very interesting subject. Thirty years ago this country spent approximately $140,000,000 a year on education, while today we spend more than $1,000,000,-000. Those seem like very large figures at first thought, and yet they do not represent so much by a very large amount as we spend on automobiles and motors; alas, they do not represent so much as we spend on tobacco, and not nearly so much as we formerly spent on intoxicating drinks. We have banished the latter, and I wish with all my heart we might have a strict observance of the Constitution and the law and add what we spend for intoxicants to further the cause of education in our Republic. [Applause.] We even spend quite as much on soft drinks, on nut sundaes, pop, ginger ale, near beer, and I know not what all as we do on education. However, we are doing well. I believe we have the finest public schools in the world. I told an audience of prospective teachers in Montana several mornings ago that I myself before the World War encountered a commission which came from Germany to study the American public school system. At that time most of the world thought Germany was the most efficient country so far as education was concerned, and perhaps she was. It is one of the supreme tragedies of the war that a great, efficient and thoroughly educated people should have come to such grief by their own folly. It was a great testimonial, however, to education in America to have them send a commission to study our educational system.

Futile Without Practical Application

It may not be inappropriate to add that education does not amount to a great deal if it is not put to a practical purpose, and that is the lesson you must teach. The teacher prepares the youth of the land for the duties and obligations and battles of life, and then the result is measured by the application which the scholars make of their advantages. It is one of the beautiful things of this land of ours, where there is no caste, aye, where we are without class—except that we are a very fine class—that, under the Constitution and laws of the Republic, every boy and girl is presumed to have equal advantage and to find opportunity beckoning. Education is the equipment we supply to enable them to embrace that opportunity.

There devolves upon you not only the responsibility of training the mind of the young, but, in our modern educational system, there rests upon you much of the responsibility for character building. I believe every young man and young woman in this company has formed some of his habits and gained some of his impressions from his appraisal of the character of the teachers who instructed him in the schools. I know that has been my experience, and I believe it has been the experience of everyone. We are very unconscious of our influence on the lives of others. There is not one among you—I care not who—that has not influenced the life of some younger person somewhere. If you are extremely modest and retiring, that quality alone is somehow taken up by someone to whom it appeals, and you are made an example. So there comes a very great responsibility upon the teaching body of the Republic.

Teachers Finding Their Responsibility

Alas, too much of the responsibility that belongs in the home is nowadays placed upon the teacher in the public school.

Somehow in our modern life we have turned to others to perform the duties which I sometimes think we ought to perform ourselves. The influence of the public schools in character building can never be substituted for that of the mother and the home; but the teachers of America are finding the responsibility thrust upon them. I hope you will meet such responsibility well. I hope you will not only prove efficient in improving the mind of the young, but I hope with all my heart that you will impress the necessity of moral character. We need it in order to insure a better America. No nation has ever survived that has not developed a high moral character and has not clung to spiritual ideals. I am quite practical. I know the necessity of sustenance; I know the desirability of material welfare, but if we are going to fulfill the destiny which I believe Providence has in store for this splendid representative democracy of ours, we must be a religious people; we must have moral and spiritual ideals.

I commend these thoughts to you, and I not only wish you well in your personal affairs, but I wish you that compensation which comes with the knowledge of having performed well a good and noble work. That is perhaps the greatest compensation that can come to a professional life of teaching, and no greater compensation can come in any other walk of life. You have a fine prospect before you; you live in a wonderful country; and I want you to play your part in ever making it a better one. I thank you for your greeting. Good-night. [Applause.]

PRESENTS OLD OREGON TRAIL FILM

Remarks at Meacham, Ore., When Presenting to the Old
Oregon Trail Association the Original Film of "The
Covered Wagon," Donated by the Laskey
Corporation, July 3, 3 p. m.

Mr. Chairman and Ladies and Gentlemen:

IF I may address myself to the president of the Old Oregon Trail Association, I will perform what is to me the very agreeable service of placing in his hands the original film of "The Covered Wagon." I take a great deal of satisfaction, sir, in saying that I have sat under the spell of this wonderful picture, and I know how accurately, how thoroughly, and how impressively it preserves the story of the trials and triumphs of the pioneer empire builders who blazed the trail to this western land and made a greater United States. It is a treasure worthy of preservation. It is a picture of history that could not have been portrayed in times gone by, and I congratulate your association that you have become the possessors of this fine story, to be handed down to generations which are yet to come, who shall learn so impressively the story of the making of the wonderful West. [Applause.] I present to you, sir, as president of the Old Oregon Trail Association, the original film of "The Covered Wagon."

POETIC PRAISE OF THE PIONEERS WHO BLAZED THE WAY TO EMPIRE FOLLOWING THE OLD OREGON TRAIL

Address on The Oregon Trail at Meacham, Ore.,
July 3, 3:15 p. m.

My Countrymen:

AS I stand here in the shadow of the great hills, my mind reverts to the placid banks of the broad Potomac. There, as here, to an American proud of his country and revering her traditions, there is much of patriotic interest, and between these rugged mountains and those fertile lowlands I find much in common. Living history records many indissoluble links, to one of which it seems fitting that I should direct your attention today.

Of the many rooms in the White House, which possess the peculiar charm of association with epochal happenings, the one most fascinating to me is that which formerly comprised the Cabinet room and the President's study. Through its high windows one's gaze is drawn irresistibly to the towering granite shaft whose very grandeur, exceeded by no other monument in the world, admirably symbolizes the matchless character of George Washington. The beautifully carved mahogany bedposts are those upon which fell the eyes of Andrew Jackson when opened from the troubled slumber which even to this day occasionally falls to the lot of an over-weary President. Sunk into the marble mantel piece is a bronze tablet recording the circumstance that it was in this room that Abraham Lincoln signed the great emancipation proclamation, which struck the shackles of slavery from millions of human beings.

Poetic Picture of Historic Scene

Yet another episode of hardly less importance in the building of our mighty Nation took place within those walls. Before my mind's eye as I stood in that historic chamber a few days ago appeared the vivid picture. I beheld seated at his desk, immaculately attired, the embodiment of dignity and courtliness, John Tyler, tenth President of the United States. As the story goes, facing him, from a chair constructed for a massive frame, his powerful spirit gleaming through his cavernous eyes, was the lion-visaged Daniel Webster, Secretary of State.

The door opened and there appeared before the amazed statesmen a strange and astonishing figure. It was that of a man of medium height and sturdy build, deep chested, broad shouldered, yet lithe in movement and soft of step. He was clad in a coarse fur coat, buckskin breeches, fur leggings, and boot moccasins, looking much the worse for wear. But it was the countenance of the visitor, as he stood for an instant in the doroway, that riveted the perception of the two chiefs of State. It was that of a religious enthusiast, tenaciously earnest yet revealing no suggestion of fanaticism, bronzed from exposure to pitiless elements and seamed with deep lines of physical suffering, a rare combination of determination and gentleness— obviously a man of God, but no less a man among men.

Whitman, Pioneer Oregon Missionary

Such was Marcus Whitman, the pioneer missionary hero of the vast, unsettled, unexplored Oregon country, who had come out of the West to plead that the State should acquire for civilization the empire that the churches were gaining for Christianity. [Applause.]

Many of the exploits of America's resolute sons are recounted in prose and verse. How often in our youth, and even in later years, have we been thrilled by the story of how "on through the night rode Paul Revere, through every Middlesex village and farm" to call the Minute Men to embattle at Lexington and fire "the shot heard 'round the world!" How many times we have shuddered at the impending fate of the Shenandoah Valley with "Sheridan twenty miles away!" I loved the martial notes of those stirring verses as a boy. I love them still.

But, when I stood in that historic room in the White House and my imagination depicted the simple scene, I could not but feel that the magnificence of Marcus Whitman's glorious deed has yet to find adequate recognition in any form. Here was a man who, with a single companion, in the dead of winter, struggled through pathless drifts and blinding storms, four thousand miles, with the sole aim to serve his country and his God. Eighty years and eight months ago he was pushing grimly and painfully through this very pass on his way from Walla Walla to Fort Hall, thence, abandoning the established northern route as impassable, off to the South through unknown, untrodden lands, past the Great Salt Lake, to Santa Fe, then hurriedly on to St. Louis and finally, after a few days, again on the home-stretch to his destination, taking as many months as it now takes days to go from Walla Walla to Washington.

More than a Perilous Adventure

It was more than a desperate and perilous trip that Marcus Whitman undertook. It was a race against time. Public opinion was rapidly crystallizing into a judgment that the Oregon country was not worth claiming, much less worth fighting for; that, even though it could be acquired against the insistence of Great Britain, it would prove to be a liability rather than an asset.

It is with sheer amazement that we now read the declarations of the leading men of that period. So good an American, so sturdy a frontiersman, so willing a fighter, as General Jackson, shook his head ominously in fear lest the National domain should get too far outspread, and warned the country that its safety "lay in a compact government." Senator McDuffie, of South Carolina, declared he "would not give a pinch of snuff for the whole territory," and expressed the wish that the Rocky Mountains were "an impassable barrier." Senator Dayton, of New Jersey, said that, with very limited exceptions, "the whole country was as irreclaimable and barren a waste as the Sahara desert," and that malaria had carried away most of its native population. Even so far-seeing and staunch an advocate of western interests as Thomas Benton protested that the ridge of the Rockies should be made our western boundary, and avowed that "on the highest peak the statue of the fabled God, Terminus, should be erected, never to be thrown down."

Firm in Face of Webster's Opposition

Webster, although not definitely antagonistic, was uninterested and lukewarm. Years before he had pronounced Oregon "a barren, worthless country, fit only for wild beasts and wild men," and he was not one who changed opinions readily. But neither was Whitman one easily dismayed. Encouraged by the manifest friendliness of President Tyler, he portrayed with vivid eloquence the salubrity of the climate, the fertility of the soil, the magnitude of the forests, the evidences of ore in the mountains, and the splendor of the wide valleys drained by the great rivers. And he did not hesitate to speak plainly, as one who knew, even like the prophet Daniel.

"Mr. Secretary," he declared, "you would better give all New England for the cod and mackerel fisheries of Newfoundland than to barter away Oregon."

Manly Appeal to President Prevails

Then, turning to the President in conclusion, he added quietly but beseechingly:

"All I ask is that you will not barter away Oregon or allow English interference until I can lead a band of stalwart American settlers across the plains. For this I shall try to do."

The manly appeal was irresistible. He sought only the privilege of proving his faith. The just and considerate Tyler could not refuse.

255

"Doctor Whitman," he rejoined sympathetically, "your long ride and frozen limbs testify to your courage and your patriotism. Your credentials establish your character. Your request is granted."

Finds Inspiration in the Story

I have recited this story mindful of the fact that its accuracy is challenged. Since this address has been prepared, on numerous occasions friends, with kindly and thoughtful interest, have said I ought not to relate it because it cannot be justified in history; but, my countrymen, I have recited this story of Dr. Marcus Whitman because from my intimate association with the White House, I have come to believe that this story, whether literally correct or not, affords the finest inspiration for the highest possible type of American patriotism and devotion. I like accuracy in history; I love truthfulness in biography; I like the dependableness of tradition; but I do not like the iconoclast who would seek to destroy faith in those things which have inspired the most enthusiastic devotion to America.

I referred earlier in my address to the ride of Paul Revere. Only a few days ago an iconoclastic American said there never was a ride by Paul Revere; that he started out with Colonel Dawes, an ancestor of the recent Director of the Budget, to give the warning to "every Middlesex village and farm," but was arrested, so it is said by a British sentry, and never made the ride. Suppose he did not; somebody made the ride and stirred the minutemen in the colonies to fight the battle of *Lexington*, which was the beginning of independence in the new Republic in America. I love the story of Paul Revere, whether he rode or not. [Applause.]

Likened to Barbara Frietchie

There is another much disputed story which I greatly like and which has been preserved in the splendid poem of Whittier. I refer to Barbara Frietchie, of Frederick. In these days when one visits Frederick he is told that

256

no such incident as that recited by Whittier ever took place. But I like the observation of the old keeper of the cemetery who was pointing out one day the grave of Barbara Frietchie, and said: "There was such a person in Frederick. Perhaps it is true she was an invalid when Jackson's troops marched through the town, and perhaps there was no such defy as the verse recites; but Barbara was there and the flag was displayed from her window." Whether or not she defied old Jackson or uttered the words—

> "Shoot, if you must, this old gray head
> But spare your country's flag—"

She put Frederick on the map, and the story relates an example of patriotism that may well be passed on to generations ten times ten yet to come, because it is a story of American devotion that stirs the heart and adds to our love of flag and country. So, if the story I have related of Whitman is not literally true, it ought to be true.

Whitman's Strategy True Statesmanship

Whitman's strategy was true statesmanship. Substantial occupation would make good the claim of the United States, and that was what he had initiated during his few days in St. Louis. A few months later he had completed an organization of eager souls, and led the first movement by wagon train across plains and mountains along this unblazed trail.

What a sight that caravan must have appeared to the roaming savages! And what an experience for the intrepid pioneers!

More than two hundred wagons, bearing well-nigh a thousand emigrants, made up the party. They traveled by substantially the same route that Whitman had taken when he first went out to Oregon; from a rendezvous near what is now Kansas City they moved due northwest across northeast Kansas and southeast Nebraska to the Platte River; followed the Platte to the middle of what is now Wyoming, thence crossing the mountains by way of the

257

Sweetwater Valley and the South Platte; and from Fort Hall, following the well-known route, roughly paralleling the Snake River, into Oregon. The difficulties of the trip, involving beside the two hundred wagons, the care of women and children, and of considerable herds of livestock, were such that its successful accomplishment seems almost miraculous.

Theirs by Right of Occupation

But stern determination triumphed and the result was conclusive. Americans had settled the country. The country belonged to them because they had taken it; and in the end the boundary settlement was made on the line of the forty-ninth parallel, your great Northwest was saved, and a veritable empire was merged in the young Republic.

Never in the history of the world has there been a finer example of civilization following Christianity. The missionaries led under the banner of the cross, and the settlers moved close behind under the star-spangled symbol of the Nation. Among all the records of evangelizing effort as the forerunner of human advancement, there is none so impressive as this of the early Oregon mission and its marvelous consequences. To the men and women of that early day whose first thought was to carry the gospel to the Indians—to the *Lees*, the Spauldings, the Grays, the Walkers, the *Leslies*, to Fathers De Smet and Blanchet and De Mers, and to all the others of that glorious company who found that in serving God they were also serving their country and their fellow men—to them we pay today our tribute; to them we owe a debt of gratitude which we can never pay, save partially through recognition such as you have accorded today.

We may reasonably do more today than rejoice in possession of the imperial domain which they revealed, and the life they made possible to the virile, aspiring, and confident Northwest. I find new assurances in recalling the heroism, the resolution, the will to conquer of these pioneers.

I wish I might more effectively visualize them. Not very long ago I saw "The Covered Wagon" in the moving picture. I sat entrancèd. There was more than the picturesque, more than sorrow and discouragement, more than appealing characters and enthralling heroism. There was more than the revelation of the irresolute, who failed in fitness to survive, more than tragedy and comedy in their inseparable blend. There was more than the scouts who surpassed our fancies, more than nature's relentless barriers revealed. Everywhere aflame was the soul of unalterable purpose and the commanding sturdiness of elemental greatness. Still more, there was determination to do for themselves, not asking the government to do, but for government only to sanction or permit.

Same Spirit in Central West

Much the same spirit was revealed in the making of the Central West, where the determined pioneers builded in the confidence which they had in themselves. They battled with nature and against every obstacle which they encountered; heroes perished without fame's acclaim; but .they conquered and wrote big their part in the making of the greater Republic. Their victory proclaimed the strength of resolute purpose, and the resourcefulness of human genius, confident in itself and eager to achieve on its own account.

The lesson can not fail to impress itself. In this test of self-reliant citizenship there came the rugged, militant, wholesome West. Greater things were wrought, larger accomplishment was recorded, greater victory was won in this wholesome, inspiring individualism than will ever attend paternalism or government assumption of the tasks which are the natural inheritance of the builders who may better serve for themselves. [Applause.] Government may well provide opportunity, but the worth-while accomplishment is the privilege and the duty of men.

The Wonderful "Trail of Love"

I thank you from the bottom of my heart for permitting me to participate in doing homage to those brave souls. I rejoice particularly in the opportunity afforded me of voicing my appreciation, both as President of the United States and as one who honestly tries to be a Christian soldier, of the signal service of the martyred Whitman. And finally, as just a human being, I wish I could find words to tell you how glad I am to see you all, reflecting as you do, from untroubled eyes and wholesome faces, the happiness of spirit breathed by your own best song:

"There are no new worlds to conquer—
  Gone is the last frontier,
And the steady grind of the wagon-train,
  Of the sturdy pioneer.
But their memories live like a thing divine,
  Treasured in Heaven above,
For the Trail that led to the storied West,
  Was the wonderful Trail of *Love*."

[Applause.]

DEDICATION OF OLD TRAIL MONUMENT

Remarks on the Occasion of the Dedication of the Stone Marking the Old Oregon Trail near Meacham, Ore., July 3, 5 p. m.

Ladies and Gentlemen:

YOU have witnessed the unveiling of this monument dedicated, as the tablet says:

"To the memory of
the intrepid pioneers
who came with the
first wagon train
in 1843 over the
Old Oregon Trail
and saved the Oregon Country
to the United States."

I am glad to participate in these dedicatory exercises. It is a fine thing for this generation to express its gratitude and appreciation by this monument to a heroism, a romance, and an empire-making which is worthy of a place in the history of any people in the world. I only hope that those who follow after and enjoy the lands which they gave to this Republic and embrace the opportunity which they left for us shall be worthy of the sacrifices they made; shall inherit the devotion and courage which they manifested, and that we shall all be worthy citizens of the greater Republic which they bequeathed to us.

I am glad that there are representatives of the pioneers present on this occasion, and, inasmuch as one of the ladies present has a water-bottle which came overland with the earliest pioneers, I think, perhaps, it would be appropriate, in addition to the dedication, in a way, if I may so call it, to baptize this stone in the name of the Creator and of those who love and revere our common country. [Applause.]

ACCEPTS *LIFE* MEMBERSHIP CERTIFICATE

Remarks Near Meacham, Ore., July 3, 5:15 p. m., on Being Presented with Certificate No. 1 of *Life* Membership in the Old Oregon Trail Association

Mr. Meacham and Ladies and Gentlemen:

I AM somewhat embarrassed to speak again, because it seems to me I have already said enough; but I cannot be unmindful of this added expression of the courtesy, the thoughtfulness, and the cordiality with which you have greeted us. It is a pleasing reminder to me, not alone of this testimonial to the Pioneers and the work you have performed in preserving the lessons of early history, but it is a splendid reminder of the joy we have had in associating with you today. I cannot tell you what a pleasure it has been.

I do not think that we are different from others, and I speak only the truth when I tell you we love contact with the people we are seeking to serve. It is the greatest pleasure in the world to know people. I find a greater comfort, a greater joy, a greater inspiration, nay, a greater consecration to the purpose of serving in an official way the more I come in contact with the people who make up this great country of ours.

Someone said today that this splendid Northwest territory, this inland empire, out of which has been carved the States of Oregon, Washington, Idaho, and Montana, is made up of the best people in the world. Of course I cannot say just that, for I am President of all the United States, but I will say there are no better people in the world. It is a very great pleasure to come into this most agreeable and intimate contact with you. You have given us a sweet memory to cherish, and you have given us a new satisfaction in the assurance that you are doing your part to preserve the traditions, the lessons, and the inspirations which attended the making of this empire Republic of ours. I know we shall all go on seeking to do our part in bringing about the fulfillment of the destiny which belongs to this great Nation. I thank you, sir. [Applause.]

PREDICTS FUTURE FARM PROSPERITY

Speech at Pendleton, Ore., July 3, 7 p. m.

My Countrymen:

I FEAR Senator Stanfield has been a little extravagant in his introductory remarks. I think I will try to return the compliment by saying that from appearances Pendleton is the largest city in the State of Oregon. [Applause.] It is very good of you to come to greet us while we are passing through your beautiful city. There has been a continual offering of greetings and good wishes all the way across the continent. We have had a wonderful experience, one which I wish might be the portion of every American, for I know that no one could see what we have seen, appreciate the spirit and the attitude of the people of our country as we have appreciated them, without being a more proud and hopeful American than he was before. It has been especially a joy to note the marvels of this wonderland of the Northwest.

We have had an exceedingly busy day celebrating the dedication of a monument to the pioneers who opened the trail to Oregon and who gave of their confidence, their courage, their capacity, and their faith in order to insure that this great northwestern empire should be a part of the Republic. It was a tremendous offering to make. It was a fine thing to wrench from other powers the great territory out of which we have carved four of the wonder States of the Northwest. We have also experienced that glad realization that the genius and the determination of man have wiped out the barriers of the mountains. There is no longer any frontier in the United States. We find mountains dividing, rivers separating, conditions varying and ideas to some extent differing; but, after all, throughout the United States we are just one common people, with a common purpose and universal pride in this great land of ours. Everywhere there is the same American spirit, and I believe that everywhere there is the same confident, American hopefulness and pride in this great Republic of ours.

Return of Farm Prosperity Predicted

We have heard nothing in the way of complaint today. Rather, we have heard words of tribute to those who have contributed so much to the expansion of American territory and American influence. We know, of course, that the aftermath of the World War, the reaction from that great upheaval, and the inevitable deflation that followed inflation have brought hardships, discouragements and trials to all the people. That has been notably true in the case of agriculture; but it is not limited to the farming community alone. I have been learning something of the problems of the farmer, and I have been happy to tell those engaged in agriculture that their government, and Congress in particular, have been doing everything they know how to do in order to make the lot of the American farmer more fortunate. That is not because he is so numerous as a voter; it is not because he is more clamorous in his demands for assistance; it is because the farmer represents the fundamental industry of the Republic. We are dependent upon him for our sustenance and we want him to be in a prosperous and thriving condition, because upon his good fortune depends the good fortune of the people at large. I do not think that the government can cure all the ills which afflict the farmer; some of them are going to require time and inevitable readjustment; but we have provided means for financing; we have provided all the conditions which the government has authority to provide, and we hope ultimately to add the encouragement of a diminution in the cost of transportation. When that is accomplished, I am sure that there will be a return to normal and prosperous conditions in agriculture.

In Heart of Wheat Region

I am told that we are now in the finest wheat producing section probably in the world. I congratulate you, and I hope that, in addition to an abundant crop, you may also have a production which will bring an adequate compensation. Out in Ohio we rejoice when we can make 20 or 25 bushels of wheat to the acre. I believe in this section of the country you raise rather more than that. As a farm hand, I was satisfied with 25 bushels when I followed the binder. Nowadays we do things in a somewhat different way. The day of mechanism and of improved machinery has brought a change in conditions. I hope for the good of our country that we may be able to bring about such readjustments in the distribution of the profits of production as will insure to you your full and complete share. I say to you, as I would say it anywhere in the United States, that one class of citizenship, or one community, cannot prosper at the expense of another; that

264

is impossible. In order that we may have a happy, contented and prosperous people, it is necessary that universal good times should prevail. Good fortune must be more or less shared by all alike.

The government is interested in doing everything it can to bring about proper adjustments, but the government cannot do the things which men must do for themselves. I hope never to see the day of a paternalistic or a socialistic United States of America. That would mean the paralysis of every ambition that we cherish. Men and women must strive for themselves in this land of American opportunity.

Impressed by West's Progress

One of our great problems—and I speak of it because I see so many boys and girls before me—is to equip the growing citizenship of the country so that we may embrace the equal opportunity which we always boast.

I am glad you came to greet us, for it heartens us, and it enables you to know me a little better. I shall be your President for some months more, I am sure, and I am glad to know you, see in your faces the look of confidence, and be reassured that you constitute a happy portion of the great American public. I wish I could tell you—and I think I could if it were not for the appearance of boasting —how wonderfully I have been impressed by the marvelous development I have seen in the West. I wish those who live in the East could visit the West and see you, and I wish you could go East and see the people of that section. If you could come into more intimate contact, if you could know each other better and could come to an understanding, I feel confident that we should be an even happier people than we are.

We are doing pretty well in America. I wish that the other nations in the world could do as well. We have made more progress than any other people in the world since the cataclysm of the World War. We mean to go forward, and I believe, my countrymen, if we hold fast to the fundamentals on which we have builded this Republic, a certain and glorious triumph will be our portion. I thank you sincerely for coming out to extend this cordial greeting. [Applause.]

NEW VIEW OF NATION'S RESOURCES

Speech at The Dalles, Ore., July 3, 11:30 p. m.

Ladies and Gentlemen:

YOUR representative in Congress was not quite accurate in his statement in introducing me. I did not "consent" to greet you; I said I would be happy to greet you, because anybody who will come out at this late hour of the night to extend a welcome to a traveler who is passing through is thoroughly entitled to a very cordial and ready response. I am only sorry that we are not passing through this section in the day time. I know something of you as an agricultural community, and I am beginning to learn about your fruit production. Your Congressman brought us a consignment of cherries today that made us wonder that Eve did not use cherries instead of apples when she offered the great temptation. [Laughter.] I know we are going greatly to enjoy the cherries.

We have been having a wonderful trip across the continent. We are now, as you know, nearing the coast, and are about to embark for Alaska. Everywhere we have met a confident and a seemingly happy people, although as yet they may not be wholly satisfied with conditions, which require correction after the deflation incident to the war. Everywhere, however, they are hopeful and confident of the future and manifestly glad to live in this wonderful Republic of ours and proud to be Americans.

Pride in Nation Growing

I am very much more proud of our country than when I started westward. It is not given to many of us to know how vast and wonderful this land of ours is. Even

266

on our trip, somewhat hurried as it is, we get only a cursory view; but I have come to a new realization of the measureless material wealth, the vast extent of this Republic, and the quality of its citizenship which in the West needs no apology anywhere I have been.

It is a pleasure to see you. I can only wish you the very best of good fortune. I wish it personally and officially, because the government is always concerned with the good fortunes of its people everywhere throughout the Union. One of the chief businesses of the government is the adjustment of our relationships so that good fortune may be shared by all the people more or less alike. I wish you a full measure of good fortune, and I trust that your cup of happiness may be filled to the utmost. [Applause.]

WE ARE WITHOUT CASTE IN AMERICA

Remarks at Reviewing Stand, Portland, Ore., July 4, 10:15 a. m.

Young Ladies and Young Gentlemen, Boys and Girls:

WE ARE grateful to you indeed for painting for us this morning this picture of marvelous youth, symbolizing this great floral city. Somehow I lack the words to say what is in my heart when I look down and see immediately in front of me these Boy Scouts, now youthful Americans, who are sure to be the country's stalwarts on the morrow. Then I see these boys and girls in brilliant and fascinating raiment, emphasizing a picture which I have tried to portray many times. One cannot tell by looking upon them which come from palatial homes and which come from modest homes; they are all children rich in American inheritance. They give forth the same rollicking laughter; they are clad in the same raiment; they have marched this morning in the light of the same opportunity, and they grow up to manhood and womanhood in this country of ours with precisely the same chance to achieve and triumph in life.

What a privilege it is, boys and girls, to be children of the great Republic! Here in America we are without caste; we are without class distinctions; we are just free Americans, with each one having the right to aspire to the best there is in life, and to be rewarded according to his or her merits. I like to stand before you, boys and girls, this morning, and tell you that above all aspirations I have in official life is to continue to hold secure the Republic which we all today enjoy, so that it may be yours on the morrow to carry on to greater glory and power.

It is a very great pleasure to see you. You have pleased the eye; you have thrilled the heart; and you have added to the splendid welcome we have received in this wonderland of the West. I wish you the best in the world, young ladies and young gentlemen, and I hope the fullest measure of happiness in life may be yours. [Prolonged applause and cheers.]

OBLIGATIONS OF CITIZENSHIP URGED UPON ALL WHO COME TO OUR SHORES IN SEARCH OF LIBERTY AND WEALTH

Address at Multnomah Field, Portland, Ore.,
July 4, 2:50 p. m.

Ladies and Gentlemen of Oregon, My Fellow Americans All:

I WOULD not be true to my own sense of gratitude if I did not in my first utterance thank you most sincerely for the very hearty, cordial, and heartening reception which you have given us this day. We have come to love the "Rose City." [Applause.] You have delighted our eyes and have warmed our hearts and stirred our pride in the great State of Oregon. [Applause.] I cannot quite subscribe to what Chairman McDougall said about Oregon being the greatest State in the Union because I see the Ohio Society on guard in the stand on my left. [Laughter.] Quite apart from that, if one is fit to be President, he is President of all the United States and he must not play any favorites. [Applause.] As spokesman for the United States, however, I am quite willing to say that we are indeed proud to have Oregon occupy a conspicuous place in the Union.

Omen of Peace and Good Will

I do not know whether or not you realize it, but there has been recorded today in Portland an historical event. Never before in the history of the American Republic has a contingent from the British Navy marched in a Fourth of July celebration in the United States. [Applause.] I am glad our British friends have shown us that distinc-

269

tion because it symbolizes the progress which has been made during the last one hundred and forty-seven years and brings to us once more the realization that the English-speaking world is of one kin and has common aspirations. [Applause.] I hope from this day on the representatives of the British navy and the representatives of the American navy may always march together in the proud processions of peace. [Applause.]

Some men sneer at the suggestion of destiny in National life, but those who do so give scant thought to actualities. One who doubts our destiny might as well believe that the well-ordered universe is an accident of creation; that the fixed stars in the heavens and the planets in their evolutions are a mere jumbling of creative fortune. I myself believe in destiny, and I believe that the destiny of this New World Republic was written by an Infinite Hand in the consciousness of Divine intent. . How else could we explain the marvel of the founding and development of the American Republic?

Birth of the Constitution

Mr. Idleman has just read the Declaration of Independence. Did you note that there was nothing in it that gave the slightest suggestion of the Nation which was to follow? The war for American independence was not fought for nationality; it was fought to strike at oppression; but in the chaos of American victory we turned to nationality as the only means of preservation. Likewise, it was in the chaos of the great beginning that we called on the loftiest statemanship in the early life of the Republic. The colonists, spent and wearied in their victory, having conflicting ideas, threatening jealousies and varied demands, at that time had no thought of becoming a Nation; they were seeking to go the way of separate States. But somehow the divinity of the Republic asserted itself; union was established, and the Constitution adopted. I believe, my countrymen, with all my heart there was destiny in that.

My countrymen, two schools of politics were in conflict from the very beginning of the Republic. One was the nationalist school, led by Hamilton, believing in strong Federal power, and National control over all that is of direct concern to the Republic's welfare. The other was the Jefferson school, believing in the larger sovereignty of the States, and only a Federal authority for National defense. Jefferson was an outstanding champion of independence, but he did not have the broad National conception.

Destiny in Division of Minds

The fight between these two schools was persistent and unending, and was so bitterly waged that we began with an ambiguity in the Constitution, which had, ultimately, to be wiped out in blood. At an immeasurable cost of lives and treasure, that dispute and that ambiguity were settled in the great Civil War, and, thank God, the settlement was in favor of Union and nationality. I think there was destiny in that.

Then came the processes of reconstruction and restoration. The wounds of war had to be healed. The South had to be won to a new concord of Union to permit the Nation's greater and grander development. The process was necessarily slow. War's wounds are always difficult to heal. That is the chief hindrance to world recovery today. The wrecked timbers of the broken State are poor material from which to build anew, when pride is suffering and humiliation is blended with hate. But we started in high confidence after the Civil War, and the North gave the world a fine example of tolerance and brotherhood, and the South gave the same world an inspiring application of good purpose and of faith in the new order.

Blended in the Cup of Peace

We came to understanding, the one supreme solution in which to blend the cup of peace. A half-dozen Presidents came and went before the healing was completed. It remained for the gentle and tactful and sympathetic McKinley fully to understand the South and lead the South to understand him. A new consecration of the whole people to a National defense helped him mightily. Sons of the South joined the sons of the North and West in a war of conscience against oppression at our very door—the most striking instance of unselfish warfare in all human history. [Applause.] Out of it came new freedom and a new Republic, new concord at home and new faith in our America. I have said before, and I choose to repeat now, that if in the crowning wreaths of immortality there is separate bloom for every noble achievement, then the angel of the South will have placed on William McKinley's grave the sweetest garland that may bloom there.

There was destiny in that reunion. It equipped us to go on; to grow in strength; to expand in influence; to plant American ideals of liberty in the Orient. We planted the flag across the seas. We had made sure of the flag at home, with every glittering star fixed, fastened by popular faith and brightened by popular hope, and then we held it aloft in the Philippines and Porto Rico as the emblem of the same liberty and the guaranty of the same justice that we cherish for ourselves.

Progress Without Parallel in History

The progress from the day of reunion for a full half century is without parallel in the recital of human progress. The march westward of the Star of Empire illumined forty-eight States. We saw the frontier disappear, until the ocean bounded our mainland civilization and attending development, and Old Glory was afloat in reverence at the crossroads of the Pacific.

We made ourselves foremost in industry and commerce; we progressed in education; we notably advanced in art; we had reared new standards of living; and out of our example of representative democracy the stars of many new republics were aglow above the horizon of human hope and happiness.

We passed the vicissitudes of social evolution, from organized resources, so essential to development but, unhappily, attended by the greed that conscience had not inhibited, to the reaction and reasserted freedom. Amid the solution of the problems of recovery, correction and preservation, we maintained the great fundamentals, and we grew in population, in wealth, aye, in the finer attainments, beyond our fondest dreams.

But we had been guilty of one gross neglect. We were so eager to explore our boundless National wealth, we were so keen for that development which makes communities and in their aggregate makes the greater Nation, that we called to the man-power of the world to come and participate. And the men of the world came.

"Hyphenism" Wiped Out

They came from the lands of the oppressed, to drink, and drink freely, of the waters of our political life. They came from the lands of caste and classes, to stand erect in the invigorating air of American freedom. They came from the realms of hopeless struggle to embrace the freedom of our beckoning opportunity. They came, not by hundreds or by thousands, but by unnumbered millions, in the floodtide of human migration to a new home of hope in the land of the free. They joined in the development and we wrought the miracle of American accomplishment; but we omitted the consecration at the altars of our freedom. The gates at the port of entry swung inward and no conditions were prescribed. We invited inhabitants, without demanding citizenship. We bestowed the privileges and advantages of citizenship without demanding the assumption of its duties and its obligations. We enlarged numerically, but neglected the declaration of American faith.

The World War brought the great awakening. With our variety of nativity, and no racial entity, it required the threat of a National peril, and the endangering of civilization itself, to bring us to a realization. But when 5,000,000 of our manhood were equipped for war and 10,000,000 were enrolled in readiness, and 90,000,000 were answering every call of duty and ready for every sacrifice, we found the American soul, and we discovered those who knew it not. Then, hyphenism disappeared. [Applause.] In a Nation-wide reconsecration we firmly resolved that every man embracing American opportunity must pledge American loyalty; that every man wearing the habiliments of an American citizen must be an American in his heart and soul. [Applause.]

Quality, Not Quantity, in Immigration

No, we do not forget that the colonists came from varied lands, that essentially all of Europe was represented in our war for independence, nor that in the blend of peoples was developed our best and strongest citizenship. It was undeniable that up to the time of the World War there was none but the Indian whom we could call distinctly American; but from this time on we shall all be Americans, citizens of the United States, subscribing to the American concept of freedom and justice and pledging devotion to this Republic before any other power on earth. [Applause.]

We are having our problems in handling immigration right now. Congress has placed a restriction on the number of foreigners to be admitted, and there is assault everywhere to break down the barriers. Doubtless there is need for larger man-power in renewed industrial activities, and our more fortunate conditions ·in America are attracting the longing gaze of millions in the Old World. But I prefer waiting jobs to idle men [Applause], and I choose quality rather than quantity in future immigration. [Applause.] Thousands are finding their way across our borders or through our ports every month in defiance or evasion of the law, because of our insufficient regulations or inadequate provisions for enforcement of restrictions provided by the law. The aspirant to American citizenship who breaks the law to gain admission, makes a poor beginning, and gives little promise of useful citizenship. I would like to acclaim the day when there shall be no room in America, anywhere, for those who defy the law, and when those who seek our hospitality for the purpose of destroying our institu-

274

tions shall be deported or held securely behind prison walls. [Applause.]

It is a great thing, my countrymen, to build up the surpassing Republic, but it is a greater thing to preserve it. This land of ours has little to fear from those who attack from outside our borders, but we must guard very zealously against those who work within our midst to destroy the very institutions which have given them hospitality. [Applause.]

A Republic worth living in is worth living for; and a Republic worth defending is worth our patriotic vigilance, so that it shall not be undermined by those who preach the gospel of envy and hate or destroyed in experiments against which forty centuries of human experience cry out in protest. One hundred and forty-seven years ago today, the inspired fathers proclaimed the American freedom on which our people have builded to the wonder and astonishment of the world. Let us, my countrymen, duly resolve today that in our grateful appreciation it shall be sacredly preserved. [Applause.]

Triumph of Nationalist Schools

A little while ago I made reference to the two contending schools of American politics. It must have been destined that the nationalist school should triumph. Every new experience, every larger aspiration, confirms the National viewpoint. I know of none in all the land who is desirous of abridging the rights of the States. Few, if any, could be charged with Federal responsibility for any considerable period without wishing to diminish that responsibility. Traveling across the continent one may hastily survey States ample in domain and resources to be empires within themselves. If they were content to wall themselves within their borders and diversify their productivity, they could live and prosper within themselves alone. But nobody in America wishes to live in that way. We are National in our vast areas, in our larger aspirations, in our practicable helpfulness for each other; we are National in our common destiny.

The broader viewpoint is not limited to defense alone, because we mean so to deport ourselves, and so appeal to honor and love and justice among others, that we shall never again be called to wage armed warfare.

Only the broadest National viewpoint makes possible, through Federal aid, the vast projects of irrigation, reclamation and power development in which the West is so deeply interested. The immediate gain is within the State or the group of States concerned; but the added wealth and the larger achievement is a National triumph.

Only the broadest National viewpoint could sanction the expenditure of $75,000,000 annually to be paid out of the Federal Treasury for improved road construction. Many of the States have largely improved their roads at their own expense, as they were well prepared to do, and, from the strictly State viewpoint, there is little concern in New York or New England about road-improvement in Idaho or Oregon, but the Nation is concerned about improved communication, cheapened and efficient transportation; and out of the National wealth we contribute to aid the newer States, and to make a greater land and a happier people.

Nationalist Viewpoint Compelling

We are confronted with no greater problem than transportation, both by rail and water. Only National solution is possible. We can have no merchant marine if that problem be left to those States alone which border the salt seas; we can hope for no inland waterways where the States directly interested are to assume the cost. The railway problem is especially National in scope, and only a Federal plan will provide an ample solution. Everywhere the nationalist viewpoint is impelling, and compelling. In our closer ties, our inter-dependent relationships and common aspirations and purposes we are forty-eight for one, and one for forty-eight; and we are all for our territories, because our flag is there, and wherever it floats it must represent the conscience and the faith of the whole Republic.

My countrymen, I think on this natal day of the Republic it is wholly becoming—surely it will not be considered unseemly boasting—to refer again, as I have heretofore referred, to the wonderful progress made in this land of freedom.

Recites Favorite Story

I believe I can best illustrate what I have in my heart at the moment if I tell you my favorite story. Some years ago, before the world became engulfed in war, on a beautiful autumn morning, I stood upon the deck of a great ocean liner approaching the port of New York. It was at that indescribable moment when the sun was lighting up a path of emeralds and sapphires in the sea, that indescribable moment when the heart beats quicker because of the approach to home and native land. We had outridden the storms; we had passed through unending fogs; we had wearied of the long journey at sea, and everywhere on board ship, on which there were 3,000 living souls, there was rejoicing at our near approach to a home port. I cannot quite convey to any of you who have never experienced it just what that feeling is, but there is nothing else like it ever to be experienced. We may dwell on the marvels of a trip to foreign lands; we may revel in their traditions, and rejoice in their accumulation of art and antiquity and history and what not; but in all the Old World and its fascination there is no enjoyment to be found so keen as that of getting back home again to the good old United States. [Applause.] I suspect that the band on board the ship had learned these emotions of travelers, and just as we were getting in to the quarantine station the band struck up the stirring strains of—

"My country 'tis of thee,
Sweet land of liberty."

As I stood out on the forward promenade deck looking at the human freight on the forward main deck, which had stepped out on that deck to pass the quarantine examination, I saw a picture that is not presented anywhere else in the world except at a port of entry like

New York or some other great American port. On that deck were more than 2,000 immigrants, with everything they possessed in the world in bags or bundles, awaiting the medical examiner's edict as to whether they could land. Mothers were fatigued; children were crying; men had been ill. They afforded a very sorry looking spectacle, I must confess. As I stood on the deck making a study of that human picture, my heart was touched, and I saw little of promise in that gathering of humanity. With the consciousness of the sympathy in my heart, I turned to a stranger at my side and said: "Look at that picture; things are all wrong in this world; there is not any justice in the uneven division of the fortunes of the world."

Case of Misplaced Sympathy

The man turned to me and said: "Well, my dear sir, do not worry about those people down there. This is the greatest moment of their lives. They are traveling in hardship, to be sure, because they are journeying from lands where hard conditions have faced them, to this land of opportunity. To some of them it is the greatest moment that will ever come, and, probably, sir, the next time they travel across the sea, after living in America, they will travel as you and I in the first-class accommodations of the ship. Do not waste your sympathy on them, sir, for this is the day of their awakening. I know whereof I speak," said he. "I came over that way myself six years ago." [*Laughter and applause.*] I found myself talking to a man who, with his widowed mother and $15 in money, had come to the United States only six years before, but when I met him he was receiving $30,000 a year as a mining engineer and finding himself able to command more day by day in the urge of American opportunity. Such are the accomplishments, my countrymen, resulting from the blessings of this land of freedom. It is worth while to make American in every way those who come amongst us to enjoy the opportunities afforded within our borders.

If we can do so much for the individual, whencesoever he may come, I think there is one thing more which

America may righteously, conscientiously, and honorably contribute to the world. I know, my fellow Americans, that you never want to participate in another war. [Applause.] You are interested in the practical steps to be taken to avoid war. I have suggested to the United States Senate that it give its consent to American adherence to the International Court of Justice. In view of the judgment of our people against entrance into the *League* of Nations, with its super-powers and assumption of world governments, I have thought our adherence to the World Court the most practicable and logical step which may be taken by the United States in contributing to the maintenance and promotion of peace. [Applause.]

I believe we can enter that Court without the slightest entanglement in the affairs of the Old World. I am sure that we will give only of American influence, prestige and support to the establishment of a judicial body which shall have power to settle disputes of a justiciable character among the Nations and thus eliminate the irritations and disagreements which ultimately lead to war. I cannot urge too strongly 'my belief that this is the one logical step to which the best civilization of the world should be committed; and I want America heart and soul to give its support to this fine promise for the maintenance of peace throughout the world. [Applause.]

"In the Morning of Our National Life"

We are just in the morning of our National life, my countrymen, for in the story of the world one hundred and forty-seven years is but a brief span of time. We Americans have wrought so marvelously in that short time that I wonder who can venture, quaffing the cup of optimism, to say what we shall be when the sun of National life has passed the meridian, when we of America have gone on to the fulfillment of the destiny which I believe to be ours. It is easy to conceive that the 100,000,000 of today will be the myriads of the future. I like to think of this great free Republic clinging to the fundamentals which made us what we are, dispensing justice with an even hand and

279

insuring a fair distribution of the fortunes of life. I do not say "an equal distribution;" I never preach that, because if all the fortunes of life were precisely equal there would be no inspiration to achieve. God Almighty never intended such a condition, but I do want a fair distribution of the fortunes of life. I want to maintain American opportunity; I want this Republic of ours to go forward, and I like to think, my countrymen, of the future when myriads of Americans shall have their faces to the front as we have ours today; I like to think of them as an onward marching army of peace gathering at the campfires at night, rejoicing in the accomplishments of the day, and singing from their hearts until the strains echo from the heavens: "Glory to God in the Highest, and on earth, peace, good will toward men." [Applause.]

GREETS MAIL MEN AS FELLOW WORKERS

Speech at the Oregon Postal Conference Convention, Auditorium, Portland, Ore., July 4, 3:50 p. m.

Mr. Chairman, Senator McNary, and Fellow Workers for Uncle Sam:

I AM very glad to come and greet you as one who is engaged in precisely the same occupation that you are, namely, attempting efficiently to serve the government and thereby serve the American people. I am rejoiced to be able to come to your convention. For a time there was some doubt about my coming, because when the President travels it sometimes seems as though everybody is thinking of something for him to do, and it requires a few to think of the things that he cannot do.

I think it is extremely patriotic that you should meet on a National holiday to discuss questions which involve the improvement of the service of the Post Office Department. After all, service is the highest manifestation of patriotism that we can have in our country. You represent the nerve lines of the Republic. The Post Office Department is the greatest peace institution that we possess and I suspect that it is the closest of all the departments to the American people. I know in a broad way of the tremendous activities and the wide scope of your work. You represent the largest business institution of its kind in all the government; and I believe in no place in the world is there a better postal service than in the United States of America. [Applause.]

Happy to Have Been Able to Help

Perhaps you have not always been entirely satisfied, and I speak the truth when I say that for a time you had reason to be dissatisfied. [Applause.] I think the men employed in the postal service were the longest neglected of any men serving in any branch of the government. Since I am only on an official mission, I dare to tell you that I rejoiced during the last portion of my term in the Senate to be able to assist in doing something towards making your compensation more nearly adequate to the service you render the government.

It is a splendid thing for you to come together, and I think it is an excellent thing that some of the higher officials of the postal service have come to meet with you. One of the things we are trying to do in the government administration, for its everlasting betterment, is to bring about a more intimate contact between the heads of the departments, those who are in the more responsible positions, and those who really do the work.

We have in Washington a business organization of the government under the Director of the Budget, to whom the President gives the most cordial cooperation imaginable. We have this business organization, which, with your cooperation, is proving the efficacy day by day of putting business practices into the affairs of government. A couple of evenings ago, at Spokane, I had the pleasure of reading a telegram from the Director of the Budget which reported a saving of more than $290,000,000 for the past fiscal year in the ordinary expenses of running the government as compared with the year before. Of course a sum such as $290,000,000 does not create much of a thrill nowadays [Laughter], and that is the trouble with the world. The mention of $290,000,000 ought to be heard with awe and not with contempt.

"Billion-Dollar Congress" Days

It was only a few years ago that we thought that $500,-000,000 annually was an enormous expenditure for all governmental purposes. The expenditure of such a sum was made a political issue, as we had come to a period when we had a "billion-dollar Congress," or a Congress which appropriated $500,000,000 each year. Now the government is costing annually more than $3,000,000,000, and I regret to say that the American people will probably never again know the day when the cost will be much less. We cannot diminish public expenditures which relate to the interest charges on the public debt until that debt is substantially reduced, and it takes nearly a billion dollars a year to pay the interest on what we owe. Then there came to us the tremendous obligations which followed the war. I think we are expending more than $500,000,000 a year in seeking to care, as we ought to care, for the veterans who were disabled in the war.

Government has become a very expensive thing, my countrymen, and you who are in the service are the only men who can do anything towards lifting the burden. It is the man who comes in direct contact with the people, it is the individual who is the initial unit in the service who can begin building up the bulwarks of economy and efficiency. If as a result of your deliberations you are finding methods of bettering the service at less cost, you are rendering very great service to your country, and in the end you are bringing not only higher compensation to yourselves but you are bringing to your breasts the one great compensation which comes in life—the consciousness of having done something worth while.

282

It is a pleasure to greet you men of the postal service. I wish I might stop long enough to participate in the deliberations of your convention and come in contact with some of the problems you are seeking to solve. I hardly suppose that my efforts would be of any great practical value, but it would be a delight to me to know more intimately of the work you are carrying forward. I may say to you, however, that the President learns more about you than you think. Since this administration came into power the direction of the Post Office Department has been under the control of excellent officials. Mr. Hays was a fine Postmaster General. Dr. Work was a fine successor to Mr. Hays, in fact he was so good that I was delighted to enlist his services in solving the problems of the Department of the Interior. You have in Postmaster General New a mighty fine fellow-American as the head of the department now, and you have an Assistant Postmaster General—and I am glad he is with you today—who is fit at any time to be Postmaster General of the United States. I congratulate you on his presence. I renew the expression of my pleasure at the opportunity of greeting you, and I wish you well not alone in your affairs of official character and in your service to the government, but in all the personal affairs of life which are of concern to your welfare and your happiness. [Applause.]

PLEDGES GOVERNMENT AID TO VETERANS

Remarks at United States Veterans' Hospital, No. 77, Portland, Ore., July 4, 4:15 p. m.

Service Men and the Service Force of the Hospital:

IT IS a pleasure to come to greet you. Nowadays no government activity is of greater interest and concern to those who are in a position of responsibility than that which has to do with the care of the men who were injured in the service. I know how deep in the hearts of the Members of Congress is the desire to provide proper care for and to bring about the rehabilitation of the injured service men. I know how sincere is the wish of the executive branch of the government to provide the most ample relief. We do not always do things perfectly, I am frank to say, and we do not always understand the real conditions. The undertaking was such a tremendous one that nobody at first appraised the magnitude of the task; but we have been building and equipping hospitals throughout the land; we have been trying to get the best service, the best talent, and the best appliances and appurtenances and equipment of every kind. We are sincerely trying to be of real, thoughtful, grateful service to you men. If conditions are not right, then we are going to keep at work until we make them right, for I know that the government means to do all that it properly can to assist you.

Supreme Tragedy of War

In addition to that, I hope there may come to you that spirit, that hopefulness and that confidence that enables men to fight their way back to health and usefulness. I know there are not any of you who do not long to get back to the activities of normal life, and I know you want to be useful. The great, the supreme tragedy of war is not that it sacrifices so many lives, but that it impairs men for the active service of life. Your big fight is to rise above the impairment.

I wish you the best ever, men, and I desire to assure you that if matters are not going right with you, and the government learns of it, it will make an honest effort to try to correct conditions, because in the grateful heart of the Republic is the determination to do the best that can be done to bring you men who offered everything back to a full participation in active life. I am glad to see you and I want to greet each of you personally before I leave and to offer a personal suggestion of good wishes. [Applause.]

AMERICA *LEADS* WORLD IN PROGRESS

Speech at Vancouver, Wash., July 4, 11:30 p. m.

Ladies and Gentlemen:

I APPRECIATE your thoughtfulness in making us a present of what I am sure are most excellent prunes, and I thank you.

It is very good of you to come out at this late hour of the night to greet us. I am sorry our train is late and you have been kept up. We knew that you expected a short stop, and I am glad to have the opportunity of expressing to you our gratitude for your kind and cordial greeting. I hardly believe you quite understand how impressive it is to travel across the country and meet everywhere a cordiality, a hospitality, and a cheer that heartens us and brings to our journey a series of new delights. Notably has that been true of the reception which has been accorded us in this boundless, wonderful and wholesome western land. [Applause.]

I presume you in the West do not differ greatly from those of us who live in sections farther east, but there is something so free, so wholesome and so generous about your greetings, that, after all, I think that there must be something in the atmosphere that makes you a little different —and that is not amiss. I have been more proud than ever of this great country of ours since I have been getting the impressions which have come from my official journey across the continent. It has brought a new realization that, after all, we are just one people, with common aspirations, a common purpose, and a common love of country. We are all living for the same purpose and striving for the same end.

Happiness the Greatest Possession

In all of us, perhaps, there is the desire to acquire; but, after all, my countrymen, the greatest possession in life is happiness. The man who has acquired a measurable degree of happiness is the richest man in the world. I care not how you measure his material fortunes, if there

285

is the glow of happiness in his heart he has not lived in vain. I wish you all the greatest happiness that can come to any people. Your government alone cannot bring happiness to you, but it hopes to maintain conditions under which men may strive and have an equal chance to attain the good things of life. We cannot expect that there will ever be an equal division of material good fortune. God never intended that there should be such a distribution. If He had so intended, He would have made us all precisely alike, and then this would have been a miserable old world. The desire to acquire is the inspiration of all endeavor, and all we can ask is that the government shall be so conducted that one man shall not acquire unjustly or at the expense of his fellows. I should like to see good fortune be the lot of everyone in America.

We have been passing through a period when normal conditions were dislocated and put out of plumb by the aftermath of the World War. Misfortune came, first of all, to those engaged in agriculture, but it came not alone to them. It affected business; it affected finance; it affected all forms of industry, and it thrust upon us very serious problems. In the difficult process of readjustment, the government has been trying to help speed a restoration to normal conditions, and I am very happy to tell you that I think we have made better progress and gone further in the United States of America than have the people of any other country in the world. [Applause.]

Decries the Boastful Spirit

I do not mean by that to boast a good fortune for us which other peoples do not share, but we have better conditions because we have more quickly gotten down to hard work and evinced a resolute purpose of bringing about a restoration after the great upheaval caused by the war. It is impossible after a world-wide calamity to recover by any easy processes; it requires work, sacrifice, and still more work; but, after a while, I know we shall be completely on the right track again, and I hope to see America go forward as it never has gone forward before. I hope there will come to you of the West a full and abundant share of the good things which we believe are in store for our common country.

I thank you again for coming out to greet us. It makes the burdens of government more easy to carry, and I am happy to tell you it makes me more anxious than ever to serve you well. Good-night. [Applause and cheers.]

EQUALIZE PROFITS OF PRODUCTION

Speech at Centralia, Wash., July 5, 7:30 a. m.

Ladies and Gentlemen:

YOU are very kind to come down on an inclement morning to greet us, especially at this early hour. Perhaps I ought not to say "early hour," for I remember when I was a young man and more or less identified with agriculture, we did not consider 7:30 in the morning an early hour. I may add that it is not such an early hour to me, for the President many times is up and at work before that hour. I may also add that the boundlessness of your Western hospitality has caused him to be up very late at night in order to receive the manifestations of your cordiality; in fact, almost from sunrise until well toward midnight, in this wonderful western land, I have been receiving expressions of kindliness and interest. The President really does not find much time to sleep; but it is a wonderful experience.

We are today closing a program of 15 days' travel across the continent. The journey was undertaken primarily and specifically in order to visit Alaska; but when the President travels it seems that the people desire him to stop and make report as to what he is doing, and I have been glad to do so. Consequently, with our stops to make such report and to receive expressions of interest and courtesy we have been 15 days coming from the city of Washington, to the State of Washington. That is almost as long as it would have taken in pioneer days. A private citizen can make the trip in four days. However, it has been a fine experience; it has brought to us a new vision of this land of ours, and I believe it has brought to us a new understanding of the aspirations and desires of the American people. It has been inspiring and heartening in every way. Everywhere we have met with kindness and courtesy and, in this western section, the most delightful cheer and evidences of the most manifest hopefulness and confidence that one may see anywhere in the world.

After Effects of the War

I know, we all know, that those who live in the agricultural sections have been hit hard by the after-the-war adjustment, but that does not apply to agriculture alone. General business, commerce, and industry have also been hard hit; but the former was hit first and the hardest. We have been doing everything that we know how to do in Washington to provide a remedy. We cannot do it all; it cannot all be done in a moment. In our attempts to correct an unhappy situation we are not going to overturn certain fundamentals of human society, for if we did we would be left a wreck after the miserable experiment. [Applause.]

I am sure we will find the way to an adjustment which will equalize the profits of production. That is always a problem in life. Ages ago, as a result of the system which prevailed for a long time, there was virtual enslavement, but there is no enslavement anywhere in America. We shall find a way to a righteous adjustment so that the producers of the essentials of life may have a fair share of the profits resulting from their labors. The government is just as much interested in a righteous adjustment of the problem for the State of Washington as it is for any State in the Union. I like to say to you, because in saying it I speak the truth, that the Federal government has the same concern for a Pacific Coast State or a Mountain State or a Southern State as it has for a Northern or a New England State. The government is concerned in the common welfare of the American people. [Applause.] We want you who live in the great Northwest to assist your government to make it the best on the face of the earth.

Stop for Specific Purpose

I have stopped at Centralia for a specific purpose and I wish to tell you what that purpose is. All the world was horrified when four *Legion* boys were sacrificed here by those who would destroy the very government itself. The incident illustrated the readiness of America, on the one hand, to defend her institutions, and, on the other hand, the boldness of those who would destroy them. So I have chosen to stop here; and we are going to drive to your cemetery to place some wreaths of tribute on the graves of the boys who were sacrificed in the parade to which I have reference. We are going to do it because we know how much of the security of our institutions is dependent upon the service men who fought in the World War, who have organized the American *Legion*, and who are the first ready spokesmen of the Republic for law and order and the institutions which we Americans cherish. We are going to pay our tribute to those boys, and I want you to know it. [Applause.]

NATION'S INTEREST IN SICK VETERANS

Remarks at United States Veterans' Hospital, No. 59, Tacoma, Wash., July 5, 12:15 p. m.

Service Men and Personnel of the Hospital:

IT IS a great pleasure for me to come and greet you. I am glad to visit the hospitals when I can, because the government is just as deeply interested in your welfare as are your own families and you yourselves. It is fine to get out among the hospitals and see that everything is going well. The government is deeply and sincerely and affectionately concerned in having you boys who were impaired in its defense restored to health and capacity for activity. I just wish you the best in the world, and I know that I speak for all of the American people. Good morning, and good-bye. [Applause.]

THE MAKING OF A BETTER REPUBLIC SEEN IN THE ADVANCE OF EDUCATION AND REDUCTION OF WORKING HOURS

Address at Washington Stadium, Tacoma, Wash., July 5, 1:15 p. m.

Governor Hart and My Countrymen All:

I WOULD not have missed this picture for anything in the world. [Applause.] I know of no other place in America where one may witness such a scene as this, and I should like you to know that it is both a joy and an inspiration. I am sorry that the weather is inclement, not for myself entirely because we Baptists are not greatly moved by a downpour of water [*Laughter and applause*], but I am sorry for you, and I am also sorry for a selfish reason. I had hoped while here to get a view of Mount Tacoma, for I am afraid that when I get to Seattle I will not see it. [*Laughter and applause.*]

It has been fine to come among you and it has been a great pleasure to greet you and to be greeted by you. It has been a great satisfaction to come into a little closer contact with this cross-section of American life, to know how interested you are in the affairs of the Republic, and to tell you in return how interested the government is in the common welfare and the good fortunes of all the American people.

Proof of School Advancement

The presence, my countrymen, of these schooling children, on whom is centered every interest in our daily activities, in whom is the highest inspiration of our varied pursuits in life, leads me to inquire to what end we are striving. We boast our American freedom and we mean

290

to maintain it. We cherish the reign of justice and we mean to sustain it. We glory in the equal rights of all Americans and the equality of opportunity under which our people strive for attainment. We are ever doing the things which are meant to equip our citizenship to embrace that opportunity. Hence the public schools and the ever more determined purpose to educate the youth of our land. There is no denial to the children of the humblest home. The proof of our accomplishment is strikingly impressed by the fact that today we send ten times more working men's sons and daughters, and twenty times more farmers' sons and daughters to colleges and universities than we sent rich men's sons and daughters a half century ago.

Nation of Home Owners

In the better operation of this equipment we are building a Republic of communities in which the American masses are acquiring and owning their own homes. I understand Tacoma is strikingly a city whose people own their own homes. No wonder you are the "City Beautiful." Nothing finer can be said of any city. No better bond can ever be written to guarantee the progress of the community and the security of the Republic. No better defense will ever be organized to halt the destroyers from within— the traitors who seek our hospitality for the purpose of rending the very temple of representative democracy.

I know the predominant aspiration. Parent citizens of today wish a better Republic on the morrow for their sons and daughters. They wish less of the toil and drudgery and sacrifices of life, they hope for less of the inequalities which come of varied capacity and the abuses of opportunity. I fear the ambition sometimes leads to impractical programs. Under old-time conceptions of fancied ease in professional life, and the manifestly larger rewards of commerce, there has been a tendency to get away from the trades and the tasks out of which are wrought the very essentials of all attainment. We must, we do, recognize that the wage-earner is quite as essential as the professional man, and the nobility of righteous employment is the same in either pursuit. Our aim ought to be, not to rescue the oncoming generation from the essential pursuits and activities, but to equalize their rewards. We cannot cease work, for there is no life without labor. It would not be endurable if there were.

We are making fine progress in the great social evolution. Long ago we set up new standards of living and new conditions of industry in this land. We are constantly striving, not for conditions which tend to paralyze, but conditions of greater inspiration and fit contentment.

Forward Step in Industry

I am able today to give promise of a very notable forward step. It is my firm belief that one of the great avenues of progress in American life lies in the constant recognition by American industry of its obligations to our society as a whole, and that many of our most successful steps in social progress are made through the voluntary action of industry itself in amelioration of those hardships that have grown from the rapid development of industry. It is very gratifying, therefore, to be able to announce an important step in such progress. I have received a joint communication from the large majority of steel manufacturers of America in which they have undertaken to abolish the twelve-hour day in the American steel industry at the earliest moment that the additional labor required shall be available. [Great applause.]

Early in the administration, feeling that a working day of 12 hours' length was an anachronism in American life, that regardless of any other consideration, it did not permit of the proper development of citizenship and family life, I suggested to the steel industry that they should appoint a committee to develop methods for its abolition. After an investigation extending over some eighteen months, the steel manufacturers came to the conclusion that, in view of the present shortage of labor, such a revolution in the industry was infeasible. Upon the receipt of this report, I still felt that a pledge on the part of the steel manufacturers that they would undertake to respond to manifest public opinion in this matter would be welcomed by our people as a whole and would be received as a great boon by American workers. It is in response to this suggestion that I have received today the pledge to which I have referred.

Congratulates the Steel Industry

I wish to congratulate the steel industry on this important step. It will heal a sore in American industrial life which has been the cause of infinite struggle and bitterness for over a generation and it marks an accomplishment from the conscience of industry itself, a recognition of responsibility from employer to employee that gives us faith in the rightful solution of the many tangled problems that are the concomitant of the rapid growth of America. It is an example that I trust the few other continuous processes in industry which still maintain the twelve-hour shift may rapidly follow. I should be proud indeed if my administration were marked by the final passing of the twelve-hour working day in American life.

There is another American aspiration on which I have wished to touch today. You of Tacoma are proud of your harbor and dock facilities. You provide the dock facilities and the government improves the harbors, but of what value is either without shipping? A merchant marine is the worthy aspiration of every commercial nation. [Applause.] There can be no dependable commerce without carriers, and there can be no eminence in American commerce without American carriers. Friendship among nations does not demand of them the promotion of a competitor's trade. [Applause.]

Great American Merchant Marine

So, this administration has been earnestly striving for a great and efficient American merchant marine. We had it once, when the sails of our clippers whitened the seas of the world. But there came a recession, and the World War found us an inconsiderable maritime power. I have always believed that there would have been no war, certainly it would have been of less duration, if we had possessed a merchant marine comparable to our commercial aspirations. [Applause.] In the exigencies of war we builded ships as no nation ever built before. We expended approximately three billion dollars extravagantly, inefficiently, and without a program for service in peace. We turned the energies of the Republic to the making of ships, we builded yards and trained our builders, and we produced marvelously, until we owned twelve million tons of merchant shipping, ample for the greatest merchant marine ever dreamed of for America.

But it is government property, builded for an emergency, rather than for competitive activity in carrying world commerce. This administration has cleaned up the vast work of settlement; we encountered the paralyzing slump in shipping; we have settled the enormous claims—more than $150,000,000—for something like 12 cents on the dollar, and liquidated the stupendous failures. But Congress did not respond to the request for legislation calculated to dispose of our shipping to private owners and encourage the upbuilding of a permanent merchant marine. I had hoped to turn one extravagance of war to permanent and practical utility. The House of Representatives approved. The Senate was prevented from expressing itself. So the government is confronted with the possession of vast tonnage, but without market in which to sell or inspiration to private enterprise to operate.

Vital to National Defense

I do not for one moment believe in government ownership and operation as a permanent policy [Applause], but, frankly, I prefer that hazardous venture to the surrender of our hopes for a merchant marine. [Applause.] So we mean to operate until we establish, though it cost far more than it was contemplated to expend in promoting private enterprise. It is vital to our National defense; it is necessary to our foreign commerce; it is necessary to maintain American eminence. So we mean to maintain the flag on the seas, hoping for the day when Congress may rise above the obstructionist, when the reflective sentiment of all the country will sense the great necessity and compel the legislation required to turn to the rational way of triumph on the seas. [Applause.]

Only yesterday there sailed from the port of New York the flagship of the American merchant marine, the great Leviathan. Idle since the days when she was used as a transport during the war, she has been reconditioned until she stands out conspicuously as the finest merchant ship afloat on any of the seas of the world. She sailed from New York under the American flag to establish what I hope may be a new record for crossing the Atlantic.

Significant of a "New Independence"

Let us hope, my countrymen, that the departure on July 4 of the reconditioned Leviathan, "mistress of the seas," on her first trans-Atlantic trip after the war may be significant of a new American independence on the seas and of a renewed American determination to live up to the worthy and highest aspirations of the Republic. [Applause.]

It has been good, my countrymen, to see you. In conclusion, I wish to give my pledge to these young men and young women who stand before me that the government means with every commitment possible to hold for them and hand on to them in their majority the splendid American liberty and the substantial American institutions which they have inherited and which have made us what we are, and I hope that we may make for them an even better and grander country in which to live. [Great applause.]

CORRESPONDENCE WITH STEEL OFFICIALS RE-
SULTING IN THE ELIMINATION OF THE
12-HOUR DAY FOR MILL WORKERS

[The following correspondence, referred to by President
Harding in his address at the Washington Stadium,
Tacoma, Wash., July 5, 1:15 p. m., was given to
the press for publication with his address.]

"New York, N. Y.,
"June 27, 1923.
"Honorable Warren G. Harding,
   "President of the United States.
"Dear Mr. President:
   "Careful consideration has been given to your letter
of June 18th by the undersigned directors of The American
Iron and Steel Institute comprising all of those whose
attendance could be secured at this time.
   "Undoubtedly there is a strong sentiment throughout
the country in favor of eliminating the twelve-hour day
and this we do not underestimate. On account of this sentiment and especially because it is in accordance with your
own expressed views we are determined to exert every
effort at our command to secure in the iron and steel
industry of this country a total abolition of the twelve-
hour day at the earliest time practicable. This means the
employment of large numbers of workmen on an eight-
hour basis and all others on a basis of ten hours or less.
Without an unjustifiable interruption to operations the
change cannot be effected overnight. It will involve many
adjustments, some of them complicated and difficult but
we think it can be brought about without undue delay when
as you state it 'there is a surplus of labor available.'

"The iron and steel manufacturers generally of the United States outside of the directors referred to are expected to concur in the conclusion reached by the directors as above stated.

"With highest regard, we are,

"Cordially yours,

Elbert H. Gary,	Willis *L.* King,
John A. Topping;	James A. Burden,
W. A. Rogers,	*L.* E. Black,
W. H. Donner,	Severn P. Ker,
W. J. Filbert,	J. A. Campbell,
E. A. S. Clarke,	A. C. Dinkey,
James A. Farrell,	Charles M. Schwab.
E. G. Grace,	

"Directors, American Iron and Steel Institute."

———

THE PRESIDENT'S LETTER TO JUDGE GARY

"The White House, June 18, 1923.

"My dear Judge Gary:

"I have now had an opportunity of reading the full report of the Committee of The Iron and Steel Institute on the question of the abolition of the twelve-hour day in the steel industry.

"As I have stated before I am, of course, disappointed that no conclusive arrangement was proposed for determination of what must be manifestly accepted as a practice that should be obsolete in American industry. I still entertain the hope that these questions of social importance should be solved by action inside the industries themselves for it is only such solutions that are consonant with American life and institutions.

"I am impressed that in the reasoning of the report great weight should be attached to the fact that in the present shortage of labor it would cripple our entire prosperity if the change were abruptly made. In the hope that this question could be disposed of I am wondering if it would not be possible for the steel industry to consider giving an undertaking that before there shall be any reduction in the staff of employees of the industry through any recession of demand for steel products or at any time when there is a surplus of labor available, that then the change should be made from the two shifts to the three-shift basis. I can not but believe that such an undertaking would give great satisfaction to the American people as a whole and would indeed establish pride and confidence in the ability of our industries to solve matters which are so conclusively advocated by the public.

"With very cordial expression of personal regards, I am

"Very truly yours,

(Signed) "WARREN G. HARDING."

ASKS ALASKANS TO SAY "OUR COUNTRY"

Speech at Metlakatla, Alaska, Sunday, July 8, 9:15 a. m.

Governor Bone, Mr. Mayor, Ladies and Gentlemen:

THIS is to me a very pleasing and happy experience. I think it is altogether appropriate that on this Sabbath morning we should meet with those who have constituted one of the ideal missions in the progress of Christian civilization, and that we should receive your welcome and obtain here our first view of this wonderful Territory. I have had just one disappointment, and I must tell you of it: I am sorry to hear you say "your country;" I want you to say "our country." [Applause.] If under the opportunities afforded by the United States government, if under the considerate treatment accorded you, you have been able to work out so much of progress for yourselves on this island, then I think surely the United

States ought to make available to the older ones of you citizenship under the flag, just as it comes to your children who are born under the flag. I do not know whether I am entirely reliable as a judge of human nature, but I am happy to say that I should like to see all of you citizens of the United States. [Applause.]

I am not unmindful of the grievance so feelingly expressed relating to the fisheries. I regret I cannot make the response which the address would seem to invite. We cannot return to primitive days in Alaska; but there ought to be some righteous solution of our relationships under which the native shall have everything that he needs to enable him to live and prosper. Such conditions, however, will not be brought about by a reversion to the primitive, because that would be against the law of God and the best interests of human society.

Island a Part of the Republic

It is a very great pleasure to greet you; it is a joy to hear your band and to hear you sing, and it is an inspiration to look into your faces. I am glad that we have such an island under the American flag; I am glad that you are a part of this Republic of ours and are doing your share to develop it and make it better; but, above all else, I am glad to see this wholesome manifestation of what the good Doctor referred to as the "Christian teaching." It shows the mollifying, uplifting and refining influence of religion, and to you as pioneers in this section I pay my tribute for bringing about such a softening and elevating influence in this great Northwest. I wish you all well.

I desire to say a word more on a subject to which reference has not as yet been made. There have come impressions of inconsiderate treatment and some injustice in government dealings. I do not pass upon them hastily; but, if there is aught of neglect or injustice in the relationship of the government with the people of this island, it would be worth coming to Alaska to be able to correct it. We want every condition of that kind speedily corrected.

So, if there is anything that we should know, while we will not have time now to give to further public expression, I should like to be advised before I leave Alaska, so that we may understand your situation. In return I should like you to understand that your Federal government wants to do everything that is just and righteous toward the promotion of your welfare and at the same time the promotion of the welfare of our common country. It is good to see you all. I wish you the fullest measure of happiness. I love the Indian smile, and I hope it will wear with you forever. [Applause.]

NEED FOR RELIGIOUS REVERENCE

Speech at Ketchikan, Alaska, Sunday, July 8, 3 p. m.

Mr. Mayor, Governor Bone, and Fellow Americans:

I AM sure it affords me just as much pleasure to greet you as it affords you to receive a visit from the President. We have had a wonderful experience. We have come to know more about the great Territory in which you live, and already it is a source of wonderment to us, as well as a source of constant and growing admiration. As I see you before me, I take a great deal of pleasure in saying that I do not know where one would go in the United States of America to find a finer assemblage on a Sunday afternoon. I am proud of you as fellow Americans, and if this official visit of ours results in making Alaska better known to the mainland of the United States and contributes somewhat in proper form to expedite the development of this measureless Territory, then I am doubly delighted to have come.

It is not our custom in traveling to make public addresses on the Sabbath day, although I presume that anything good enough to say on a week-day is good enough to say on the Sabbath. I remember some years ago I was starting out on a lecture engagement and had only one address. I discovered that I was going to be called on occasionally to speak upon the Sabbath, and I asked a minister friend of mine: "What am I going to do on the Sabbath with my week-day address?" "Well," he said, "if your speech is good enough for week-days, it ought to be all right for the Sabbath."

Impressed by Religious Spirit

I was particularly impressed today with the little meeting we had a short distance south where we were welcomed by the Indians and where in all that was said there was a deeply impressive religious tone. One of the spokesmen uttered his words in great humility; he referred to the white man as the agent of the superior civilization, but in all he said was a spirit of religious reverence which I should be glad to see the white civilization of the United States of America emulate, because I believe it would be helpful to them. [Applause.]

I like to hear of your patriotic devotion. I read a little story of an Alaskan who was not of American descent, which made a deep impression upon me and which, perhaps, will impress you if you love dogs, as I do. I love a dog; I love him for his fidelity; and I remember early in the war when the French government was sending in all directions to recruit its armies an agent visited some place in Alaska, and, among others, found an old Frenchman who was too well along in life to be fit for service. His heart was with the allies, and when he found he was too old to serve he wanted to do the next best thing, and, with tears streaming down his cheeks, he sent his favorite dog into the service. I can understand what that meant to a Frenchman who loved his dog and who, of course, had greater love for his country.

I do not know the reason, but I imagine the life you live in this great out-of-doors, in this picturesque and inviting land, probably makes you a little more enthusiastic in your patriotism and more cordial in your greetings, and, perhaps, more earnest in your friendships. I can well understand all that.

Government's Interest in Territory

I merely want to say to you today that the Federal government is deeply interested in the affairs of Alaska and the welfare of the people of Alaska. We hope to know more intimately about your lives and your possibilities, commercially, agriculturally, and industrially. We are interested because you are a great big part of the United States of America, and concerning your possibilities of development no one may venture a forecast. I like to see your healthy and seemingly happy appearance; it is a joy to greet you, and I wish for you the most and the best of all good fortune in the world.

Inasmuch as ours is an official party, I take it that you will be interested in meeting some of those who are conducting the affairs of government and hearing just a word from them, since they are taking part in this official journey. I will say to the governor that I will now take the liberty of acting as presiding officer. All the members of the Cabinet are deeply interested in the progress of Alaska, but the one who has probably more intimate relations with your Territory than any other is the Secretary of the Interior, Dr. Hubert Work, and I take pleasure in presenting him to you. [Applause.]

ACCEPTS TROWEL USED IN MASONIC RITE

Remarks on the Occasion of Laying the Cornerstone of
Masonic Temple, Under Auspices of Ketchikan Lodge,
No. 159, and in Acknowledgment of Gift of
Silver Trowel Presented by the Lodge
at Ketchikan, Alaska, Sunday,
July 8, 1923, 4 p. m.

Mr. Mayor, Brother Masons, Ladies and Gentlemen:

I THANK you for this gift; it will be a treasured souvenir of my visit. The suggestion which has been made that you desire to make use of the President is not peculiar to Alaska [Laughter], for, apparently, there is the same wish everywhere in the United States, and it is all right that it should be so, because the President is naturally the servant of the people and desires to be such.

In the most serious vein of which I am capable, I wish to say that I hope this little ceremony today may convey the suggestion of the splendid influence of the principles taught by the Masonic Order, every lesson of which is calculated to make men better citizens. I wish, too, that it may be an augury of larger fraternalism and finer and more effective and more sincere brotherhood among men. I have said on many occasions—and I am glad to repeat now—that I know of nothing the world needs so much as a sincere brotherhood. It needs brotherhood among the men of Ketchikan, among the men of Alaska, among the citizens of the United States, among the men of the world, and, particularly, fraternity among the nations of the world. If we can only have a little more of the spirit of brotherhood everything will be better in the world and conditions on earth will more nearly conform to the design of the Creator.

I am glad to participate with you on this occasion, symbolic of the soul of American fraternity. It is a joy to be with you, and I shall greatly treasure this souvenir of my visit. [Applause.]

DESIRE FOR A CLOSER KINSHIP

Speech at Wrangell, Alaska, Monday, July 9, 8:30 a. m.

Ladies and Gentlemen:

IT AFFORDS me great pleasure to receive so cordial a welcome at Wrangell and to be able to greet you. One thought expressed by your spokesman a moment ago appealed very strongly to me. He said we would find here a happy and more or less contented people. I wonder if that is not about the greatest thing in life. Men may acquire riches; they may attain fame; they may exercise great power and sometimes great influence, beneficent or otherwise; but I know of nothing in the world to be so cherished as the possession of happiness. If your happiness in Alaska is comparable to the sunshine this morning and is in any way a reflex of the beautiful scenery through which we have been traveling you are a most fortunate people.

I cannot see very much difference between Alaska and other portions of the wonderful West. When we get off the boat we find bearing the colors ahead of us a splendid representation of the American *Legion*. You in Alaska probably did more in the Nation's hour of trial in the effort to preserve civilization than did some of the States. It is good to know that up here are legionaires who will be the spokesmen and sponsors for American patriotism for a generation or more to come. It is a delight to enjoy this magnificent view.

Came to Get Better Acquainted

I believe I will merely bring a message of congratulation and leave all promises until we are better informed about conditions obtaining in the various sections of Alaska. The simple, honest truth is that we have come in order to know you better.

If I may be credited with one desire more than another it is to act as an apostle of understanding. I have been trying to preach understanding ever since I came to the Presidency, for I believe that understanding is the remedy for nearly all our ills. If there are conditions which ought not to exist we need only to understand them in order to correct them; if there are relationships which are not fortunate, then we need only to understand them and the remedy will be easy. If the nations of the world could have a complete and ample understanding each with the other, there never would be war. Intelligent understanding is the most desirable possession among peoples and nations of which I can conceive. So officers of your government have come to this wonderful land, first of all to understand conditions better and to ascertain what is essential here in order to promote progress and add to your happiness and to your opportunity. I do not mind confessing to you that we have come just a little bit selfishly also, for we wanted to enjoy this matchless scenery, these tremendous expanses of mountain and water, to breathe your invigorating air, and to absorb something of the strength and the wholesomeness of the lives you in this territory live. Thus far we have been more than delighted.

It has been a pleasure to meet you, fellow citizens; it has been good to look upon you; it has been good to drink in the wonders of nature; aye, and it is good to feel that there is before you and before our country a glorious and inspiring future. I want to thank you for the cordiality of your greeting and to wish you the best of good fortune in all your undertakings. [Applause.]

I take it that you would like to greet and hear from some of the members of the official party who are traveling with us, and I shall ask Governor Bone to introduce them.

NEW VIEWS OF "FROZEN NORTHLAND"

Speech at the Governor's Mansion, Juneau, Alaska, June 10, 11 a. m.

Ladies and Gentlemen, My Countrymen All:

I THINK there must be many Baptists in Juneau; at any rate, people who would turn out in such great numbers on a rainy morning like this to extend a greeting ought to have some measure of return, and I wish I might offer it to you. I can only say how grateful we are to have your cordial greeting, how pleased we are, and how heartened we are to come here and find such a fine people so kindly and cordially disposed. I do not know how it affects you, but during the course of my journey amidst the wonderful scenery of Alaska, certain adjectives have been constantly recurring to me. I think of the words "sturdy," "majestic," "stalwart," and "immovable" as expressing but in poor fashion the marvels of this wonderland of ours. If it be true, as I believe it to be, that we are largely constituted in harmony with our environment, you of Juneau must be a very sturdy and stalwart people, and I may say to you that you look the part. I am proud of you as citizens of the United States of America. [Applause.]

It is very good to come here and to be able to know Alaska better. Some of us have had miserable, petty ideas about Alaska. Some of us had the notion that it was in the frozen and locked-up North; but we are having a most delightful awakening. The purpose of our visit is to know you better and, if possible, to have you know your government better and to come into closer relationships, so that we may jointly cooperate in making your wonderland a greater part of an even greater Republic. [Applause.]

Pleased to Greet Children

I love to see these children. Unhappily, perhaps, children are never allowed to choose where they are to be born; but I believe, if I could have had my choice, I would have chosen the West, where one may grow amidst such freedom and such boundless possibilities, and where the youth are rosy-cheeked, healthy, and hopeful. It is a fine thing to see these children coming on because, if you should fail to make an empire of Alaska, I know they will succeed, and I am happy to say I believe the government is going to be more helpful to them than it has been to you. [Applause.]

For your sake I am sorry it is raining, but for our sake I am rather glad. We have heard about rainy Alaska, but this is the first time rain has fallen while we have been within your borders, and I rather think it accentuates the sincerity of your wecome to have you come out in a rain such as this to extend to us your cordial and smiling greetings. The reception you have accorded us has made us all very happy.

I did not come here to make you a speech. I have come to Alaska to learn and not to talk; but I do want you to know how rejoiced we are to be here and how compensated we feel for the long journey we have undertaken. Perhaps I shall not speak to the citizens of Juneau again, and therefore, I desire at this time to assure you that, as President, I wish you the best of good fortune and the utmost happiness that can come to any people in all the world. [Applause.]

FRIENDSHIP THE SWEETEST THING
IN THE WORLD

Speech at the Pullen House, Skagway, Alaska,
Wednesday, July 11, 11:15 a. m.

Mr. Mayor and Ladies and Gentlemen:

IT IS a very great pleasure to come ashore at Skagway and have the opportunity of meeting you in this intimate way. Originally Skagway was not on our itinerary. Alaska is so vast that it is difficult to reach all the settlements en route, and even more difficult to meet everyone, no matter how much pleasure it would afford me to do so; but when we found we were within a short sailing distance and recalled the fame of Skagway and the romance interwoven with its history, we thought we could not go by without taking advantage of the opportunity to look in upon you and greet you.

The visit to Alaska has afforded very great pleasure to me and to all the members of the party. There is nothing we do that affords us so much comfort and happiness as coming in direct contact with the people. One may speak at length of God's bounteous bestowal upon Alaska and the natural marvels of this wonderland, but, after all, the charm is in meeting the people, and I do not know

307

where there can be found in all the world a finer people than we have encountered in Alaska. Some may think I am saying that to be genial and courteous, but, really, environment plays an important part in molding character, and there is something in the freedom of the great out-of-doors, there is something in the limitless possibilities of a domain such as Alaska that cause those who breathe such atmosphere to develop in harmony with it. It is a joy to come in contact with such a wholesome, free, hopeful, kindly people as we have met thus far in our journey through Alaska.

Valuable Experience for Anyone

It is a valuable experience for anybody in public life to visit this vast territory. We have come to learn; we have come in order to know Alaska better; we have come to find out wherein the government is remiss—if it is remiss—in aiding you in the development of this tremendous and resourceful land. I think it is a splendid thing for the government to get a little closer to the people and to know their problems more intimately. Washington is far away, and it is not always possible to secure dependable information from such a long distance. It is not altogether convenient for many of you to come to Washington; so we have come to you, and we are learning; we are beginning to know you better. It is a very great satisfaction to be able to study conditions at first hand, and I know the knowledge we shall acquire will equip us better to perform the duties which you have entrusted to us.

I become somewhat philosophical as I travel. We may wonder what is the great end of life. Men make their plans and try to adhere to them. Skagway, a port located in a mountain pass, was developed and made notable in the rush of men seeking to acquire material substance. That is a motive which is inherent in us, but the longer I live and the more I see of communities and human beings, the more firmly is my belief established that the sweetest thing in the world is the friendship of a few dependable friends and happiness that makes a life of contentment. Apparently you have much of that here, as much as may be found anywhere; and you also live in an atmosphere that tends to cultivate ambition and lofty aspirations. I only hope that the worthy ones will come to full realization.

I imagine you will not expect me to say more; but let me wish you the most abundant happiness that can come to any community in all the United States. I want you to be fortunate and happy, and I want you to experience as great gratification over the part you may play in the building of a greater Republic as shall be experienced by any community in all the land. It is a very great pleasure personally to meet and greet you. [Applause.]

ACCEPTS GIFT OF IVORY VASE

Remarks at the Pullen House, Skagway, Alaska, in Acknowledgement of Gift of Fossilized Ivory Vase Presented by the Mayor on Behalf of the People of Skagway, July 11, 11:30 a. m.

Mr. Mayor:

I THANK you, sir, and the good people of Skagway for your beautiful gift. It makes manifest again one of the striking attributes of the people up here, that of boundless generosity and kind thoughtfulness. This gift only adds to our knowledge of the considerate thoughtfulness of the people of Alaska, and we shall cherish it greatly, for anything that reminds us of the happiness of this trip will always be greatly treasured.

CHRISTENING OF "HARDING GATEWAY"

Remarks on Leaving Seward for Fairbanks, Friday, July 13,
and also Statement of Governor Scott C. Bone, of
Alaska, as to Christening of "Harding Gateway"

Citizens of Seward:

IN TAKING leave of Seward for the time being I wish
to say that I have greatly enjoyed the few hours I
have spent in your midst, and it has been an especial
pleasure to meet and greet those who live here. I appreciate their hospitable and cordial welcome.

I may add that Seward appeals to the eye as a jewel
in one of the most beautiful settings that may be found
anywhere in the world.

Governor Bone: I want the people of Seward to know
that on entering Resurrection Bay this morning we chris-
tened the entrance "The Harding Gateway," and always
hereafter it is to be known by that name.

It will interest you also to know that the distinguished
visitors aboard this train are agreed that nowhere in all
the world have they seen more beautiful scenery than at
the magnificent entrance to your harbor.

President Harding: The governor might have said
further that the President has not seen anything in Alaska
that he would rather have bear his name than the entrance
to this splendid harbor. [Applause.]

"EMPIRE" AND ALASKA SYNONYMOUS

Speech at Anchorage, Alaska, Friday, July 13, 10:30 p. m.

Mr. Mayor and Citizens of Anchorage:

MRS. HARDING and I accept with the greatest pleasure
this splendid gift which, on behalf of the people of
Anchorage, you have so generously presented to us.
We shall treasure it and look upon it, picturing, as it does,

NOTE: The President was introduced by the Mayor, Mr. J. C. Conroy, and
presented by him with a painting of Mt. McKinley by Sydney Laurence, of Anchorage.

the loftiest mountain on the American continent, as a symbol of the high ideals and the sterling, rugged character of the people of Anchorage.

It is quite as great a pleasure for the President to visit Anchorage as it is for Anchorage to have a visit from the President. This is the first "baby" city I ever called upon in my life, and I must say it is the healthiest "baby," the best nine-year-old that I ever saw. Manifestly you have built for the future, and I hope your most enthusiastic expectations of the future may be completely fulfilled.

I have come to know a new meaning of words since undertaking this wonderful journey. I have come to know a new and enlarged meaning of the word "hospitality," and nowhere in all America has it been more bountifully shown than in this wonderful land of Alaska. I have also come to know a new meaning of the word "empire" in its loftiest and best sense. Hereafter whenever I hear the word "empire" I shall think of Alaska, an empire within itself. Then I have come to know a new meaning of "majestic," "mighty," and "wonderful," and adjectives fail me when I try to describe the marvelous vision which has come before us during our travels in this astonishingly wonderful land.

Cheerful, Hopeful Communities

I do not know that I have ever encountered communities surpassing in cheerfulness, in hopefulness, and in confidence those I have been privileged to visit in Alaska. If anybody is dissatisfied with Alaska, it must be for some reason that I have yet to find, for everyone seems to be happy and measurably fortunate—and that is very difficult to say of any other section of the world—and you have the finest women and the best children I ever laid my eyes upon. [Applause.]

I wish I could convey to you what an inspiration it is to see these bright-faced, smiling, happy children of yours. I have not seen them brought together in one place, as they were at Seward earlier in the day, but I never saw a more fascinating picture in my life. I am very sure, my countrymen, that the children of today will at some time experience the fulfillment of the aspirations which you older people are cherishing.

I have doubt that Alaska will come into its own, as you hope, in this generation. It is so big, it is so little understood, it has such tremendous possibilities that the development which you hope for is not going to come with the wave of a magician's wand—it is not possible to do things in that way—but here at Anchorage you have built a city on a foundation which contemplates a great and wonderful future. I think you have done well. You are here in the open way to the center of this great empire, and I tell you that truly I think you are destined to have a notable and highly successful future. Certainly, you have started admirably.

The official trip which brings us here was designed to enable us to understand Alaska better and, at the same time, to give you an opportunity to understand your government better. The government is at your service. There is nothing wrong about its intent. If we have been remiss at Washington, it is because your long distance from the seat of government has made it difficult for us to understand your problems as we wish to understand them. So we have come to learn. We have not come to promise; we have not come to make speeches, for we are not as yet sufficiently informed to enable us to reach final conclusions, but we are distinctly settled in our minds as to a number of things. There is no division amongst us as to the wonders of this empire of ours and as to the pride we feel in the quality of American citizenship which we have found here.

"Vision Has Been Broadened"

My visit to Alaska has afforded me great pleasure; but, quite apart from that, my vision has been broadened; I have been heartened and cheered, and upon my return to Washington I know I shall be better equipped to discharge the duties which have been imposed upon me and to serve the public weal so far as it is in my capacity to serve.

I thank you for coming out at this late hour of the night to extend to us this cordial greeting. It is a new experience to us to be received by such numbers at an hour approaching midnight and still be able to see the glow of daylight on your faces. It is all a novelty, and is quite delightful indeed. You have given us joy by the cheer and cordiality of your hearty greetings, and I thank you. [Applause.]

RELATIVE VALUE OF *LIFE'S* VIEWS

Remarks at Anchorage, Alaska, July 13, 10:50 p. m., in Acknowledgment of Gift of Paper-cutter Presented by C. J. Lincke, of the Anchorage Times

Mr. Lincke and Ladies and Gentlemen:

I WISH you to know how deeply grateful I am for this very beautiful gift. I think, perhaps, I cherish an evidence of thoughtfulness on the part of the members of the "Fourth Estate" more than would the average person. I have been in newspaper work for thirty-nine years, and I love it today no less than when I began.

I thought we could do something in the way of publishing newspapers down in the States where there are communities ranging from 20,000 inhabitants up to the great metropolitan cities, but I come to Alaska and find thriving daily papers in cities of 1,000 and 2,000. So I have concluded that we do not know anything about the business back in the States and should come to Alaska to find out.

A very amusing thing happened to me a few days ago at Ketchikan. I will tell the story on myself. At that place a newsboy came running by our car offering newspapers for sale. I thought I would buy a couple, and, inasmuch as we were in the habit of selling our newspapers for two cents, I reached in my pocket for some change and said: "I will take three." Not finding anything less

than a half a dollar—I had felt for a quarter—I gave it
to the boy, and thinking that would be the only time we
would ever meet I told him to keep the change. He said:
"Thank you." I learned after he had disappeared that
if I had offered him twenty-five cents for three newspapers,
I would have been in extreme disfavor in Alaska. You
treat a quarter up here about like we do a nickel in the
States. All things, however, are relative. I do not intend
to make another speech, but I should like to say that
when I was a boy and my father gave me a nickel to spend
it looked as big as a full moon. That was what we thought
of a nickel. But nowadays when I come to Alaska I find
that a dollar does not look any bigger than a flyspeck. It
illustrates the relative value of many of our views of life.

It is a great pleasure to have seen you. I again thank
you and wish for you all the good things that can come
to any people in all the world. [Applause.]

ALASKAN RAILROAD WORK OF GENIUS

Remarks at North Nenana, Alaska, Sunday, July 15, 4:50
p. m., on the Occasion of Driving the Golden Spike,
Marking the Completion of the Alaska Railroad

*Mr. Secretary, Governor Bone, Col. Steese, and Fellow
Citizens:*

BEFORE performing the last act in the program which
symbolizes the completion of this railway, I wish to
add my word of tribute to those who "pioneered" it
and contributed of their genius and courage to the making
of this steel highway through an almost impassable land.
We have been traveling now between four and five thousand
miles over marvelous highways, and one thought has
occurred to me everywhere, namely, that the outstanding
genius of it all is the man who found the way, who had

314

the conception, the perception, and the confidence to find an open pathway through the mountains, the wilderness, and the canyons, and to surmount the various other physical difficulties which necessarily had to be encountered.

I do not suppose any individual or set of individuals would have undertaken the construction of such a railway as this one in Alaska. It had to be left to the government itself. I am frank to say that when the enterprise was first proposed I was rather inclined to oppose it; but, having seen the empire of Alaska and the possibilities which this railway opens up, I am glad a generous government undertook and carried to completion the construction of the Alaska railroad. It is not possible to liken a railway to a magician's wand, but the effect to me is the same, for the whole problem of civilization, the development of resources, and the awakening of communities lies in transportation. So the government has come into this wonderful land and opened up a steel highway which makes possible an inestimable development. I hope the development which will accrue will be all that the people of Alaska are hoping for and more, but I hardly presume it will come in any hurried way; I cannot see how it may.

I was very much impressed by a remark made by the president of the Pioneers Association, in which I was admitted to honorary membership a little while ago. He referred to the sturdiness, the industry, and the confidence of the pioneers in developing this country. In my humble judgment, the qualities of the pioneers cooperating with the transportation line, which has now been opened, will do more to work out the development of this wonderland than anything which the great government of the United States can do. I hope that the greatest expectations of the people of Alaska may be completely fulfilled.

Now, Mr. Secretary, in conformity with your suggestion, and in commemoration of the completion of the railroad, I take pleasure in driving the golden spike.

ACCEPTING TANANA BRIDGE SOUVENIR

Remarks at Nenana, Alaska, July 15, 5 p. m., Acknowledging Gift Presented by Mayor Teufel, Emblematic of the Bridge Across the Tanana River

Mr. Mayor and Citizens of Nenana:

I THANK you very much for this gift which will be a very treasured souvenir of this happy day. I think you of Nenana are to be congratulated upon having the distinction of being at the site of one of the most wonderful bridges in the world. I hope it will be suggestive of the thought that there may never be a gap which you cannot bridge, and that there will never be a break in any connection which has to do with your welfare. I am glad to accept the gift as a memento of this happy occasion. It is a pleasure to greet you, and I thank you very much.

ALASKA A REAL "HOME COUNTRY"

Speech at Fairbanks, Alaska, Monday, July 16, 10:15 a. m.

Mr. Mayor and Fellow Americans All:

I WONDER if you know what has most impressed us on our most interesting and enjoyable trip to Alaska. You have a sample of it here in Fairbanks. One who comes to Alaska from the States, even though measurably well read, usually has an impression that this is a man's country, that it is the home of the itinerant adventurer and prospector and sometimes of the "rough-neck." He does not stop to think, as I myself did not, of the charm of Alaska as a home country. I had no idea of the incomparable American childhood which I have seen here, and of course that implies also the matchless American woman-

hood. [Applause.] While Alaska is majestic and boundless and mighty, an empire in itself, it is also strikingly
a home land, and that is the finest thing that may be said
of any section of any nation in the world. [Applause.]

I presume the reason for the magnificent specimens
of youthful Americans that I see everywhere in Alaska
may be found in the open life which is led here, in the
inspiration of environment, in the boundlessness of their
hopes, and in the wonders of the Alaskan climate, with
its long nights in the winter during which they may grow
and the long days of the summer during which they may
play. There are compensations in all things. God must
have worked it all out. I have come to the conclusion
that you need your long winters. We have come in the
summer and found your hospitality so generous and the
sun so deceptive and so constantly "on the job" that we
do not want to go to bed. I am sorry to say, however,
that Mrs. Harding was obliged to go to the hotel in order
to rest, for the lure of Alaska, the charm of the new surroundings, and the invitation to be doing something all the
time have really so worn her out that she has had to
seek rest.

Sympathy with Genuine Settlers

If I may digress for a moment, what is the great
object in life? I think a little philosophy might well be
applied to Alaskan conditions. I do not know of any aspiration that is more desirable than that to enjoy health and
happiness. What do we live for? For the compensations
of friendship, the delights of association, and the happiness
and contentment of home; and you have all of those in
Alaska as much as any people in the world. [Applause.]
I have a suspicion that most of the complaint which comes
from Alaska must come from those who are commercially
disposed, who have a desire to acquire more than the
average share of this world's goods and then to take it
somewhere else. [Applause.] From this day forth my
official as well as my personal interest in Alaskans will be
in those who are trying to make a real empire of Alaska

317

and who intend to abide in the empire which they have helped to create. [Applause.]

I share the ambition that seeks to develop this wonderland. It is a very natural ambition for men of talent, genius and industry. Men like to take the tremendous bestowal God has made and turn it to practical use; but frequently they are not patient; they are not willing to await natural processes—and that is a perfectly normal tendency—but as surely as the sun shines this beautiful morning, just so surely will Alaska attain the fullest development that God must have intended for her. [Applause.] I do not think that the government can do it for you, but it probably can be helpful, and it wishes to be helpful. That is why we are here. We want to know Alaska better from first-hand information and from intimate contact. The knowledge we have acquired has been a revelation, although some of us perhaps thought we knew a great deal before we left Washington. But, whatever the government may wish to do, whatever it may do, after all, I would rather trust the fortunes of Alaska to the sons and daughters of the pioneers here than I would to all the politicians that ever assembled together at any place. [Great applause.]

Tribute to Pioneer Parents

I pay my tribute to the pioneers. They constitute the reason for these fine children. It takes a good deal of a man to be a pioneer. He has to have strength of character, sturdiness, and determination of purpose. It is very natural that men of that type, after doing the work of pioneers, should leave a very fine and sturdy race to follow them. [Applause.] I wish the pioneers could all live to see the fruits of their efforts.

I am the nearest to a Presidential "sourdough" that was ever known. [Applause.] If the first President to come to Alaska is entitled to be called a "sourdough," I may justly claim that title. I know how you feel about a Presidential visit. I know how I should have felt when I was a "Main Streeter" in Marion, Ohio, if the President at that time should have come to my home town; but I should like you to know that this experience is just as wonderful to the President as it is to you. [Applause.] I have come to have an expanded pride in our Republic, and it is a fine thing to know what a splendid part of it you are. It is good to realize what a magnificent, wholesome American citizenship there. is in this great Northland. [Applause.] I would be willing to trust the fortunes of America to a popular verdict in Alaska. [Applause.] I have every confidence you will work out your problems, with such help as we can give, to the ultimate satisfaction of the aspiring people of this Territory. Alaska is a wonderful land and I say with all the sincerity I can put into my words that you are a wonderful people. [Applause.] While there are not so many of you as you hope to have, and undoubtedly will have, do not worry about that; but consider the quality and the prospects that lie before you.

I want you to know the members of our party and they will be introduced to you in a few moments by your distinguished mayor. I want you to know that we have come to Alaska to learn, to understand and to be understood. In conclusion let me repeat that it is a very great pleasure to have seen you and greeted you and to know what a magnificent body of citizens dwell in this great section of the American Republic. [Applause.]

KINDNESS TO DOGS COMMENDED

Remarks at Fairbanks, Alaska, July 16, in Acknowledging Gift of Collar for "Laddie Boy," Presented by Mayor Marquam on Behalf of the Citizens of Fairbanks

Mayor Marquam and Citizens of Fairbanks:

HAVING spoken once, I had not thought to say a word more, and I dare not trust myself to talk about dogs.

The popularity of the dog in Alaska is, I think, one of the reasons why I like the Territory so well. I took an oath before one of the pioneer secret orders the other

319

day never to kick a dog. I like that spirit and I admire those who are unwilling to kick a dog. I like dogs, and I was pleased to hear what the mayor said about "Laddie Boy's" courage, confidence, trust and fidelity. Of course when I speak of "Laddie Boy" I merely speak of him as one typical dog. I cannot understand anybody who does not love a dog. I like his unfailing fidelity and his unquestioning confidence and his ever-willingly expressed admiration and love and his utter restraint from ever saying anything unkind about one.

The gift which you have presented to me is a beautiful souvenir of my visit. Oh, you are too generous in Alaska! It is not necessary to carry away some trophy or memento in order to remember you. You could give us nothing to surpass the cordiality of your greeting this morning, but, none the less, the gift is treasured, and I think I will take the time to say that I do not believe you could have done anything that would have more appealed to Mrs. Harding.

Womanlike, she did not want to receive "Laddie Boy" when he was presented to me on the morning following my inauguration as President, for the very same reason that we had lost a very beautiful dog and it was difficult to recover from the sorrow that came from the broken association. So Mrs. Harding did not want to have a renewed attachment that must inevitably be broken because of the short life of the dog. However, I thought the President ought to have a little authority and so I insisted on receiving "Laddie Boy." [Laughter.] When he first came Mrs. Harding barely noticed him, but, like all good dogs—and "Laddie Boy" is a fine gentlemanly dog—he won his way to Mrs. Harding's heart, and wherever she has seen an Airedale on this trip she hails him as "Laddie Boy."

This is just an added expression of your generosity, your thoughtfulness and your kindness and I am as grateful as I can be. [Applause.]

ALL IN UNITED STATES "FELLOW AMERICANS"

Speech at Cordova, Alaska, July 20, 3:30 p. m.

Mr. Mayor, Mr. Hazlet, and Fellow Americans:

I THINK, since I am the first "sourdough" President, I might say "fellow Alaskans" [Laughter and applause], but it is more agreeable to me just to say "fellow Americans," because we are all Americans everywhere throughout the domain of the United States of America.

Mr. Mayor, I deeply appreciate any token which is a reminder of one of the happiest and most enjoyable journeys of my life. I have not had opportunity to satisfy my curiosity concerning the gift which you have presented to me and so cannot speak explicitly, but it is always gratifying to have a token of the friendship and the esteem of any body of the American people. However, one needs no token to retain sweet memories of Alaska, for there is a lure about this wonderland that will bring back any man who has once come here. [Applause.] That is why you older men are here; and these younger folks may rejoice that they are here.

Beauty in Alaskan Homes

We have been paying tribute to the pioneer, to those who came to develop the gold fields and the other mineral wealth and the possibilities of this great Territory. But there are those among you who are deserving of higher tribute. I give my reverence to the American women who brought the American home into Alaska [Applause], because the development of this Territory is dependent upon homes. I will say—and I know that I speak truly—that there are no homes in the world that produce more beautiful flowers than the homes of Alaska, as I see them before me in these children. [Applause.] No one in the world ever saw a finer picture than the one we encountered as we motored up the hill where the boys and girls had ranged themselves in the form of the letter "A" and sang

"Alaska" to us. You may talk about your wonderful mountains and their fascination, your waterfalls and their charm, and your lakes and rivers and bays—all wonderful and unsurpassed anywhere in the world—but even they are not so fascinating and so inspiring as the picture of American childhood in the glow of Alaskan health and in the strength of your wonderful surroundings. It is the finest picture in the world.

There is something else about Alaskans that ought to make them very well satisfied. I have yet to see a single manifestation of poverty in the Territory. If there is anyone here who is extremely poor he is an artist in hiding it from the view of everyone else, and wherever poverty can be hidden its existence is not a serious matter.

Covets an Alaskan Log Cabin

Mr. Hazlet made some statements as to what is the matter with Alaska. I do not see anything very much the matter with it, to tell you the truth. Perhaps, it is not developing as fast as the more ambitious among you would wish; perhaps, there are some who come here occasionally but live elsewhere who are not making money as rapidly as they would like; but there cannot be anything very much wrong with a Territory so rich in resources and so ornate in happy and fortunate American homes. We human beings are a strange lot; we are always wanting the things we do not have. There is not a thing in Alaska that I have coveted so much as one of the things you are trying to kick aside. I would give a month's Presidential salary if I could own one of your log cabins on a little farm I have down in Ohio. [Applause.] They are attractive to look at, and they must be delightful to live in, and I wonder that you seek to get away from them. So much came from the log cabin of America that I think it would be well to cherish it and continue its possession in this wonderful Territory.

My countrymen, I did not intend to speak so long. We have had a wonderful visit in your vicinity. The trip to the Childs' Glacier was more than fascinating; it excited our wonder and our admiration; but the greatest pleasure of all, apart from the new experiences that come from a visit to a wonderland, is to know the people who inhabit it and in whose hands the fortunes of the Territory and the Republic lie. I could not wish for a finer people than I have found in Alaska. When I say that I but express to you my pride as a fellow American in the splendid citizenship of this Territory who are making it a helpful and most admirable part of the great American Republic.

I hope the Mayor will take it upon himself to present to you the members of the Cabinet who are in the party and also the Speaker of the House, because our journey was intended to bring you a little closer to the government and to bring the government a little closer to you. I want you to know them, because whatever of good comes out of the present administration, leaving out of consideration for the moment the responsibilities of Congress, comes largely through the excellent men who are at the head of the various departments of the government. I am glad to have you know them and I am thrice glad to have the privilege of knowing you. [Applause.]

ALASKA'S RESOURCES BARELY TOUCHED

Speech at Sitka, Alaska, Sunday, July 22, 10:50 a. m.

My Fellow Countrymen All:

TWO weeks ago today for the first time I set foot on Alaskan soil. During the intervening days I have visited many Alaskan coast towns and have penetrated the interior to Fairbanks. I have found it difficult to find words to express my admiration as scene after scene of wondrous beauty has been unfolded before my eyes. After a few days in Alaskan waters it seemed that nature, even in Alaska, could not offer more sublime scenery than had already met my gaze, but each day something new, something perhaps still more inspiring, was revealed. And on this glorious Sabbath morning I awoke in the beautiful bay of Sitka, studded with wooded islands rising from the blue waters of the placid sea, and saw your historic city nestling between its majestic hills. It occurred to me then, since the time had come when I must say farewell, that there could be no better place in which to speak the parting word, nor one whose beauty would longer command a grateful memory. When I come ashore I am met with your generous welcome; I see the smiling faces of the children of Sitka, who are the promise of this great Territory; and once more I am glad that Alaska is part and parcel of the great American Republic and that her people have the same loyalty and the same devotion to the flag as have those of any other section of the United States.

Then I was reminded, Sitka having been the seat of the Alaskan government for many years, of some of the incidents which mark her history, especially in connection with the purchase of Alaska by Secretary Seward. I recalled that Russia, not appreciating the resources and wealth of Alaska, as, indeed, many of our own countrymen did not, had prior to the Civil War offered to sell Alaska to the United States for $4,000,000. Then this Nation became engrossed in the mighty conflict between the States, and Alaska was forgotten for a while; but during the war Russia showed her friendship for the Union cause by sending one fleet of warships to New York and another to San Francisco. The moral support thus given was of great value to the Republic, and was one of the events which inspired the goodwill which has so long subsisted between the people of Russia and those of the United States. But Russia had incurred great expense in fitting out and sending her fleets to American waters; and so when negotiations for the purchase of Alaska were resumed it was agreed that there should be paid for this great Territory the sum of $7,200,000.

Seward's Foresight Justified

It is worth while noting in this connection, as a justification for the action of Secretary Seward and as a tribute to his foresight and statesmanship, that Alaska has proved such a storehouse of treasure that she has added to the National wealth an hundred times more than the price paid to the Russian government, and it may be said, truly I think, that as yet her vast resources have barely been touched.

In one respect, perhaps, I think I may say that our visit to Alaska has been agreeably disappointing. If we have diagnosed the situation even half correctly, there is much less the matter with Alaska and much less the matter with the relations between the Federal government and Alaska than has been widely proclaimed. The simple truth is I cannot see anything the matter with Alaska. It is probably not developing in harmony with the ambitious desires of many of you, but a great empire like this cannot be developed by the wave of a magician's wand. Development must come from citizenship. What is needed in Alaska is more citizens, like those I see before me this morning, who will make this Territory their treasured home.

I have said in many places, and I am glad to repeat here, that a prettier picture than that presented by such representatives of the childhood of Alaska as I see before me now cannot be found anywhere in the world. Clearly, it matters little whether they are native or white, for they represent a promising, hopeful childhood in either case, and I am sure that if there can be provided in Alaska adequate educational facilities the way will be lighted for the development to which you aspire.

Sincerity in Religion Urged

My countrymen, we are met on the Sabbath morning. How good it is to believe that the hungering for the promotion of religious influence throughout the world first brought civilization here and that you are striving for its high fulfillment. I wonder if it does not occur to you that, in appreciation and in reverence for God over all, we ought to be just a little more devoted, a little more sincere, and a little more earnest in our own religious activities, so that we may "carry on" as God must have intended.

It is good to see you; it is a delight to see these children; it is a pleasure to feel the charm of your wonderful scenery. It is a regret that we must leave Alaska tonight, but we go away with fine impressions, after having received many suggestions which will be helpful to you and helpful to the government in its relations with you. I should like you all to know that we go away wishing you the best that can come to any community of the great human family. [Applause.]

"CANADA OUR VERY GOOD NEIGHBOR," FOLLOWING THE PATH TO PEACE AND LIBERTY ALONG A PARALLEL HIGHWAY

Address at Stanley Park, Vancouver, B. C.,
July 26, 12 noon

Citizens of Canada:

I MAY as well confess to you at the outset a certain perplexity as to how I should address you. The truth of the matter is that this is the first time I have ever spoken as President in any country other than my own. Indeed, so far as I can recall, I am, with the single exception of my immediate predecessor, the first President in office even to set foot on politically-foreign soil.

True, there is no definite inhibition upon one doing so, such as prevents any but a natural born citizen from becoming President, but an early prepossession soon developed into a tradition and for more than a hundred years held the effect of unwritten law. I am not prepared to say that the custom was not desirable, perhaps even needful, in the early days, when time was the chief requisite of travel. Assuredly, too, at present, the Chief Magistrate of a great Republic ought not to cultivate the habit or make a hobby of wandering over all the continents of the earth.

Canada Our Good Neighbor

But exceptions are required to prove rules. And Canada is an exception, a most notable exception, from every viewpoint of the United States. You are not only our neighbor, but a very good neighbor, and we rejoice in your advancement and admire your independence, no less sincerely than we value your friendship.

327

I need not depict the points of similarity that make this attitude of the one toward the other irresistible. We think the same thoughts, live the same lives and cherish the same aspirations of service to each other in times of need. Thousands of your brave lads perished in gallant and generous action for the preservation of our Union. Many of our young men followed Canadian colors to the battlefields of France before we entered the war and left their proportion of killed to share the graves of your intrepid sons. This statement is brought very intimately home to me, for one of the brave lads in my own newspaper office felt the call of service to the colors of the sons of Canada. He went to the front, and gave his life with your boys for the preservation of the American and Canadian concept of civilization. [Applause.]

Saluted as "Fellow Men"

When my mind reverts and my heart beats low to recollection of those faithful and noble companionships, I may not address you, to be sure, as "fellow citizens," as I am accustomed to designate assemblages at home, but I may and do, with respect and pride, salute you as "fellow men," in mutual striving for common good.

What an object lesson of peace is shown today by our two countries to all the world! [Applause.] No grim-faced fortifications mark our frontiers, no huge battleships patrol our dividing waters, no stealthy spies lurk in our tranquil border hamlets. Only a scrap of paper, recording hardly more than a simple understanding, safeguards lives and properties on the Great Lakes, and only humble mile-posts mark the inviolable boundary line for thousands of miles through farm and forest.

Our protection is in our fraternity, our armor is our faith; the tie that binds more firmly year by year is ever-increasing acquaintance and comradeship through interchange of citizens; and the compact is not of perishable parchment, but of fair and honorable dealing which, God grant, shall continue for all time. [Applause.]

An interesting and significant symptom of our growing mutuality appears in the fact that the voluntary interchange of residents to which I have referred, is wholly free from restrictions. Our National and industrial exigencies have made it necessary for us, greatly to our regret, to fix limits to immigration from foreign countries. But there is no quota for Canada. [Applause.] We gladly welcome all of your sturdy, steady stock who care to come, as a strengthening ingredient and influence. We none the less bid Godspeed and happy days to the thousands of our own folk, who are swarming constantly over your land and participating in its remarkable development. [Applause.] Wherever in either of our countries any inhabitant of the one or the other can best serve the interests of himself and his family is the place for him to be. [Applause.]

Evidence of Increasing Interdependence

A further evidence of our increasing interdependence appears in the shifting of capital. Since the armistice, I am informed, approximately $2,500,000,000 has found its way from the United States into Canada for investment. That is a huge sum of money, and I have no doubt is employed safely for us and helpfully for you. Most gratifying to you, moreover, should be the circumstance that one-half of that great sum has gone for purchase of your state and municipal bonds,—a tribute, indeed, to the scrupulous maintenance of your credit, to a degree equalled only by your mother country across the sea and your sister country across the hardly visible border. [Applause.]

These are simple facts which quickly resolve into history for guidance of mankind in the seeking of human happiness. "History, history!" ejaculated Lord Overton to his old friend, Lindsay, himself an historian; "what is the use of history? It only keeps people apart by reviving recollections of enmity."

As we look forth today upon the nations of Europe, with their armed camps of nearly a million more men in 1923 than in 1913, we can not deny the grain of truth in this observation. But not so here! A hundred years of tranquil relationships, throughout vicissitudes which elsewhere would have evoked armed conflict rather than arbitration, affords, truly declared James Bryce, "the finest example ever seen in history of an undefended frontier, whose very absence of armaments itself helped to prevent hostile demonstrations;" thus proving beyond question that "peace can always be kept, whatever be the grounds of controversy, between peoples that wish to keep it." [Applause.]

Causes Making for Enduring Peace

There is a great and highly pertinent truth, my friends, in that simple assertion. It is public will, not public force, that makes for enduring peace. And is it not a gratifying circumstance that it has fallen to the lot of us North Americans, living amicably for more than a century, under different flags, to present the most striking example yet produced of that basic fact? If only European countries would heed the lesson conveyed by Canada and the United States, they would strike at the root of their own continuing disagreements and, in their own prosperity, forget to inveigh constantly at ours. [Applause.]

Not that we would reproach them for resentment or envy, which after all is but a manifestation of human nature. Rather should we sympathize with their seeming inability to break the shackles of age-long methods, and rejoice in our own relative freedom from the stultifying effect of Old World customs and practices. Our natural advantages are manifold and obvious. We are not palsied by the habits of a thousand years. We live in the power and glory of youth. Others derive justifiable satisfaction from contemplation of their resplendent pasts. We have relatively only our present to regard, and that, with eager eyes fixed chiefly and confidently upon our future.

Therein lies our best estate. We profit both mentally and materially from the fact that we have no "departed greatness" to recover, no "lost provinces" to regain, no new territory to covet, no ancient grudges to gnaw eternally at the heart of our National consciousness. Not only

330

are we happily exempt from these handicaps of vengeance and prejudice, but we are animated correspondingly and most helpfully by our better knowledge, derived from longer experience, of the blessings of liberty. [Applause.] These advantages we may not appreciate to the full at all times, but we know that we possess them, and the day is far distant when, if ever, we shall fail to cherish and defend them against any conceivable assault from without or from within our borders. [Applause.]

"Bugaboo of Annexation" Gone

I find that, quite unconsciously, I am speaking of our two countries almost in the singular when perhaps I should be more painstaking to keep them where they belong, in the plural. But I feel no need to apologize. You understand as well as I that I speak in no political sense. The ancient bugaboo of the United States scheming to annex Canada disappeared from all our minds years and years ago. [Applause.] Heaven knows we have all we can manage now, and room enough to spare for another hundred millions, before approaching the intensive stage of existence of many European states.

And if I might be so bold as to offer a word of advice to you, it would be this: Do not encourage any enterprise looking to Canada's annexation of the United States. [Laughter.] You are one of the most capable governing peoples in the world, but I entreat you, for your own sakes, to think twice before undertaking management of the territory which lies between the Great Lakes and the Rio Grande. [Laughter and applause.]

Traveling Parallel Roads

No, let us go our own gaits along parallel roads, you helping us and we helping you. [Applause.] So long as each country maintains its independence, and both recognize their interdependence, those paths can not fail to be highways of progress and prosperity. Nationality continues to be a supreme factor in modern existence; make no mistake about that; but the day of the Chinese wall, inclosing a hermit nation, has passed forever. Even though space itself were not in process of annihilation by airplane, submarine, wireless and broadcasting, our very propinquity enjoins that most effective cooperation which comes only from clasping of hands in true faith and good fellowship. [Applause.]

It is in precisely that spirit, men and women of Canada, that I have stopped on my way home from a visit to our pioneers in Alaska to make a passing call upon my very good neighbor of the fascinating Iroquois name, "Kanada," to whom, glorious in her youth and strength and beauty, on behalf of my own beloved country, I stretch forth both my arms in the most cordial fraternal greeting, with gratefulness for your splendid welcome in my heart, and from my lips the whispered prayer of our famed Rip Van Winkle: "May you all live long and prosper!" [Great applause.]

PEACE EXAMPLE TO ALL THE WORLD

Speech at Luncheon Given by the Civic Government at Vancouver Hotel, Vancouver, B. C., Thursday, July 26, 2:30 p. m.

Mr. Mayor, and Ladies and Gentlemen:

I HAVE only remained upon my feet to give expression to the gratitude which is in my heart for your more than cordial and most neighborly reception. We had anticipated with very great pleasure coming to Canada and to Vancouver in particular. We had rather expected to meet just such a citizenship as we have encountered here, but we did not expect such an overwhelming manifestation of your very friendly neighborliness. It has been so genuine and so outspoken that I know it is a new assurance that the United States of America and the Dominion of Canada will continue to go along side by side and, if I may say so, hand in hand in the fulfillment of the destinies of the two great and free democracies. [Applause.]

It is said that it is a very common human trait to measure others as we measure ourselves. If I may adopt that method for a moment, I can understand your neighborliness and your cordiality because I know we come as visitors in precisely the same spirit which you have made manifest in receiving us. [Applause.] We like you as neighbors. [Applause.] We like you as fellow North Americans. We like you as exemplars and promoters of one of the freest and finest democracies in the world. [Applause.] We also like our cotemporaneous development of the resources and possibilities of the New World. You in Canada are doing precisely what we have been doing and mean to continue to do in the United States. If many of our citizens are joining to help you, many of your citizens are joining to help us. There is not a reason in the world why we should not continue along the same path, keeping our faces to the front, confident of bringing about a great accomplishment for humanity in the Western World. [Applause.]

Lesson for Other Nations

I do not know anything in the world better than a good neighbor. That is true of the individual neighbor to whom one may go and borrow a couple of eggs if there are none in his pantry and make other practical exchanges. If it is well for an individual to have good neighbors, it is even better for nations to have good neighbors.

It may seem much like repetition, but I like to say that the United States and Canada are doing more at this moment for humankind by their example of fine neighborly, peaceful relations than any other contiguous nations in all the world. [Applause.] If I knew how to bring it about, I would invite humankind this afternoon to look upon the ways of friendship which are free from suspicion, upon the neighborliness that is without envy, and upon the mutuality of interest in human advancement that contemplates no selfish end which mark the relationship between our Republic and your great Dominion. When all the nations of the world can be made to see the desirability of maintaining a similar relationship there will never be another war with its shadows and sorrows. [Applause.]

It is good to have seen you and to have been with you. Please accept from me, and from me as spokesman for our party, the gratitude of your neighbors for the cordiality and friendship of your greeting. [Applause.]

BOND OF LANGUAGE AND BLOOD

Speech at Dinner Given by the Government of the Dominion of Canada, Vancouver Hotel, Vancouver, B. C., Thursday, July 26, 8:30 p. m.

Mr. Minister and Ladies and Gentlemen:

HAVING been assured that I would be expected to speak but once in Vancouver, and accrediting Canadians with essentially the same human qualities which we confess or boast in the United States, I have come prepared for the call you make upon me. [Laughter.]

It has required only a survey of your splendid citizenship and contact with your fine people to be newly assured of the mutuality of American aspirations, though we are ever pursuing our respective and wholly independent ways. And I am sure I may say becomingly that the aspirations of the English-speaking peoples are as noble as human impulses have inspired anywhere on earth.

I have rejoiced to find here so large a representation of former citizens of our Republic, sharing in the development of your vast domain, participating in the fruits of British Columbian progress, and cherishing and reverencing your institutions no less than they did ours when citizens of the United States. I very much suspect our kinship is so manifest and our ideals and purposes so much alike that there is little realization of transferred allegiance. I unfailingly observe that former Americans of the United

States are very happy in their Canadian habitation and habiliments, and have their eyes to the front in confident anticipation of a glorious future.

If the evidence of likeness had been lacking in the general aspect, I should have had ample proof in finding here one of my former political associates in the General Assembly of Ohio, Mr. Thomas F. McConica, with whom I carried the same banner and fought the same fights. Leading here as in Ohio, he is an effective and patriotic contender for Canadian progress.

The Anglo=Saxon Concept of Liberty

I made allusion this afternoon to the participation of Canadian sons in the Civil War for our preserved Union, and the later eagerness of our youth to enlist under your flag in the World War, prior to the time when our Republic made common cause with the allied nations. General Sam Hughes once told a friend of mine that up to 1915 sixty thousand Americans had attempted to enlist in the Canadian army, and thousands of them succeeded in doing so, even though they had to "perjure themselves like gentlemen and patriots" in order to be accepted. We can all understand the motive—it was the irresistible appeal to do or die for the Anglo-Saxon concept of liberty and its civilization.

I am sure we share the same fundamental convictions about world peace and the human obligation to promote and maintain it. We may differ as to the practicability or effectiveness of this or that program, but we are in complete accord about the end to be attained.

No finer example of peace in confidence and honor has ever been recorded than the growth of our two Anglo-Saxon-Celtic democracies side by side, without jealousy or friction, and the glorious century of neighborly progress was never marked by more of neighborly confidence and good will than it is today. We rejoice with you in the archway of comity which spans the Vancouver-Seattle highway, dedicated to eternal friendship, and I hope there will be erected others to symbolize our cherished neighborliness and good will. I would rejoice if we might coordinate a due proportion of our work in constructing good roads, so as to facilitate international intercourse and neighborly fellowship.

Mutual Desire for Understanding

It is our mutual will to understand our joint problems, though we confessedly sometimes go amiss. Commissioners representing our two governments some time ago agreed upon a treaty to protect the fish in our bordering waters, and our Senate ratified, but added a reservation making the compact apply to Australia. It has hindered the consummation of protective measures, but it is rare tribute to the lure of your fishing to invite Australia to conform to a Canadian-American compact.

We have found inspiration in such leading Canadians as Sir Wilfred *L*aurier and Sir Robert Borden, and are everlastingly grateful to you for the late Franklin K. *L*ane and the late James J. Hill. You will not deny that we have aimed at reciprocity in sending to you Van Horn and Shaughnessy, and on either side of the border are constantly developing the stalwarts of New World leadership, who honor the continent no less than they do our neighboring states.

I would never seek to diminish pride in National allegiance, or reverence for the National emblem, and soul devotion thereto. I would ever have righteous and honorable competition among peoples to excel in their attainment and attending contribution to human progress. We shall strive as we always have for highest National eminence, but we do not seek it at your cost. On the contrary we yield becoming tribute to your every worthy achievement, and we feel the inescapable ties of blood in our confidence in Anglo-Saxon-Celtic fitness for lofty human achievement. More, there is the bond of the same language, and in Canada and the United States we speak it the same way. [Applause.]

336

ALLEGIANCE TO THE FLAG AND THE HOME

Speech at Woodland Park, Seattle, Wash., 3:30 p. m., July
27, at the Annual Picnic Given by the Elks to the
Boys of the State of Washington

Boys, hold up your right hand and repeat after me
the pledge of allegiance:

**"I pledge allegiance to my flag and to the Republic
for which it stands, one Nation indivisible, with liberty
and justice for all."**

Mr. Chairman and Boys:

SOME time ago it was my good fortune to be present
at a meeting of a lodge of the Elks in the Southland.
A class of neophytes were being initiated into the mysteries of the order and the exalted ruler did me the very
great distinction and afforded me the unusual satisfaction
of allowing me to present at the close of the initiation
a tiny silk flag to each of the new members of the order.
I do not know when I have been so pleasantly impressed,
because I tell you boys of Washington, every consecration
to the flag, every renewed expression of allegiance, every
manifestation of your respect and devotion is a new promise
for a greater and better Republic in these United States of
America. [Applause.]

I do not think I could improve upon the "pledge of
allegiance." I like the work which the Elks are doing in
promoting patriotism and in fraternizing with American
boyhood. It is the key to the open way of making the
finest manhood in the world and at the same time retaining
the finest manhood in the world. Wherever you find a father
and a son who are chums you have discovered the ideal
relationship. If I were going to preach at all,—and I
am not—I would admonish the fathers of America never
to do aught which they could not have brought to the
fullest attention of their sons; and I would counsel the

337

boys of America never to do anything that they could not explain fully to their fathers. Whenever we can have that sort of a moral relationship in America, we shall have come to a state of ideal manhood and womanhood. I do not want a nasty good or a goody goody boy. I like a boy who enjoys sport, who wishes to have fun, who craves athletics, who loves the outdoors, and who relishes a trick and a prank. I want him to be a real boy, but he can be all of that and yet be everlastingly on the square with his dad at the same time, providing, of course, that his dad is everlastingly on the square with him. [Applause.]

Allegiance to the American Home

There is only one further consecration I should like to have at the hands of American boyhood, and that is a pledge of allegiance to the American home. During the course of my travels I have become more and more impressed with the relationship that home bears to a worth while civilization. Somehow, God has put love of home instinctively into the hearts of all living creatures; but perhaps we of the human race are less considerate of home than the animal life which lacks our refinement and ideals. If we could have greater devotion on the part of men to the home and could better safeguard and preserve the ideals of the family relationship, then I know we would have an ample guaranty that America would become the ideal Republic. I want the boyhood of the State of Washington and the boyhood of the United States to grow up believing that the American home is the finest institution in it, not excepting the flag itself, because if we do not have ideal and happy homes the Nation is not very much worth while. I want our Republic, this wonderful America of ours, this free America, beckoning with equal opportunity to all its children, to be a land of homes, where every man is a sovereign at the fireside of happiness and hope. I wish for such a state in America, and I wish for the boys and girls in Washington a continuation of the careers which are suggested by this splendid meeting here today. I never knew a young man to preside with greater dignity and propriety than your chairman. He is fit to preside over the United States Senate or the House of Representatives now. [Applause.] Better still, boys, to every one of you born in the United States the Presidency of the Republic is just as available as to any one else though, perhaps, I should caution you to think twice before accepting it.

No Suggestion of Caste in America

What a wonderful land ours is! There is nowhere in America the suggestion of caste. A boy may come from the humblest home of the humblest toiler of the Republic and yet hold his head erect and know that to him comes every opportunity afforded to any other boy. There is no social distinction. I will correct that by saying that there is a little social distinction in society life among some of your parents, but there is not any among you, thank God, and when you grow up the difference disappears. I do not think that you quite appreciate the significance of that. I have seen in older communities the lines drawn in society life, but I have seen the boys and girls mingling together in the rollicksome hopefulness of youth, without regard to the society lines which divided their fathers and mothers; and when the youth developed into manhood the lines had disappeared and probably the working man's son of today became the society dictator of the morrow. Some may like such a position; I would not give much for it myself; but, at any rate, in this beckoning land of opportunity we do not know today who will be the foremost citizen of the morrow. It may be that the apparently least promising and the humblest boy in the ranks before me will occupy that position. That is one reason why I love this Republic of ours; there are no marks of distinction except as they are earned. There are no restrictions of class and must never be in these United States of ours. There is not anything to impede the progress of the ambitious and the worth while young man in America.

I bid you boys who have renewed your pledge of allegiance this afternoon to go on hopefully, and I know, in the fulfillment of the aspirations of your parents and of your own natural desires, you will make a greater State of Washington and in the making of it you will also make a greater Republic of the United States of America. [Applause.]

HARDING AN OPTIMIST ON ALASKA; NO NEED OF "HOT HOUSE" FORCING OR GOVERNMENT MANAGED EXPLOITING

Address on the Territory of Alaska at the Stadium, Seattle, Wash., Friday, July 27, 4 p. m.

Governor Hart, Mr. Mayor, My Countrymen All:

I WOULD be false to the promptings of my heart if I did not thank you with all the sincerity of my being for the cordiality of your welcome and the very fine tribute of courtesy shown by this wonderful gathering on this rather heated afternoon.

People sometimes think that the President of the United States ought not to travel, but they think many things about the President which are wrong. [*Laughter.*] Some of them even believe he ought not to have any fun; but who would want to be President if he could not enjoy a little amusement occasionally? So far as travel is concerned, however, I wish to convey to you the profound conviction which has come to me that I am better equipped to serve and more resolved faithfully to serve the Nation than when I left Washington last June. [Applause.] One finds a new pride in this Republic of ours and gains a new confidence in the unalterable determination and the patriotic devotion of the American people from the intimate contact with them made possible by seeing them in their homes. That is the impression which has been given to me today by the people of Washington and of the wonderful city of Seattle. [Applause.]

Fresh Impressions of Alaska

We are returned from Alaska, fresh with the impressions received in that great Northwestern Empire. It is

341

a great, measureless, and marvelous part of our cherished Republic. Nature has been prodigal in the bestowal of resources, and incomparable in her artistry. I wish I had language to convey the lure and fascination which grow on one during every hour of a constantly wondering visit. Nature must have been in a lavish mood, not alone to create incalculable resources, but to adorn them with mountain and lake, and the streams and the waterfalls which connect them, until one may fancy the Festival of Creation, celebrating the mysterious miracle, with God himself making merry and tossing ribbons of falling water, five hundred to two thousand feet long, like confetti at the carnival.

Words seem inadequate to portray the grandeur, to measure the magnificence, to express the mightiness, or acclaim the glory of monumental mountains and their jewelled valleys. Then, as though magnificent profligacy were a fit revelation of God's bounty, nature reared the outstanding sentinel of North America, to stand guard on the top of the world, and in its serenity we call it Mount McKinley. [Applause.] About its towering head there is never-ending sunshine in the summer, and in the long winter its unchanging garb of white reflects a sheen of glory no darkness can wholly dim. We saw it at eleven o'clock at night, one hundred and sixty miles away, a revelation of glory that can not be dwarfed by distance. Somehow Mount McKinley is distinctly typical of Alaska, so mighty, measureless and magnificent, resourceful and remote, with some great purpose, yet unrevealed, to challenge human genius.

Empire of Scenic Wonders

There can be none to dispute to Alaska preeminence as the empire of scenic wonders. One never wearies of them, but I confess that one engrossing picture so constantly follows another that it is difficult to duly appraise them. It brings upon one a new conception of the mightiness of creation, and proves nature's plan of blending might and magnificence. Since the water journey by the inside route is very little less wonderful and impressive than the vast domain of Alaska itself, it would seem that we need only to have our people understand its fascinations and compensations on the one hand, and develop hotel facilities for entertainment on the other, to make Alaska a favored destination in summer travel. There is no sea trip in the world to equal it. There is no lure of mountain, stream, valley and plain to surpass it anywhere. [Applause.] There is ample development of the transportation service essential ꓳ travel, and there is comfortable accommodation now, which demand will make luxurious whenever it is expressed.

Moreover, the traveller will find his contact with the finest, most hospitable people in all the world. The people of Alaska of today give no suggestion of the population which formed miracle settlements in the old gold-rush days. The ruggedness of the Territory is reflected in their vigorous health, and the freedom of the great out-of-doors is seen in their wholesomeness and their cordial hospitality, but otherwise Alaskan people are precisely the same as those back in the forty-eight States whence they came. There is no finer citizenship in all the United States, no more promising a childhood anywhere. Indeed, in this citizenship and in this vigorous childhood, both devoted to Alaska as the land of their homes, lies the solution of the Alaskan problem. In them is the assurance of Alaska's ultimate and adequate development. No magic wand made from Federal Treasury gold may be waved to effect the grand transformation. The processes of development and the establishment of permanent and ample civilization lie in a citizenship with homes in Alaska, not in investors who are seeking Alaskan wealth to enrich homes elsewhere. [Applause.]

Appropriate Setting for First Report

On one point of propriety regarding the official trip of inquiry to Alaska, there has been agreement everywhere. That is, that the first report on our observations and judgments might most appropriately be rendered here. Puget Sound has been from the beginning the gateway to the Territory. The cities of the sound, American and Canadian, stand as international sentinels over the continent's interest in the North Pacific. In that international role they will serve the ends of two imperial democracies, typifying the common aspiration for friendship, cooperation and peace, as media wherein to work out the problems of our Western World and its civilization.

Because of this international character, the noble waterways of Puget Sound must always be the base of a commerce as wide as the spaces of the Pacific. Here will be the seat of a group of cities with interests common as to every essential, and with an assured future in which their population, trade and influence will expand beyond all our imaginings. Standing thus, twin sentinels over the North World's gateway, their joint authority will be among the sure guarantees of peace between the great nations to which they give allegiance.

Our American cities of the sound represent the closest touch between the body of our mainland, and our newest commonwealth of the far Northwest. Theirs is the last farewell to the departing Alaskan, the first greeting to him on returning. They have known Alaska, have been interested to nurture and to develop it, have prospered by its prosperity, and shared in its misfortunes.

Alaska a Potential State

Let me say that I shall undertake no more than a preliminary report at this time. He who undertakes to forecast the future of Alaska and formulate a program for its realization, on the strength of such a fleeting glimpse as has been permitted to us, will be a wiser, and a far bolder, man than I. We have seen much, but it is only a little of the stupendous whole. We have learned something, but its first effect has been to impress us that nobody yet knows Alaska. We have been astounded at the immensity of resources and possibilities. We have wondered at the variety of its riches, at the luxuriance of its glorious vegetation, at times at the almost tropic heat of its night-long summer days. We have thrilled to its wonder, and felt the charm which holds to it the affections of all who once have breathed its air and lived its life. More than all, we have enormously strengthened our faith in the future of Alaska as the home of a great State in the American commonwealth. [Applause.] A brave, hardy, enterprising, uncomplaining people are building for Alaska's tomorrow precisely as our forefathers in the older communities built for our today, and I am sure that they will, in their time, bring another great State into the Union.

There has been disposition in many quarters to assume that Alaska has lately been experiencing a serious backset. This seems to be based on a loss of rather less than 15 per cent in population from 1910 to 1920, and on some curtailment of the Territory's production of wealth. Judgments adverse to Alaska will not be based on such adventitious conditions, save by the unintelligent or by those who would deliberately cry down the country's availability as a land of homes, in the hope of getting it turned over to wholesale exploitation on a scale that would ruin it for all the future. Against a program of ruinous exploitation we must, and we will, stand firmly. [Applause.] Our adopted program must be a development of Alaska for Alaskans. [Applause.] To plans for wise, well-rounded development into a permanent community of homes, families, schools and an illuminated social scheme, we must give all encouragement. Few similar areas in the world present such natural invitation to make a state of widely varied industries and permanent character.

A Parallel and a Contrast

Let me present a parallel—and a contrast. Fully three-fourths of the area of Alaska is south of the Arctic Circle. There are found most of its resources in forests, metals, minerals, fisheries, and agricultural lands. Within the temperate-zone Alaska has an area nearly three times that of Finland. Its climate is milder and more equable. Its forests far exceed those of Finland, and likewise its fisheries. Its coal deposits are among the world's greatest, while Finland has no coal. Its wealth in gold has scarcely been scratched; Finland has no gold. There is copper in Finland, but there is a thousand times more in Alaska.

Now come with me for a little journey of exploration along the sixtieth parallel of north latitude. We find that it boasts two of Europe's great cities, Christiania and Petrograd. Trace it westward, across the Atlantic, and we find that it also passes through Seward, Alaska. That means that most of the present wealth and population of Alaska are farther south than either of these two European capitals. Stockholm, "the Venice of the North," with its 400,000 people, is in the same latitude as Juneau, our Alaskan capital. Glasgow, one of the world's greatest workshops with over a million inhabitants, if translated in its own latitude to the Pacific Coast of America, would be the metropolis of Alaska! Copenhagen, with its 600,000 guardians of the Baltic portals, is in almost exactly the same latitude as Wrangell, Alaska!

Possibilities Exceed Those of Finland

This study of latitudes and locations seems likely to help us in projecting a picture of the future Alaska. Let us now follow our sixtieth parallel eastward on a return trip to Finland. We will be amazed to find that all of Finland lies north of this latitude. Helsingfors, the capital, in the extreme south of the country, would be an interior city of Alaska; yet it is one of the fine cities of Europe, with well nigh 200,000 inhabitants. From this capital northward extends Finland—far into the Arctic Circle. Is it possible that in such a latitude a great State can exist? Not only is it possible, but it is the fact, for Finland has the same population as Missouri, and is one of the most advanced countries of Europe. If the Finns owned Alaska, they would in three generations make it one of the foremost states of modern times. It is not possible that Americans, who in three centuries have builded the greatest country in the world, will fall into error about such an empire as Alaska. I cannot speak of comparative rainfall, but the climate in Alaska as to temperature, is no more severe than in these largely developed European sections; indeed,

346

it is not more severe on the coast than in the greater part of our northern mainland. The snow is more evident, but in most of the coast cities the extremes of cold are often no more trying than in Washington, D. C., and we actually saw three prostrations from heat during a public meeting in far away Fairbanks.

Why, then, are there so any misgivings about Alaska? Why the questionings as to its permanent usefulness for a homeland? True, it lost 15 per cent in population in the decade wherein the great war demoralized the entire world. But one province in Canala lost 80 per cent and another 60 per cent. Alaska is once more gaining in everything which testifies prosperity; but from the agricultural provinces of Western Canada comes report of a still continuing exodus. Some of our foremost States lost notably in population between 1910 and 1920. The other day I read that 77,500 colored and 29,900 white people had left Georgia farms. There are like reports from all over the South, and the farming sections of the West are not far behind. Australia and South Africa are offering direct money inducements to immigration, and failing to get it. If we would take down our immigration bars, there would be a tidal wave of emigration from all Central, Southern and Southeastern Europe. Evidently Alaska is not alone in feeling the effects of the war on her population. However, we have come, in these later days, to appraise population by quality rather than quantity, and Alaska will loom big in any quality test. [Applause.]

Gold Production Comparatively High

But, we are told, gold production in Alaska has fallen off discouragingly. Let us see about that. In 1915 Alaska produced $16,000,000 of gold, and in 1921, $8,000,000. That is a loss of one-half. But the United States as a whole fell off in gold takings by almost the same percentage: from $101,000,000 in 1915 to $50,000,000 in 1921. The world never needed new gold supplies more than now, to rehabilitate ruined financial systems. Yet from 1908 to 1920, Australasia lost over two-thirds of its gold production; and since the war began in Europe, the world, as a whole, has lost just about one-fourth. We all know perfectly well that this has been the result of world-wide economic conditions. Gold is worth just about one-half as much, in buying power, as before the war. The wonder is not that Alaska's gold production has fallen off, but that it has fallen relatively so little. There is every reason to believe that its gold crop will be restored, just as soon as the world resumes a normal economic balance.

Precisely the same story is told by the figures on copper. Since 1916 the Alaska copper product has fallen off 44 per cent, which looks grave; but when we turn to the other side, we find that the total product of the United States fell off 41.6 per cent: and still our country holds its place as chief copper source of the world. The shrink in copper prices was a discouraging fact, it is true; but Alaska's copper did not lose in price so much as Minnesota's wheat, or Iowa's corn. Look at it as you will, Alaska is simply going through the wash along with the remainder of the world. It will come out with the rest, and then, able to realize on its natural riches, will be second to no community in prosperity. [Applause.]

Importance of Fish Industry

It may be said now, as well as later, that there is no panacea for Alaska; largely because Alaska needs none, but also because Alaskan troubles flow from the same general causes which make troubles elsewhere. The world has burned up so much of its capital that there is not enough to go around. When the stocks of liquid capital are restored, Alaska will come in for a better share than ever before has fallen to its lot, simply because our country, if it clings to stable ways, will be the greatest capital Nation. [Applause.] It imposes no strain on credulity, to believe that when that time comes Alaska will go forward at such a rate that the ground recently lost will soon be more than regained.

The greatest Alaskan industry stands in an entirely different relation than either gold or copper. I refer to the fisheries, which in present wealth-producing potency far exceed the mines. In fact, the fisheries product is now in value more than double that of all metals and minerals. It is too great for the good of the Territory, for, if it shall continue without more general and effective regulation than is now imposed, it will presently exhaust the fish, and leave no basis for the industry.

Natural History of the Salmon

One must know the natural history of the salmon, the supremely important Alaskan fish, to appraise the fisheries problem. It is not necessary to enlighten Pacific Coast people, who understand the subject, but many others lack understanding. The salmon normally begins and ends his life in fresh water, but grows and lives in the ocean. A school of small fish, hatched in a particular stream, go out to sea, and are lost for a period of years. In that time they grow into the magnificent creatures we all know. Then they return, with seemingly unerring instinct, to the very stream in which they were hatched, to reproduce their kind, and then to die. On their way back they congregate in great schools, plowing their way up the stream of their nativity. Full grown and perfectly conditioned, they are now ripe for the enterprise of the fisherman and the canner. Their habit of traveling in schools is their undoing, for fishermen, with their nets and traps, literally scoop entire schools into their gear, and thus gradually exterminate the entire fish population of a particular small stream. Thereafter, that stream will be barren, unless a sufficient portion of the school is permitted to escape to spawn and perpetuate it. Too often this does not happen, as is proved by the history of both our Atlantic and Pacific Coast salmon fisheries, and the record of fisheries elsewhere which depend on fish with similar life habits. The progressive disappearance of salmon along our coasts from California northward is a story whose repetition ought to warn us to protect it in Alaska, before it is too late. The salmon pack not only represents nine-tenths of the output of Alaska's commercial fisheries, but is an important contribution to our National food supply.

It is vastly more easy to declare for protection and conservation of such a resource, than to formulate a practicable and equitable program. Fish hatcheries have been established to re-stock streams, but the results are still conjectural and controversial. Argument is advanced for the abolition of one method of fishing in one spot, the condemnation of another type in another, and so on, until there is a confusion of local controversies which no specific and exclusive prohibition will solve. Even in his cruder pursuit of the fish industry, the Indian seeks for himself the device which he would have denied to the canner.

Practical Means to Save Fisheries

There is encouragement in the almost unanimous agreement in Alaska that regulation must and shall be enforced, but we must apply a practical wisdom to the varied situations as the salvage of the industry demands. Against any kind of prohibition, it is urged that the immense investment in Alaska's fisheries and canneries would be greatly injured by such a reduction of the catch. To this it may well be replied that the canneries would better have their catches restricted by government regulation for a time, than exterminated in a few years through their own excesses. [Applause.] By the establishment of reserves along sections of the coast we have already accomplished much. More restriction is necessary, and urgent. The conservation must be effected. If Congress can not agree upon a program of helpful legislation, the reservations and their regulations will be further extended by executive order. [Applause.] There is an obligation to the native Alaskan Indian, which conscience demands us to fulfill. Moreover, the salvation of the industry is no blow at vested interests; it is a step toward protected investment and promoted public welfare. We have invited cooperation, and in the great majority of cases it has been cordially and intelligently extended. If there is defiance, it is better to destroy the defiant investor than to demolish a National resource, which needs only guarding against greed to remain a permanent asset of incalculable value. Moreover, we have ever to guard against the appeal

350

of the demagogue, whose play on popular prejudice for political advantage, has no place in the solution of the great problems of National conservation. [Great applause.]

Protecting the Forests

I must confess I journeyed to Alaska with the impression that our forest conservation was too drastic and that Alaskan protests would be heard on every side. Frankly, I had a wrong impression. Alaska favors no miserly hoarding, but her people, Alaskan people, find little to grieve about in the restrictive policies of the Federal government. There is not unanimity of opinion, but the vast majority is of one mind. The Alaskan people do not wish their natural wealth sacrificed in a vain attempt to defeat the laws of economics which are everlasting and unchanging. I fear the chief opponents of the forestry policy have never seen Alaska, and their concern for speedy Alaskan development is not inspired by Alaskan interests.

I have alluded to the threatened destruction of the fisheries, due to admitted lack of regulation and protection. We have begun on the safe plan with the forests, even though we may have erred in excessive restrictions. With the lesson of forest destruction painfully learned, with the Nation-wide call for reforestation throughout the States, which will require generations and vast painstaking, it has been sought to provide for the utilization of Alaskan forests and at the same time provide their perpetuation through reproduction. The application of the policy to the proposed paper and pulp industry in Alaska will make for ready understanding.

The cutting over of vast areas of forests in the States for pulpwood, wholly without regard to reproduction, and which left the land barren, is familiar to all of us. To prevent that disaster in Alaska, the government has adopted the program of surveying out forest units to lease for pulp and paper-making. A unit for a mill of 100 tons daily capacity must contain, first, a water-power site affording, at reasonable development cost, sufficient power for the mills; and, second, timber enough to keep the plant operating for 45 years. That period is selected because it is the one in which the lands first cut over will, with proper care, reproduce their timber. Thus, after the whole tract has been cut over in the forty-fifth year, the new crop of trees on the land cut over in the first year will be ready for another cutting. Instead of removing the mill and abandoning the land as barrens, and losing the larger part of the basic investment, the business becomes a self-perpetuating one. The allowance of timber, although made on the basis of 45 years, is really sufficient for 60 to 65 years.

Cost of Pulp Wood to Manufacturer

The lessee is given two years to prepare plans and organize for business; then two more years to install his plant. A deposit of $20,000 is required; and that, plus the annual payment for timber actually cut, is all the government asks. The basic price for timber at the present time is 30 cents per cord for hemlock, 60 cents for spruce. A cord of wood produces about three-fourths of a ton of paper; that is, the manufacturer pays about 53 cents for wood and water-power rights to make a ton of paper worth about $70. Can it be charged that three-fourths of one per cent for these two raw materials is so heavy a tax as to paralyze the industry? I reply that it is not, and that no such charge is seriously made by intelligent and sincere people.

But there is another proviso which the critics protest. We reserve the right, in each fifth year, to revise the cordage price. It may be raised, but not beyond the price which has been paid for other timber of like quality and in like circumstances during the preceding year. We adjust to the prevailing market. Does that seem unreasonable? If the same manufacturer had taken his contract on the Canadian crown lands, he would be subject to an advance of his price at any time, and without such a limitation; or, if he had bought outright the necessary timber lands to operate a mill for a long period, he would have had to carry a comparatively large initial investment. I venture, with some knowledge of conditions in various paper-making countries, to state that no better contract, indeed, none so good, can be secured in any of them.

But there is also protest that "the red tape of departmental regulation and interference" makes it impossible to enlist enterprise which the government in any wise supervises. At this point the answer is easy. This very type of contract is made by the government with the timbering interests in the National forests in both Alaska and the States, and the manufacturers have been working under it for more than a decade with entire satisfaction. The delay in entering Alaska is purely an economic one: the time is not yet ripe for fruition in Alaska. With a transportation problem which complaint never solves, with the present demand and price for paper, and with the present supply of materials nearer the market, conditions have not until now called for Alaskan development. The reasons are precisely the same that caused Ohio to be settled before Nebraska or Kansas. They will no more prevent Alaska's development than they prevented Nebraska's or that of Kansas.

On the Eve of Expansion

In substance, the same considerations explain the slower development of the lumber industry. But the time is at hand for forest-product development in Alaska. Lumber is being exported, largely across the Pacific; one pulp mill has been located, and negotiations for other pulp-and-paper contracts are at the point of closing. We are, in short, on the eve of an expansion which, if not rapid, will be sound and permanent. Frankly, I do not look for rapid development in Alaska. It could only be had at the cost of sacrificing a few immediately available resources, and then abandoning the rest. That we do not desire, and will not knowingly permit.

We have been told many times that Alaska contains some of the greatest coal measures known, and I found myself asking why coal is not mined, sold, and used. Why, especially, in view of recent high prices in the States? Why, particularly, is not Alaska coal developed for Alaskan use, and such Pacific markets as are needing it? Coal is being mined, sold, and used in Alaska. It is being mined, satisfactorily and profitably, under the terms of the complained-against coal-land leasing system. Perhaps, the contracts do need slight modification. If Alaska possesses all the coal which the extremists believe, all the agents of greed ever heard of would be insufficient to grab control. The truth is we do not know the actual extent of available deposits, because nature has tossed the coal strata in all directions, and large operations remain unproven. The navy experiment, where we ventured upon building a modern town before we proved the accessibility of the coal, was a notable fiasco, with a deserted new town as a monument to folly.

Must Await Large Capital

Alaska might well be supplying coal for her own industrial and domestic needs, but participation in a big way in the world fuel supply must await large investments of capital in development and aids in reduced transportation costs which present-day conditions are slow to promise. The government has its own railroad in Alaska, and we have our own ships which may be assigned to operate in connection with the railroad, but I can see no more reason for defying the immutable laws of economics in providing transportation at excessive government cost than there is to sacrifice Alaskan resources to the same unfruitful end. Time and the normal urging of economic conditions will bring Alaskan coal into its ultimate own.

There is petroleum in the Territory. A small production is already affording a profitable return, refined in Alaska for Alaskan consumption. There are developments now in process by some of the larger commercial oil interests, and there are dreams of measureless oil resources in the most northerly sections which are expressed in terms which sound more fabulous than real.

Here is a discovery and development demanding excessively large investment, and a venture on the part of capital which the ordinarily justifiable restrictions utterly forbid. It is no project of hundreds of thousands of capital; it is the quest of the tens of millions. Long distances to ports, the making of available ports if the deposits are proven, demand that grants of leases be adequate to fair return for the big adventure. No native, no individual enterprise is to be hoped for. To uncover the suspected riches there will need be the lure of adequate return. We shall have to do whatever is necessary to encourage leasing and development or hold the vast treasure uncovered and futile.

I have left agriculture to the last, in this consideration of Alaska's leading resources and possibilities. That is because of the conviction that an examination of the others was necessary to understand the agriculutral problem. Our policy toward agriculture must depend largely on the attitude we shall adopt toward these other resources. If we are to turn Alaska over to the exploiters, to have one after another of its resources wrenched out of it by the ruthless means of mass efficiency, we will never create or need a real agriculture there. If, for example, we shall go on decimating the fisheries year by year till they have been ruined; and if, then, because a rise in the price of paper shall have made it profitable, we shall turn over the forests for a like exploitation and a like destruction; if, in short, we are to loot Alaska as the possibility of profit arises now in one direction, now in another, then we shall never have a State or States in Alaska; we shall never have a community of established society and home-tied people.

Must Encourage Agriculture

If that is to be the Alaskan policy, we need not concern ourselves about agriculture. The adventurers and casual laborers, the masters of exploitation and agents of privilege, will be satisfied to live on canned vegetables and cold-storage meat during the brief periods of their temporary stays. The slow processes and modest returns of agriculture will not appeal to them.

355

But if, on the other hand we are to make a great, powerful, wealthy and permanent community of Alaska; if we are to place its star in our flag, to shine for a land of hope and homes and opportunity for the average man, then we must commit ourselves to a program of moderation, of control, of rounded and uniform development. We must encourage the present tendency to make homes; to bring wives and raise families; to regard life in lovely, wonderful Alaska as an end, not a means. We must, if this is our aim, give especial attention to encouraging a type of agriculture suited to climate and circumstances.

Stock Raising and Grain Growing

We will learn many lessons by studying the methods of older countries with like conditions. The fine societies of Norway, Sweden, Denmark, Finland, Iceland, will all be examples for us. They have shown us the way. They have learned to make the brief summer of well nigh endless days give them ample produce from the soil. They have adapted stock-raising and grain-growing to their especial needs, so that they are actually producers not only of their own requirements, but exporters of surplus foodstuffs.

In order that we may follow in their wake in Alaska, it is necessary that we give special attention to this subject. The Federal government has done something, but all too little, along this line. We may well be generous in encouragement to the technical, scientific and demonstration work of the agricultural agencies. We will need to help the Alaskan farmers to help themselves. The Alaskan farmers are making fine progress, indeed, as we know from our samplings of the wonderful fruits and vegetables and grains they have grown; but in this one direction I would urge government interest and aid on a scale which is much more liberal. [Applause.]

In another direction there is justification for a most liberal disposition, namely, that of road and trail building. Much of the Alaska which will in another generation be rich and productive, is yet unexplored, to say nothing of being mapped and equipped with highways. There should be an organization capable of the readiest response to demands for roads and trails. No discovery of riches should be kept from rational development for want of access to it. Alaska is so vast a region that merely to prospect it thoroughly is a matter of generations, with a far larger population than it now possesses. Roads constitute a prime need in every new country, and our long National experience in pushing our highways ahead of the onrolling wave of settlement, ought to convince us that the broadest liberality towards roads in Alaska will be certain to bring manifold returns.

Aside from all this, there is the necessity to provide feeders for the railroad which the government has built and is now operating. More than $56,000,000 have been spent on this 500 miles of railroad. It was not built in the expectation of immediate or even early profit; rather, it stands in much the same relation to Alaska that the Union Pacific Railroad did to our widely separated ocean fronts, east and west, when it was constructed far in advance of economic justification. It is a pledge, a testimony of faith, a declaration of firm confidence in the future of all Alaska. It is but a beginning, as the present road system is but a beginning; and I am willing to be charged with a purpose of something like prodigality in my wish to serve Alaska generously, and more, in this matter of road building.

Tribute to Railroad Builders

To the men who built the Alaska railroad must be paid a high tribute for the skill, wisdom and patience with which, through all discouragements and multiplied obstacles, they persevered to the finish. They have given us a splendid railroad; and as they have built it miraculously, it is our determination to retain it and to operate it wisely, with a view to the broadest public interest and the sincerest concern for the Territory's future. Unless I am greatly mistaken, this gorgeously scenic route of 500 miles, through a riotous excess of nature's beauties and wonders, is destined to attract travelers from all the world as soon as report of its attractions is commonly circulated. In that

357

connection, I think our policy, in cooperation with the hospitable people of Alaska should be to invite and encourage travelers to this new domain. We can afford to make provision ahead of their coming; for I pledge you they are certain to come, and in numbers we do not now dare predict. They will carry their descriptions to every quarter of the globe, and will send others to view and marvel. Thus will be accomplished the greatest work for building the Alaska of tomorrow. Some of the visitors will love it and remain; others will believe in it, and send of their means to develop it; none, having seen it, will ever again question its place among the wonderlands of earth.

Not a "Wild West" Region

"The problem of Alaska" has been dinned into our ears a great deal, at Washington. Somehow, in Alaska, one does not hear much of it, or feel acutely conscious of its existence. In Alaska, one gets the feeling that the sturdy, vigorous and highly intelligent people of the Territory, under the leadership of our old friend, "Manifest Destiny," will solve the problem. It is the same problem that Connecticut was to the Massachusetts Bay Colony: that the Genesee Valley was to the patrons of the Hudson; that its Western Reserve was to Connecticut. The people of Ohio attended to the little matter of the Western Reserve, as Alaska will in due time attend to its problems. It is the same riddle that was once the Northwest Territory; that later was *Louisiana*, then California and Oregon. Alaska is our one twentieth-century frontier, but it will not continue such to the half-way point of the century.

There has been much misunderstanding, no little misrepresentation, and some disposition to hysteria, at times, about Alaska. It long since passed beyond the wild-west, mining camp stage and is as sobered, settled and normal a community as will be found anywhere. But the rich and picturesque literature of its earlier epoch has carried a mistaken impression even down to our times. "Soapy" Smith and White Horse Rapids, the looting of Nome and the burden of the far northern winters, give color to

Alaska's picture in minds that have not been impressed by the present community of homes and schools and churches, of railroads and roads and motor cars, of law and order. The summer time of unending daylight and glorious luxuriance in all the realm of things that grow, is entitled to be placed alongside the picture of winters no more severe than many people in the Northern States have experienced.

It has not been possible within the limits of this address to deal with many Alaska phases. The seal fisheries have been placed under regulations which assure the permanence and progressively increasing value of their output. Here we have had a fine illustration of the preservation and expansion of a rich natural resource that without protection shortly would have been destroyed. The seal herds have more than quadrupled in a few years and their perpetuation is now assured. Application of like policies to the fur-bearing animals of the Alaskan mainland is producing like results, especially as regards the highly-prized varieties of the fox. These are now semi-domesticated on the innumerable small islands, and also on fox farms in the interior, and bred for their pelts. Alaska is well on the way to an enormous expansion in its fur product, and, what is far more significant, to making this product as permanent a source of wealth as are the cotton of the South and the corn of the Middle West.

Advancement of the Indians

It would be an unforgivable omission if I should not refer to the advancement of the Indian population of the Territory. I doubt if anywhere an aboriginal people has been so fast assimilated to civilization, industry, intelligence and education, as have the Alaska Indians. Doubtless this is in part because they have had the full advantage of the more enlightened policy adopted by the government toward the Indians in recent times; but it is also due to the fact that the Alaskan Indians are a fine, peace-loving, hard-working people. They are going to be a great asset to the country and a most useful element in its citizenship.

359

*L*argely because of their faithfulness and industry, the reindeer herds which from a small beginning a few years ago now number easily 300,000 animals, have become one of the valuable resources of the country. Alaska today has half as many reindeer as all *L*apland, and in a few years its herds will far outnumber those of that motherland of this ideal domestic beast of the northland.

No Broad Alaskan "Problem"

I am altogether an optimist on Alaska and its future. I do not believe Alaska can be forced, or that it should be. There is no need of government-managed, Federally-paid-for, hot-house development. There must be no reckless sacrificing of resources which ought to be maintained permanently, in order to turn them into immediate profits. There is no broad "problem of Alaska," despite the insistence of its existence. Alaska is all right, and is doing well. It has more wealth and more population, even now, than some of the States when they were admitted into the Union.

Where there is possibility of betterment in the Federal machinery of administration, improvements should and will be effected. But there is no need for sweeping reorganization. The Federal government's processes have not paralyzed, but rather have promoted the right sort of Alaskan development. The Territory needs their continuance; some of them, as already indicated, on a more generous scale than in the past. We have been paid back many times for every dollar spent on Alaska; and the dividends have only begun. We ought to shorten the line of communication as much as possible between Alaska and Washington, and to bring about the closest cooperation and understanding between the National agencies which operate there, and the splendidly efficient territorial government which under Governor Bone has deserved and holds the fullest confidence of the people. [Applause.]

Alaska is destined for ultimate Statehood. In a very few years we can well set off the panhandle and a large block of the connecting southeastern part, as a State. This region now contains easily 90 per cent of the white popula-

360

tion and of the developed resources. It would be the greatest single impetus we could possibly give to the right kind of development. As to the remainder of the Territory, I would leave the Alaskans of the future to decide.

My feeling is one of pride and faith in Alaska. With our rational helpfulness, with our justifiable generosity, her people will work out the destiny of the enchanting empire, and turn a wonderland of riches and incomparable fascination to added power and new glory to our great Republic. [Applause.]

NAVY THE RIGHT ARM OF OUR DIPLOMACY

Address at the Press Club, Seattle, Wash., July 27, 7 p. m.

Mr. President and Members of the Press Club, Ladies and Gentlemen:

I GLADLY accept this beautiful certificate of membership, and I even more gladly accept the association which is represented by it. After all, the finest compensations in life are the associations to which a man is entitled through the fruits of his endeavors. If he has done well and has been worthy, he will have the fellowship of his friends. If he has done measurably well in his profession, he will have the respect and the fellowship of the members of that profession. While I do not claim to have been a marvel as a newspaper maker, I do rejoice in my lifetime affiliation and participation in the building of "The Fourth Estate" of America. It has been a great, a fine experience, and if I were not afraid of the futility of such a suggestion, I should be tempted to promote the idea that newspaper training should be required of every candidate for the Presidency, because newspaper work, honestly done, brings men to understanding. I like to claim the distinction of being a believer in understanding as the one great agency for the solution of all our problems, National and international.

I have been enjoying the "Marion Star" as it has been prepared by your members and now appears before me. Curiously enough, it is precisely the size of the real "Marion Star" when I purchased it for $300. I disposed of a controlling interest in it the other day, just before leaving Washington, and received rather more than that; but when I recall having started on my newspaper mission with a $300 investment in a daily journal, I think I was not very far from a certain class of endeavors which have made Alaska famous. However, it was bully fun, and the harder it is to get out a paper the more fun it is when you yourself have to do the work.

Navy as a Peacemaker

I do not know whether I ought to do what I am about to do, but, in a way, I suspected that I would participate in this meeting, and, as I had one or two things that I wanted to say in Seattle, I deliberately elected to say them to the representatives of the press. It will take me but a few moments to express the thoughts I have in mind.

When our transport brought us to your great harbor this morning, we passed in review the Pacific fleet. Ours was an impressive view, and, I may add appropriately, a very reassuring one. Within the memory of men who are still in active service, our navy, once defiant of any power on the sea, had become so inconsequential that there was none to do it homage. We were as humble with our armed forces on the seas as we were pitiable with our merchant marine. Today we saw the Pacific fleet, indexing a naval power, not second or third, or eighth or tenth, but equal to the first in all the world. Moreover, it is covenanted, in international honor, that our navy shall retain that first rank, and any failure at retention must be charged to ourselves, because the world has deliberately acknowledged the righteousness of our first-rank position.

First Line of National Defense

I make this reference because the navy is our first line of defense. It is the armed shield-bearer upon which we depend to ward off war which we mean in our hearts never to provoke. Perhaps, the day may come—I would speed it all I could—when nations will employ no armed forces. Until such a day does come, we shall find our assurance in our navy of first rank.

We were building two years ago at a rate that would have placed our armed sea-power in excess of that of any other nation; but in conviction that armament cost and competition were leading to menacing National burdens, we invited an international conference to fix limitations. We asked equality with the first rank for ourselves, and were accorded it. Let us hope our Congress, with the cordial sanction of the American people, will continue that first rank. I believe our obligation to the world means the most exacting restriction of our maintenance within the maximum limitation fixed by the conference, and I believe our clear duty to ourselves is to maintain the equality provided in that maximum until a new baptism of international conscience shall prescribe joint action toward reduction or complete abolishment.

"Right Arm of the Department of State"

We owe it to ourselves to understand that the navy is rather more than a mere instrumentality of warfare. It is the right arm to the Department of State, seeing to the enforcement of its righteous pronouncements. It guards the security of American citizens wherever they may be the world over. One could not fully reverence his flag if he did not feel that its unfolding meant security for Americans wherever they seek its proper protection.

The navy has our colors afloat today almost everywhere on the seven seas; at Smyrna to officer proper restraint and relief; in Chinese waters to make for security; in all waters to urge tranquillity and maintained righteousness; and, with it all, to emphasize our confidence in ourselves and our sense of obligation at home.

You will have observed that I have assigned myself to report on the naval review, rather than talk shop on this happy occasion. Assuming that one most readily talks upon the subject which he most lives, I should have ventured some observations on the "Fourth Estate." Ignoring the little distinction which atttended, I find a pride in nearly forty years of participation in newspaper making, and a reflective survey persuades me that the greatest satisfaction has come of a policy designed always to boost, and rarely to knock.

Compliments Alaskan Publishers

Those of us who think we know much about newspaper making may learn some very simple fundamentals by going to Alaska. I found myself involuntarily doffing my hat to the editor and publisher who succeeds in maintaining a daily issue in a town of from eight to twelve hundred people, where the circulation maximum cannot exceed from two to three hundred copies. I refrain from an attempted analysis of the relation of the value of advertising to its cost, but the community value of the publication will remain unchallenged.

There is in the Alaskan press a limited reflex of the big news of the world, with a larger relative regard for pugilism than world politics, but human interest is fairly satisfied with the tabloid story of world events. Doubtless the Alaskan community is quite as well nourished mentally with its restricted news diet as are some of us who find our nauseated way, if we read our newspapers fully, through elaborated and expatiated stories of crime and scandal, and wander through a haze of speculative politics, for which, I fear, there is frequently but little foundation.

The big asset in the successful Alaskan sheet is the home news, and, when the final analysis of the making of a newspaper is written, here is the secret of most newspaper successes. Give me a newspaper which is a true reflex of the community it serves, and I know I am reading an index to dependable public opinion as well as a potent agent in molding that opinion.

Impressed by Frankness

An impressive feature of the Alaskan press was its manifest honesty, ofttimes revealing an appealing frankness. An honest and an intelligent press, which necessitates a highly purposed press, affords a limitless opportunity for community service and the loftiest employment in life. It may preach to the larger congregation; it has every opportunity to commend and defend the law; it is the effective mouthpiece of our politics; it is the teacher which knows no vacation; it is the recording agent of human accomplishment, whose simple story is the ever-continuing inspiration to loftier achievement. Let those of us who find pride in association with the making of the American press the best press in the world, resolve upon a full appraisal of our responsibilities, and see that Conscience is maintained as editor-in-chief, and that Accomplishment writes the big "beats" which are ever giving the exhilarating thrill to the daily grind. [Applause.]

SCRUPULOUS RESPECT FOR RIGHTS OF FRIENDLY
NATIONS, AMERICA'S AIM; WORLD COURT
UNIVERSAL PEACE STEP

Address on Our Foreign Relations, Prepared for Delivery at
San Francisco, July 31; Undelivered Because of the
President's Illness, but Released for and Printed
in Morning Papers of August 1

My Fellow Countrymen:

SOMETHING in your Golden Gateway has impelled me
to speak to you of the foreign relations of our
Republic. Happily it is not a message of anxiety, but
one of satisfaction and rejoicing.

It is easy to share the feelings of home concern of
those who think first of all of our domestic fortunes; but
there can be no divorcement, in these modern days, of
home affairs and foreign relationships. Human progress
has established a relationship little short of the community
among nations, and there is and can be no great people
in a position of permanent aloofness.

The urging of commerce, quite apart from human fellowship, is fashioning intimate relationships each succeed-

NOTE: This address was not delivered by President Harding, who, at the time,
was lying ill at his hotel in San Francisco. Its publication is explained by the
following statement by George B. Christian, Jr., Secretary to the President:

"July 31, 1923.

"The President before leaving Washington and during his journey to Alaska
prepared speeches dealing with fundamental questions of policy and performance on
the part of his administration. Most of these have been delivered. One was prepared
to be delivered at San Francisco, Tuesday, July 31, and advance copies of this, like the
others, were furnished the press, awaiting release upon delivery.

"The San Francisco speech was to deal with our foreign relations, and was a
carefully considered and carefully prepared document. But for his illness the
President would have delivered the speech according to schedule; but this being
prevented he now feels that it should go to the public through the medium of the
press and for the information and consideration of the people. Therefore he has
directed that the speech be 'released,' and it is hereby released for morning papers
of August 1."

ing day. This pressure is not foreign; it is a reflex of American commercial aspirations. The Department of Commerce, newly vitalized under the administration of your fellow townsman, alone frequently receives between three and four thousand inquiries a day for information relative to foreign trade. Amid such hungering of Americans for trade relations abroad, the cordiality of our foreign relations is little less important than our tranquillity and confidence at home.

Heritage of Chaos and Discord

When the present National administration came into responsibility world affairs were in a complicated and very difficult posture. Our foreign relations presented many novel, delicate, and far-reaching problems, and their fortunate solution is no less significant than our domestic rehabilitation. We have strengthened our friendly relationships and have done much to promote peace in the world. We encountered a world condition in which peace had been covenanted, but the compact had been rejected by the United States Senate. This action left us in a technical state of war with the Central Powers of Europe, and aloof from the colossal adjustments following the World War. Many just and very necessary rights were accorded to us under the Treaty of Versailles, but these were all threatened by uncertainty and doubt. Many parts of Europe were in a pitiable destitution; small wars persisted, and widespread revolutions upset the orderly processes of civilization; so that there was a chaos of peace little less menacing than the tumult of World War.

For a little while there had been a world remorse, a penitence promising a new order, but the temporary spirit of international dedication to a common cause soon gave way to revived concern for particular National interests. The new and only partially reestablished peace was threatened and the urgent processes of reconstruction were discouragingly retarded. Our own prestige, once reaching outstanding eminence in 1919, had been greatly impaired, and we faced a situation offering little promise of satisfactory solution.

Four Main Tasks Accomplished

With faith in our own sincerity of purpose, with the consciousness of utter unselfishness, the administration promptly undertook the accomplishment of four main tasks:

First, the reestablishment of peace with the Central Powers and the orderly settlement of those important after-problems of the war which directly involved the United States;

Second, the protection and promotion, amid the chaos of conflicting National interests, of the just rights of the United States and the legitimate interests of American citizens;

Third, the creation of an international situation, so far as the United States might contribute thereto, which would give the best assurances of peace for the future; and

Fourth, the pursuit of the traditional American policy of friendly cooperation with our sister republics of the Western Hemisphere.

The eminent success and the far-reaching achievements of this program must have their ultimate appraisal by American public opinion, but I submit them with unrestrained pride, and sincere tribute to the historic services of a great Secretary of State.

The League of Nations

Few people have stopped to measure the outstanding task of reestablishing peace. The peace negotiated by my distinguished predecessor, though he was impelled by lofty purpose, had evoked a bitter and undying controversy. It was conclusive to those who had studied the public verdict that our people would never consent to assume any obligations, moral or legal, which would fetter their cherished freedom of action in unknown contingencies. If our people are ever to decide upon war, they will choose to decide according to our own National conscience at the time and in the constitutional manner without advance commitment, or the advice or consent of any other power. To revive the old controversy in any phase would have been disastrous. We do not challenge the utility of the League of Nations to others; we wish it more power in every righteous exercise of its functions; but it is clearly not for us as presented in the Versailles covenant. To have fought over again that controversy would have postponed our resumption of peaceful relations, essential to our commerce, and impaired our own tranquillity. So we took the only way, and the direct way, to peace, and we established it. We avoided controversy and recorded accomplishment. Negotiations were begun with the Central Powers, and those negotiations culminated in treaties which established peace with those countries on an equitable basis, and, at the same time, preserved for the United States the rights embodied in the Paris treaties which we had acquired through participation in the common victory. These treaties were promptly ratified, and have been in full force since November, 1921.

Our Claims Against Germany

Then, quickly followed a treaty with Germany for the determination by a Mixed Commission of the amount of American claims against Germany. The commission was promptly appointed, and the extraordinary tribute, unparalleled in international relationships, was paid to the American sense of justice by the suggestion on the part of Germany that the United States should appoint an American umpire. History has yet to record another like expression of trust by one nation in the fairness of another. In recognition of this signal tribute by the vanquished to a victor, I asked Justice Day to retire from the Supreme Bench to serve in that capacity. I know you share my sorrow that ill-health forced his retirement from this great service, and that only a little later his retirement was followed by his death.

A stupendous problem, no less important and no less difficult was the settlement of the debts owed to the United States by its late associates in the World War. This involved the funding and eventual repayment to the American taxpayers of a total sum in excess of ten billion dollars.

A freely expressed sentiment among our own people had argued for cancellation, and it was more than seized upon and urged abroad; but we believed in the sanctity of contract and that world stability which is founded on kept obligations. Settlement may enforce the hardships and details and economies which hinder the easy way to restoration, but it maintains the foundations of financial honor which must be everlasting.

The Foreign Debt Commission

Accordingly, Congress created the World War Foreign Debt Commission, and notice was sent to the debtor nations that this country was ready to negotiate an equitable adjustment. In response to this invitation the British government sent a commission to Washington; a settlement with Great Britain was soon effected and subsequently approved by Congress and by the British government. Under this settlement the British government has undertaken the discharge of an obligation of more than four and a half billion dollars, and thereby put a fresh stamp of approval on the sacredness of international obligations. When that settlement was announced there was a new assurance of stability throughout the world. More, here was the example of two great powers dealing with a sum of indebtedness unparalleled in international history, and promptly reaching a settlement without the exactions of greed on the one hand or appeal to sentimental modification on the other, thus at once committing the two peoples to the validity of international contract.

An adjustment on a like basis has been reached with the government of Finland, which awaits only the approval of Congress to become effective. Negotiations are now in progress with the government of Czecho-Slovakia; and Jugo-Slavia has given notice of its intention to send within the near future a mission to Washington for the same purpose. The advocacy of cancellation is drowned out by the advancing hosts of settlement and maintained integrity,

370

and the United States will keep faith with its own people who loaned, as they fought, with faith in the Republic.

Seemingly a trivial thing in itself, it was nevertheless a notable achievement to effect a successful settlement of the costs incurred for the maintenance of our army on the Rhine. Without adequate understanding, our own people were urging the withdrawal of our troops long before it was finally ordered, but nearly all of Europe, and Germany in particular, meanwhile were asking us to stay. There was a feeling that our military forces were immensely helpful in maintaining peace and order. We know that our military forces left behind them a fine and lasting impression of courtesy and consideration. But we were aloof from the Reparations Commission, and the payment for our army of occupation was ignored in the reparation payments made by Germany. We had received nothing up to January, 1923, though our costs had accumulated to an amount of more than $250,000,000. After discouraging delays, a definite plan for the payment of this large sum was negotiated at Paris, and the settlement was sanctioned late in May of this year. There is little about it all to make sentimental appeal, but it is a gratifying record of sane business and the seemly assertion of our just rights.

"Experiment of Mandates"

Few post-war adjustments have embodied greater potentiality of harm or exacted more careful vigilance in behalf of American interests than the new experiment of mandates, to which the United States ceased to be a direct party upon rejection of the Treaty of Versailles. We denied for ourselves any acquircment of territory, but that denial surrendered no rights of equality in industry and commerce which accrued to us along with the allied victors in the war. Under the system of mandates an effective sovereignty over former German overseas possessions was transferred to certain of the allied powers, and it was necessary for us to obtain definite assurances from those powers that our citizens should not suffer discrimination in territories which came into their possession in the bestowal of the fruits of victory. We had sought none of those fruits, but we had yielded none of our rights. So negotiations to this end were promptly begun.

Settlement of Yap Controversy

The island of Yap had special advantages as a cable center, and an acute difference developed concerning its control. A settlement satisfactory to all concerned was nevertheless reached with the mandatory power, Japan, and the treaty which was concluded and sanctioned fully secures all American rights with respect to all those Pacific islands north of the equator over which Japan exercises its mandate.

The contention that the United States is rightfully entitled to fair opportunity in the mandated regions held by other powers had been successfully presented to the governments of France and Belgium, and satisfactory treaties have been signed with those powers relating to the territories in Africa under their control. Negotiations are now in progress with Great Britain relating to the British mandated territories in Africa, and we look with confidence to a satisfactory treaty. Since I am only paying tribute to the Department of State in so saying, I may say becomingly that these adjustments of mandate difficulties constitute an outstanding achievement of inestimable importance and benefit to our America.

The outstanding historical, monumental achievement is the Washington Conference on the *Limitation* of Armament. Only a few days ago the government of France gave the ratification which makes unanimous the approval of the nations concerned, and confirms the dawn of a new era in international cooperation for world peace.

Desire for Future Peace

From the day the present administration assumed responsibility it had given devout thought to the means of creating an international situation, so far as the United States might contribute to it, which would give assurance of future peace. We craved less of armament, and we hated war. We felt sure we could find a rift in the clouds

372

if we could but have international understanding. We felt sure that if sponsors for governments could only face each other at the conference table and voice the conscience of a penitent world, we could divert the genius and the resources of men from the agencies of destruction and sorrow to the ways of construction and human happiness.

The world was needing some new assurance. The old British-Japanese military alliance was about to be extended, at a time when alliances were less needed, and common consecration at the altar of peace was a pressing world necessity. There was anxiety about the Pacific area. No one knew why, but the prophets of evil were prolific in forebodings. It is a pity we have the mischief-makers who are ever adding to the burdens of distrust, but we do have them, and in 1921 they were busy in our land, and in the East, exciting suspicion and ill-feeling. War might easily have been precipitated; but responsible government heads knew that the great undercurrent of human feelings was flowing toward peace, and that a frank discussion would reveal it. The world was weary of war burdens and armament cost, and an honest and authoritative confession would reveal that fact, so that men might act in concert to relieve the situation and make for widespread amity.

Triumph in Two Directions

The Limitation of Armament Conference was significantly triumphant in two accomplishments: It relieved and limited the burdens, and found a way to remove the causes of misunderstanding which lead to war. In the gloom and grief of the world, the conference table lighted the torch of understanding and pointed the simplest way to peace. The conference proved one of the greatest achievements in the history of international relations. Its four great treaties, now ratified, related to the limitation of naval armament, to the restricted use of submarines and poison gases, to principles and policies restoring the integrity of China, and to the regulation of Chinese customs tariffs.

Important resolutions were adopted, providing a commission of jurists to consider amendments to the laws of war, made necessary by new agencies of warfare; for a board of reference for Far Eastern questions; for international unity of action respecting various matters affecting China, such as extra-territoriality, foreign postal agencies, foreign armed forces, unification of railways, reduction of Chinese military forces, publicity for existing commitments, and the Chinese Eastern Railway. Though not a part of the conference, the Shantung treaty between China and Japan grew out of it, accomplishing for China a restoration in which Versailles had failed, and China today needs only her self-assertion to find a restored place among the nations, with her own destiny impelling and wholly in her own hands.

The Four=Power Treaty

Another achievement, not technically a part of the work of the conference as such, but which was negotiated while the conference was in session, and which was most important, was the four-power treaty between the United States, the British Empire, France and Japan, relating to their insular possessions and insular dominions in the Pacific Ocean. This treaty provided for the termination of the Anglo-Japanese Alliance, and in the pledge of respected rights it recorded a new assurance of peace. Not the semblance of war's foreboding in the Pacific remained when this covenant of good faith was signed.

Probably the most important results of this historically important conference are those which are unwritten and imponderable. I refer to the revelations of sentiment and purpose, to the manifestation of good will and the evident thirst for better understanding. New friendships were assured, new confidence revealed. Where there is friendship and confidence, treaties to maintain peace are of lesser importance. The friendly relationship and the soul of National honor are infinitely more important to peace than a written form of their expression.

If you would measure the work of the conference, contrast the present opinion as to peace in the East with the view which was widely entertained and frequently expressed before the conference was held. The mists, which had the forebodings of war clouds, have been dispelled; there is confidence today; fears have been allayed; and out of understanding has come a new feeling of friendship and respect. Quite apart from specific engagements, it was a distinct achievement to produce a new state of mind, a reign of good will, and with it new assurances with respect to our relations in the Far East. More, there has been revealed to the world the way of peace, and if humanity and its governments will only accept the indicated way, that which has been a world lament may be turned to a universal pæan of rejoicing.

Our Relations With Mexico

The preservation of the just rights of the United States and its citizens has been maintained as the basis of an American policy in respect to two very difficult situations, one growing out of revolution attending the World War, the other antedating the war itself. I refer first to the situation in Mexico. Our feeling toward the Mexican people is one of entire and very cordial friendliness, and we have deeply regretted the necessity for the continued suspension of diplomatic relations. We have no hatred toward Mexico, no selfish ends to serve at her expense. We have no promptings other than those of a neighborly friendship. We have no desire to interfere in the internal concerns of Mexico. We respect in the Mexican people the same rights of self-determination which we exact for ourselves. It is not for us to suggest what laws she shall have relating to the future, for we willingly acclaim Mexico as the judge of her own domestic policy. We do, however, maintain one clear principle which lies at the foundation of all international intercourse.

When a nation has invited intercourse with other nations and has enacted laws under which investments have been legally made, contracts entered into and property rights acquired by citizens of other jurisdictions, it is an essential condition of international intercourse that lawful obligations shall be met, and that there shall be no resort to confiscation and repudiation. We are not insistent on the form of any particular assurance against confiscation, but we do desire the substance of such protection. We would give as freely as we ask. Such assurance is in the interest of permanent friendly relations. We have sought to have this wholly defensible attitude understood by our Mexican neighbors ever since the present administration came into power. I am happy to say that we now have our commissioners in conference at Mexico City, and it is earnestly hoped that there may be definite and favorable results from their exchange of views with the Mexican commissioners. We crave not only friendly diplomatic relationship, but we wish it to be founded upon an understanding which will guarantee its permanence. Upon such an understanding we may jointly promote the most neighborly friendships which shall mutually advantage the two republics.

Problem of Russian Recognition

The problem of Russian recognition is complicated by a fundamental difficulty, because of a government regime there whose very existence is predicated upon a policy of confiscation and repudiation. No one seriously questions the continuation of the present government, or wishes to direct the expression of Russian preference. There is an unfailing friendship in the United States for the people of Russia. The deplorable conditions in Russia have deeply touched the sympathies of the American people, and we have sought to give evidence of friendship rather than dictate the course of its government. I gladly recommended an appropriation of $20,000,000 by Congress for the relief of her famine-stricken people, and, all told, America's friendly interest has been expressed in a $66,-000,000 relief expenditure, handled, in the main, by the Secretary of Commerce, in distributing food and combating disease. That this administration, supported by the strength and generosity of the American people, has saved the lives of ten millions of men, women and children in Russia, at the very door of death from famine and pestilence, is the complete answer to every charge of our ill will toward the Russian people.

It has been urged that we ought to grant political recognition to the present Russian regime because the destitution of the Russian people would thereby be put in the way of alleviation, and that this humane appeal is so urgent that all other considerations should be put aside. But the fact remains that the establishment of a basis of permanent improvement in Russia lies solely within the power of those who govern the destinies of that country, and political recognition prior to correcting fundamental error tends only to perpetuate the ills from which the Russian people are suffering. International good faith forbids any sort of sanction of the Bolshevist policy. The property of American citizens in Russia, honestly acquired under the laws then existing, has been taken without the color of compensation, without process of law, by the mere emission of countless decrees. Such a policy challenges the very groundwork of righteous intercourse among peoples, and rends the bases of good faith everywhere in the world.

A Supreme Tragedy and World Warning

If the fundamentals of our boasted civilization are based on twenty centuries of maintained error, if the Russian conception of the social fabric is the true revelation, tardily conceived after forty centuries of evolution and development, the truth will ultimately assert itself in the great experiment. I can see Russia only as the supreme tragedy, and a world warning, the dangers of which we must avoid if our heritage is to be preserved. If the revolutionary order is the way to higher attainment and greater human happiness, Russia will command our ultimate sanction. Meanwhile, I prefer to safeguard our interests and hold unsullied the seemingly proven principles under which human rights and property rights are blended in the supreme inspiration to human endeavor. If there are no property rights, there is little, if any, foundation for National rights, which we are ever being called upon to safeguard. The whole fabric of international commerce and righteous international relationship will fail if any great nation like ours shall abandon the underlying principles relating to sanctity of contract and the honor involved in respected rights.

American Influence at Lausanne

We were never technically at war with Turkey, and had no part in the Greek-Angora conflict which threatened to set the Near East aflame. But the rights of our Nationals and our Nation, long recognized by accepted civilization, were involved in the settlement, and so we had our representatives at Lausanne, not only to protect those rights, but to serve humanitarian interests and promote the cause of peace. Cynical critics sneered at our "unofficial" representatives, but the powers of the Old World thought well enough of them to tender to the United States the chairmanship of the conference. It could not be accepted, for manifest reasons, but we did not fail to voice American sentiment on behalf of Christian minorities, and we did assist in reaching a settlement calculated to assure their future protection.

I firmly believe that the American influence at Lausanne played a becoming part, and an influential part, in making for peace, when all the world stood in apprehension of an armed conflagration, the horrors of which no one ventured to predict. Unselfishness and understanding argued for the same grant to others which we would demand for ourselves, and that attitude was never successfully challenged. We supplemented statecraft with a humanitarian work and a necessary and highly appealing relief work which planted the seeds of good will in the Near East, to blossom in the years to come, and we left there the appeal of good will and mutual understanding to argue for peace for all the future so long as memory shall abide.

An achievement of a different kind in the humanitarian field has just been accomplished through the participation of American representatives in a conference at

Geneva dealing with the international traffic in opium and other narcotics. A policy of aloofness would have forbidden our presence there, but human helpfulness impelled attendance. The American representatives recorded a distinct accomplishment in obtaining the substantial acceptance of the proposals which they put forward, looking to the effective restriction of the opium traffic to the minimum required for medicinal and scientific purposes.

America's Influence Made Manifest

Out of the American example, out of confidence in American unselfishness has come a succession of incidents which reveal our influence and effective good will in the economic and political fields, as well as those of humanity. Persia gave proof of her confidence in American impartiality and integrity by inviting the nomination of an American expert for the post of administrator general of her finances. Colombia requested, and is receiving, the services of American financial experts in the study of her financial conditions; a cordial friendship with Colombia has been fully reestablished, and her people are welcoming the agents of American development and facilitating their activities.

Brazil invited an American naval commission to participate in the development of her befitting naval defense, and such a commission was named—a fine testimonial of confidence, and a deserved tribute to our navy.

Nothing can surpass the success of the maintenance and furtherance of our traditional policy of friendship and utterly unselfish helpfulness to our sister republics in the Western Hemisphere. We have given new proof of our cherishment for their independence, our desire for their peace, our wish for their unimpaired integrity and their increasing prosperity. It can not be unseemly to say that the proof of their confidence and the assurances of their reciprocated friendship are matters of especial gratification. If there was once a suspicion of intended domination or dictation, when only the most generous friendship was intended, it has been entirely dissipated.

When we found Panama and Costa Rica about to engage in war, we pointed the just way to peace, the very route we ourselves would have taken, indeed have taken. We merely asked them to join in holding sacred an agreement to accept an arbitral award. The ways of peace are in kept agreements.

We may gratefully contemplate new progress in Cuba toward stability and restored prosperity. Cuba was desperately hit by the deflation which followed in the wake of war, but out of the helpful advice which was inspired by true friendship and extended because of our peculiar relationship, Cuba is now well on the road to economic recovery and healthful restoration.

Small Nations Trust America

Where resentment once abided because of the presence of our military forces in the Dominican Republic, there are today universal expressions of approval, and the processes of setting up a constitutional government have made gratifying progress. The provisional government is in actual operation; the constitution for a permanent government will soon be voted upon, and it is expected that our troops may be withdrawn within the current year. Today there is complete trust in the unselfish aims of our government, and a new record of high purpose will soon be completed.

Progress in Haiti is giving promise of an almost unhoped for success. Peace and order have been established, and safety of life and property exists for the first time in that troubled republic. A new day is dawning in Haiti, and the foundations of security are being safely laid. Public order has been so improved in the interior that our marines have been practically withdrawn therefrom, and the day is in prospect when our complete withdrawal from the island may be contemplated. Those who little understood saw the United States embarked on a program of domination and exploitation, but the written history will recite another instance of a great Republic's insistence on order and justice, with a righteous peace attending.

Friendly Advice Bearing Fruit

The friendly offices of this Republic in furthering the settlement of a dispute, a generation old, between Chile and Peru have been attended by a most gratifying promise of success. With avowed confidence in our sense of justice, the governments of Chile and Peru have agreed to submit to arbitral settlement the long-standing Tacna-Arica controversy. Through our friendly advices and a resulting conference in Washington, these republics have agreed upon a plan of peaceful settlement of the dispute which has divided them and troubled their relations for more than thirty years. The gratifying proof of confidence in the United States lies in their acceptance of our decision in the capacity of arbitrator. This is another tribute to the way of peace, revealed in understanding.

Added proof of our deep concern for Central American stabilization was revealed in the Washington conference of the five republics—Costa Rica, Gautemala, Honduras, Nicaragua and Salvador—assembled last December. New understandings were reached; the treaties of 1907 were made effective; measures were promoted to limit armament; plans were worked out for the peaceful settlement of disputes; a general treaty of peace and amity was signed, and the establishment of an international Central American Tribunal was effected. Here was written a new and valid assurance of peaceful relations among the republics of Central America, new proof that this Republic favors conditions conducive to the best interests of the whole of the Western Hemisphere, more evidence that friendship and understanding open the avenues to peaceful progress.

Conference at Santiago

In like spirit, in the same assurance that we always may confidently look into the faces of the spokesmen of all governments everywhere, our delegates attended the

381

Fifth International Conference of American States held at Santiago, Chile. It was an occasion of most complete understanding between the United States and other participating governments. The results, tangible and intangible, are sure to facilitate commercial and other intercourse in the Western Hemisphere. While our diplomacy is not commercially inspired, we do recognize the ties of trade and the fostering of exchanges in friendly relationship. When we give precisely as we ask, we are entrenched in righteous relationship.

Frankly, trade impelled and lines of understanding urged the readjustment relating to the cable companies in various Central and South American countries, and today the way is open for the laying of one or more cables directly down the east coast of South America, which will bring these countries into closer communication with us, and facilitate commerce and the exchange of news—always the ways of understanding.

Symbol of Our World Position

Our relations in the Western World truly symbolize our position in the whole world; they reveal our friendly and peaceful intent and purpose. We have only the most genuine friendship for all. We seek nothing which belongs to another. We do not strive for aloofness; but we do not make an un-American commitment. We have shunned no obligations which duty has called us to share with others. We maintain a scrupulous respect for the rights of friendly nations in the adjustment of their own affairs not directly affecting the United States, and we have avoided their entanglements. With firmness we have asserted American rights, and have insisted upon the open door of opportunity, where Americans may enter on righteous and lawful ways, precisely as do other nationals, everywhere under the shining sun.

With the political controversies of other countries, which have often strained their friendly relations, we have had no part. In adherence to our conception of justice, with becoming dignity, we have maintained our rights; we have yielded willingly to the rights of others, and we dwell in cherished and unthreatened peace.

World Court Urged as Solemn Duty

I have thus far made no allusion to the hungering of humanity for new assurances that the world may be equally blessed. Peace ought to be the supreme blessing to all mankind. Armed warfare is abhorrent to the ideal civilization. In this enlightened day nations ought no more need resort to force in the settlement of their disputes or differences than do men. Out of this conviction, out of my belief in a penitent world craving for agencies of peace, out of the inevitable Presidential contact with the World War's havoc and devastation and the measureless sorrow which attended and has followed, I would be insensible to duty and violate all the sentiments of my heart and all my convictions if I failed to urge American support of the Permanent Court of International Justice.

I do not know that such a court will be unfailing in the avoidance of war, but I know it is a step in the right direction, and will prove an advance toward international peace for which the reflective conscience of mankind is calling.

Why should there not be a court of this character with the most cordial American support? We originated the modern suggestion of such a tribunal, and have been advocating it for years. We have proclaimed in behalf of its establishment again and again. Its origin is no hindrance, because its inspiration, growing out of conditions which we ourselves were unable to contrive, need be no less noble than our own. Our concern is not with the beginning; our interest is in the end to be attained.

Reign of Law Versus Force

There manifestly are controversies between nations, as there are between the men who constitute them, which should be decided by a court. There are controversies calling for the examination of facts and the application of the principles of law. There are international contracts, better known as treaties, now more numerous than ever, to be interpreted. I should be the last man in the United States to surrender an essential National right, or to yield the right to exercise self-determination. But there is a distinction between questions of a legal nature and questions of policy or of National honor, and there has emerged from the discussions of jurists an agreement defining justiciable disputes as those which relate to the interpretation of a treaty, to any question of international law, to the existence of facts which would constitute a breach of an international obligation, or to the reparation to be made for such a breach. A nation which believes in the reign of law, preferable to the rule of force, must subscribe to an agency for the law's just construction.

Plain and Simple Path of Progress

How else may controversies between nations be determined? Is a controversy to be left a festering sore? If it is, then there is ever increasing danger that the ultimate alternative to peaceful settlement will be the arbitrament of arms. The logical way to prevent war is to dispose of the causes of war, and the honest desire for peace must be supported by the institutions of peace. If controversies over legal rights are to be determined peacefully, there must be a tribunal to determine them. I most devoutly wish the United States to do its full part, to voice a National conscience toward making secure the provision and strengthening the agencies for the peaceful settlement of international disputes. Our own interests require the judgment of such a tribunal of international justice, and the interests of world peace demand it.

Because such a court is not able to deal with every sort of controversy, but only with those appropriate for a court to decide, is no more reason for dispensing with it than that we should cease hating war because there is no effective way to outlaw it. I would instantly subscribe to any proposal to outlaw war if someone would point to the effective way to accomplish it.

There is no immediate access to the perfected world conditions. No demand for the millennium will prevent war.

If the plain and very simple path of progress in dealing with those controversies which all countries recognize to be susceptible of settlement through judicial tribunals is not to be followed, then hope lies dead and no progress is possible.

My own sincerity of purpose has been questioned because I do not insist that we shall accept the existing World Court precisely as provided. Personally, I should vastly prefer the policy of submitting all controversies in which we are concerned to the court as it sits today, as against any other agency of settlement yet devised. As President, speaking for the United States, I am more interested in adherence to such a tribunal in the best form attainable, than I am concerned about the triumph of Presidential insistence. The big thing is the firm establishment of the court and our cordial adherence thereto. All else is mere detail. No matter what the critics may say, we have the obligation of duly recognizing constituted authority, and I had rather have the Senate grant its support and have the United States wholeheartedly favor the permanent court than prolong a controversy and defeat the main purpose. I respect the Senate precisely as I would have it respect the Presidency, and I can appraise opposition which is conscientiously inspired. In the grant of the same consideration which I would be justified in asking, I cherish the belief that fear may be allayed and hope encouraged.

Forward Step Our First Aspiration

It is the forward step to which we must first aspire. Our hopeful aspiration is to contribute whatever we can toward the elimination of the causes of war. My recital of two years of work in furthering our friendly foreign relations has had for its object the emphasis of that aspiration and the fruits of practicable application. Future accomplishment must be founded upon the combination of considered and practicable steps, and must have the support of an undivided American good will. The real hope of permanent and effective accomplishment depends upon freedom from internal dissension and international dissension.

The forward steps already taken ought to be followed by many others in our generation, but the way to a permanent world peace is a long and difficult one. Those who alleged that the suggested ways or the accepted programs of today are final are denying the ever impelling impulse to human progress. The surpassing accomplishments are progressively made, and I know that the soul of America will light the way to a gratifying victory. When that glad day shall come—I hope it may be soon—when the sincerity of our own aspirations and the sincerity of the world's convictions bring us to a united endeavor, we shall forget that there were necessary compromises which hindered but did not obstruct, and all may rejoice in the assurances which are those of peace, with all its blessings.

RECLAMATION SPEECH NEVER COMPLETED

(This portion of an uncompleted address was being drafted by President Harding at the time he became ill. It was intended for delivery at San Diego, Calif., and was to contain his views concerning reclamation problems as they affect the United States.)

THIS administration has pledged itself to the advancement of the great projects of land development and reclamation throughout the West. Indeed the creation of new homes for independent, self-supporting, and thus self-respecting, people is one of the great purposes of our National life. With the gradual utilization of our free lands, the greatest avenue for this expansion lies in vitalizing the great arid wastes of the West with the waters of our mountain slopes. The easily available projects of this kind have been to a large degree absorbed, and if we are to make further progress in this great National aim it must be by the organization of engineering works upon a larger scale than we have hitherto undertaken. One of the greatest projects of this character is near to you. I speak of the Colorado River.

Millions of Acres Undeveloped

It has been proven by the exhaustive and painstaking studies of many engineers that there lie in the drainage of the Colorado River more than five million acres of undeveloped land, to say nothing of four million undeveloped horsepower which that river is capable of producing. Thus we have a National asset as great as the whole agricultural area of the State of Maryland which may yet be added to our National wealth. This is no experimental development, for at those points where the water could be more easily distributed many substantial communities have already been organized in this great basin, and the problem before us is the expansion of these communities through greater and more extensive engineering works.

The works proposed demand the utmost genius and imagination on the part of our engineers and they must needs be upon a greater scale than any hitherto undertaken in the history of the world. Some years ago the admiration of the world was commanded by the engineering works undertaken at Assuan for the purpose of bringing under cultivation the broad areas of the Nile, and veritably here lies at our door a second valley of the Nile in its fertility and its pregnant possibilities for the future. To a people who have a proper pride in their daring and accomplishment in a great constructive effort and in the overcoming of obstacles, this is a task which appeals to National imagination and National goodwill.

Benefit to the Whole People

Such a gigantic operation may not be accomplished within the resources of the local communities. It is my view, and I believe the accepted view of a large part of our people, that the initial capital for the installation of these engineering works must be provided by the American people as a whole, and truly the American people as a whole benefit from such investment. The addition to our National assets of so productive a unit benefits, not alone the local community created by it, but also directly and indirectly, our entire National life.

The first of the steps to be taken in this tremendous engineering task lies in the construction of the great dams on the Colorado River through which the spring floods may be held in reserve for summer use and by which the great dangers which now threaten the communities of the lower river may be safeguarded. It is not my purpose to enter upon the technical discussions as to where such great works should be installed. That must be a matter for determination solely upon its engineering merits, uninfluenced by either private interests, the interest of any one State, or any one locality.

Many Obstacles to Overcome

Many obstacles must be overcome before we shall have arrived at the point of actually undertaking this great work. One of these obstacles lies in the natural conflict of State rights in the distribution of the waters of the Colorado River. Indeed, one of the primary purposes for which our forefathers created our sovereign State governments was that they should jealously safeguard the rights and interests of the peoples within their boundaries, but where these rights come into conflict with each other there is but one American way of solution, and that is by compromise and by agreement. You are well aware of the compact agreed to between the representatives of the seven States in the basin, under the chairmanship of Secretary Hoover, concluded by the sacrifice on the part of each of some part of its possible hopes and calculations, in the common purpose of removing a great obstruction to the progress of the development of this great basin. It was the hope of the Colorado River Commission and of the administration that a solution by agreement among the seven States would have substituted common sense, goodwill, and peace for warfare through our courts which must delay development for a generation.

First Agreement Among States

I, indeed, took special satisfaction in the conclusion of this compact as it represented the first agreement of any consequence between a number of States under a provision of the Constitution upon which our forefathers placed hope for the settlement of interstate conflicts. That compact has been ratified by six of the States concerned and I trust that before it shall be rejected by the seventh State and before we shall again be returned to the interminable intricacies of the law and before the hope of the advancement of this great development shall have been removed from our vision, the seventh State will consider whether she is really called upon to make undue sacrifice in common with the sacrifices of the other six States.

Another obstacle which we must overcome by the better knowledge of our people is the prejudice of our agricultural communities against opening up larger agricultural areas. It is said, with good reason, that we are already overproducing in farm products; that the prices which our farmers receive today are inadequate for the labor they perform and the capital they have invested. It may be recognized, however, that this is indeed but a temporary situation. Our population increases by fifteen million in every decade and an expansion in our agricultural production is a vital necessity for us even within so short a time ahead as ten years. The vastness of the engineering works required to accomplish this great project will not permit of competition in production by the reclaimed area for more than ten years hence and therefore any alarm or criticism in this direction may be allayed without anxiety.

I should indeed be proud if during my administration I could participate in the inauguration of this great project by affixing my signature to the proper legislation by Congress through which it might be launched. I should feel that I had some small part in the many thousands of fine American homes that would spring forth from the desert during the course of my lifetime as the result of such an act, and in the extension of these fine foundations of our American people.

PRESIDENT'S *LAST* PUBLIC ADDRESS READ A FEW HOURS BEFORE HIS DEATH, WAS *ELOQUENT* PLEA FOR CHRISTIANITY

Address Before Grand Commandery, Knights Templars, of California, at Hollywood, Calif., August 2

Sir Knights and Brothers:

I AM deeply sensible of the honor implied in my selection as the medium for the transfer of this sacred banner from the custody of the grand jurisdiction of the Commanderies of Ohio to the temporary keeping of the Knights of California. I am especially gratified that this designation has been made by my own home Commandery, composed of Brother Knights with whom I have lived in more or less intimate, neighborly association throughout the greater part of my life.

It was a beautiful idea which brought about the reproduction of the banner under which the Knights of the Holy Grail went forth to battle to the death with the Saracens for the restoration of the Holy *Land* and its shrines to

NOTE: This address, which President Harding had intended to deliver at Hollywood, was delivered for him a few hours before his death by his Secretary, Mr. George B. Christian, Jr., as explained in the following statement:

"July 31, 1923.

"CONFIDENTIAL TO THE PRESS:

"Attached hereto is the address prepared by the President before his illness, to be delivered before the Grand Commandery, Knights Templars of California, August 2, 1923, at Hollywood. It was to have been a feature in the ceremonies connected with delivering the Beauseant, which is the supreme emblematic standard of the Knights Templars of the world, from the custody of the Grand Jurisdiction of the Commanderies of Ohio to the temporary custody of the Commandery of California. The President's home Commandery at Marion, Ohio, was to have made the formal delivery of the Beauseant, the President acting as its spokesman. His illness making his participation impossible, the President desired that his Secretary, Hon. George B. Christian, Jr., who is also a member of the Marion Commandery, should represent the President and read the address the President had expected to make. Accordingly the address is released for publication, immediately upon its delivery by Mr. Christian, which is expected to be about 4 p. m., August 2, at Hollywood."

Christian hands, and to send it on a pilgrimage to the temples of the latter-day Christian Knights to reawaken or reanimate their faith and devotion. The reproduced beauseant will not encounter the storms, the fanaticism, and the romances of Knighthood which attended the original banner, but I trust its journeys will encounter no less of conscience and no less of noble purpose.

"Not Unto Us, Oh Lord, Not Unto Us"

I am sure the mission of the beauseant will be a failure if its travels are made simply a matter of symbolism and pageantry. It bears emblazoned upon it the supplication: "Not unto us, O Lord, not unto us; but unto Thy name be the glory." We should glorify the Holy Name, not by words, not by praise, not by displays at arms, but by deeds and service in behalf of human brotherhood. Christ, the great Exemplar of our order, repeatedly urged this truth upon His hearers. There was nothing mythical or mystical in the code of living preached by Jesus Christ. The lessons He taught were so simple and plain, so fashioned to be understood by the humblest among men, that they appealed to the reason and emotions of all. His words to the fishermen bore conviction to the learned men of the Roman bench. All of His teachings were based upon the broad ground of fraternalism, and justice, and understanding, from which flows always peace. "A new commandment I give unto you; that ye love one another." Surely in this was "all the law and the gospels."

I make bold to say, in reflective deliberation, there is nothing in Templar Knighthood, nothing in obligation, lecture or exemplification, nothing in practice where obligation is kept, which could not be openly, and in equal simplicity, proclamed to the world. Some one has said, in speaking of our present day civilization, that "we need less of religion and more of Christianity." This may be crudely expressed, but it contains a great truth. With the universal observance of Christ's commandment we would have the essentials of all religions. Perhaps I will best express my thought if I say we need less of sectarianism, less of denominationalism, less of fanatical zeal and its exactions, and more of the Christ spirit, more of the Christ practice, and a new and abiding consecration to reverence for God.

I am a confirmed optimist as to the growth of the spirit of brotherhood. Science and genius are lending their aid to the removal of the obstacles to intercourse and attending understanding among the peoples of the world. We do rise to heights, at times, when we look for the good rather than the evil in others, and give consideration to the views of all. The inherent love of fellowship is banding men together, and, when envy and suspicion are vanquished, fraternity records a triumph, and brotherhood brings new blessings to men and to peoples in the larger sense.

Spirit of Brotherhood Broadening

Because I am holding temporarily a position of official prominence I have been privileged in being invited into association with many of our so-called secret, fraternal societies. I find that each of them has at its foundation and the reason for its existence the furtherance of brotherhood and the Christian virtues of charity, mercy, justice and brotherly love. Moreover, the practice of these virtues has been suggested by the ways of happiness in the daily lives of men. For example—and I am sure it will be no breach of faith to relate it—I was admitted into a fraternity of Alaskan Pioneers and I was obligated never to kick a dog, or to work a horse with a sore back or shoulder. Now that was a simple thing that Christ himself would have urged; it was an expression of mercy and affection by these pioneers for the brutes who could not speak a protest, of considerate concern for a life of service. On the whole I am well persuaded that the many tenders of fellowship have come to me because men wish to have practiced in official life the teachings of brotherhood and friendship and sympathy which have sweetened their own pathways.

All Doing Helpful Work

All of these fraternities, within their spheres, are doing fine and helpful work, and adding a redolent bloom to the gardens of human fellowship. Sometimes a real purpose is temporarily obscured or defeated by jealousies, or ambitions, or too much of symbolism, or other attending developments. But the leaven imparted by devoted and enthusiastic brothers is slowly but surely raising the standard of the whole mass. We can never have too much of it. Fraternity never long conceals a wrong intent; it can harbor no crime; it fosters no wrong. Inherently it demands good conscience and worthy purpose.

First of all these great fraternities in age and dignity and power, is the great Masonic order. It is freely recognized as such. Its tap roots run into every land in which Christ is known and His teachings treasured and followed. The journeyings of this replica beauseant are strengthening the fraternal ties between Canada and the United States, even as we today feel a little closer touch between Ohio and California.

All Lands Under Christ's Law Holy

It little matters now that a mistaken idea sent the original banner at the head of armed hosts to recover by force and violence the land which had been hallowed by Christ's physical presence. Jesus Christ was the Father's gift for all the ages, and any land where His law is loved and followed is no less holy than that which His foot had trod. Christ was the Prince of Peace, and we who seek to render His name glorious must move in the ways of peace and brotherhood and loving service.

So I gladly and proudly join in sending this banner on its highly purposed journey, which is to continue probably beyond the span of the lives of those here assembled. Wherever it inspires more of real brotherhood, more of devotion to Christ's simplest teachings, it will not have been borne in vain.

I charge that it shall not be held as a banner of militant force, not as a memorial of deeds of arms, not as a mere piece of ritualistic pageantry, but as the symbol of brotherhood, raised to the glory of our Grand Commander, Whose law was love, Whose reign was peace, and for Whom the herald angels sang: "Glory to God in the Highest, and on earth peace, good will toward men."

Printed by BoD™in Norderstedt, Germany